STUDY GUIDE

Jeffrey D. Green
Soka University

Jody L. Davis
Soka University

PSYCHOLOGY

SEVENTH EDITION

Carole Wade
Dominican University of California

Carol Tavris
Dominican University of California

Prentice Hall, Upper Saddle River, New Jersey 07458

© 2003 by PEARSON EDUCATION, INC.
Upper Saddle River, New Jersey 07458

ISBN 0-13-098264-4

Printed in the United States of America

C O N T E N T S

We would like to thank Tina E. Stern, who wrote the previous version of this Study Guide. We have revised and updated it for the current edition of Wade and Tavris' *Psychology* textbook. The format of this Study Guide is user-friendly, challenging, and practical. It presents students with a variety of assessment techniques and takes advantage of what psychologists know about learning and memory. We hope that you find it to be a useful resource in your studies.

Jeffrey D. Green and Jody L. Davis

THE BEST WAY TO USE THIS STUDY GUIDE

This Study Guide has been developed utilizing psychological research findings in the areas of learning and memory. The structure of the Study Guide is designed so students can be actively involved in their learning.

LEARNING OBJECTIVES   Learning Objectives begin each chapter. Students should read the Learning Objectives **BEFORE** they begin reading the chapter. Students can also formulate additional questions on a separate sheet of paper by using headings, key terms and concepts. Students should examine all these questions before reading the text and answer them while reading that particular section of text.

CHAPTER SUMMARIES   Following the Learning Objectives, each chapter has a chapter summary. It provides a general overview of the chapter.

PREVIEW OUTLINES   Each section of the chapter is presented in a general outline format, which students are intended to examine **BEFORE** they read the chapter. Students should preview or survey a section of text before they read it.

TABLES Many chapters have tables that help students organize, categorize, and form associations to the information. The completed table will be a great study aid, but the act of completing the table is just as important; it is another way to make the information meaningful.

THREE PRACTICE TESTS   Each chapter has three practice tests that represent different testing methods. Practice Test 1 is a multiple-choice test. Practice Test 2 is a short-answer test and requires students to recall (rather than just recognize) information. Practice Test 3 requires students to apply, analyze, and synthesize information in essay or short-answer responses.

ANSWER KEYS   Answer Keys for all practice tests are presented at the end of the Study Guide. They were separated from the chapters to encourage students to try to answer the questions before looking at the key.

HOW TO STUDY

TIRED??

     * of reading a chapter and not remembering any of the contents five minutes later?

     * of fighting against drooping eyelids and losing?

     * of thinking you've studied enough only to find that you can't remember anything that's on the test?

     * of studying definitions and terms only to find that the test questions don't ask for definitions and terms; instead, they ask for examples that you never saw in the text?

     * of test scores that don't reflect what you know?

It would be nice to be able to say, "Guaranteed, 100%!!! Follow these simple guidelines and you, too, can get a 4.0! Simple! Easy! Money-back guarantee! Teachers and parents will love you, and it will change your life!!" Of course, I cannot make those claims, but I can say the following: "**YOU CAN** change the above behaviors **IF** you read **AND** attempt to use the techniques that are described in this section of the Study Guide." Changing your study habits is like going on a diet. First, you must know the details of the diet: How does it propose to help you eat healthier? However, knowing how the diet works and what you are supposed to eat will NOT cause you to develop healthier eating habits. You must implement the diet. In other words, to receive the benefits, you must DO IT! It is not enough to know what you are supposed to do...you must actually do it! It is the same thing with changing your study habits. It is not enough to know the changes you need to make...you must **MAKE THE CHANGES!**

STEP 1: DIAGNOSING THE PROBLEM

Some students have developed study skills that work well for them, and they do not wish to change their habits. Some students have many study skills with which they are generally satisfied, but they have one or two areas that need improvement. Other students have difficulty with a number of their study skills. Below is a list of some study skills. Review this list and try to identify whether you are satisfied or dissatisfied with each of these abilities. The preface to this Study Guide focuses on study skills and how to use this manual. As you read the preface, focus on the areas in which you need improvement. If this chapter does not cover that particular area, identify and **USE** the resources that are available on your campus to get assistance. **DON'T** ignore study problems. It is unlikely that they will just disappear on their own or that they will improve simply by your trying to do more of what you are already doing!

Check all of the following areas that are problems for you:

Reading the text _____
    Comprehending the material _____
    Concentrating while reading _____
    Identifying what is important _____
    Recalling what you have read _____
    Being distracted easily _____
Time Management _____
    Not planning your time _____
    Not having enough time to study _____
    Not using the time you have allotted to study _____
    Underestimating the time you need to study _____
    Difficulty saying no to other plans _____
    Not sticking to your study schedule _____
Getting the Most out of Class _____
    Trouble paying attention in class _____
    Not going to classes _____
    Not understanding what is important _____
Taking Notes _____
    Your notes aren't helpful _____
    Your notes are disorganized _____
Taking Tests _____
    Trouble recalling information _____
    Test anxiety _____
    Trouble on multiple choice questions _____
    Trouble on fill-in-the-blank questions _____
    Trouble on essay questions _____
    Trouble predicting what will be on the test _____
    Trouble going from definitions to examples _____

Identifying your problem areas should help you to focus on the skills that you most need in order to improve. Think about your problem areas as you read the preface and apply the information to your particular situation.

ON BEING A LEARNER or DON'T STOP BEFORE YOU BEGIN!

What was the last new skill you tried to learn? Were you learning to play basketball, softball, tennis, or the guitar? Or were you learning a new language? Whatever you were learning to do, it is very likely that you were not very good at it at first. In fact, you were probably **BAD** at it! <u>That is how it is supposed to be!</u> Your ability to do something well depends on gaining experience with that activity; the more you do it, the better you become at the task. This means that it is necessary to go beyond the beginning period of learning when the new skill is difficult and awkward and you are not very good at it. This can be frustrating for students who often think they already should know how to study, and if they have to learn new study skills, they should be learned quickly and easily. During the early stages of learning a new skill, a person may be tempted to say, "This isn't working," or "This will never work" or "These techniques feel so artificial." **RESIST** those thoughts. Learning these skills may be difficult at first, but no more difficult than continuing to use skills that you already know **DO NOT WORK!!** If you want to change any long-standing behavior, you will have to tolerate the early phases of learning when the new behaviors won't yet feel like "your own." In college, graduate school and employment, you will find that persistence pays. So, **RESIST** returning to your old habits and **PERSIST** with learning the new habits. Don't stop before you begin...give it some time.

MASTERING YOUR MEMORY (OR AT LEAST GETTING THE UPPER HAND!)

A great deal of the information contained in most study skills manuals and courses is based on what is known about how human memory works. Experimental psychologists study memory and how it works; therefore, it is appropriate in this course for you to understand the findings of scientific research on memory and how they apply to **YOU**. Ignore these findings at your peril! This section will present a few general findings about memory that are particularly relevant to your studying. This information comes directly from Chapter 10, which will discuss memory in more detail. Information about memory has applicability not only to your psychology class, but to all your classes.

KEEPING INFORMATION IN SHORT-TERM MEMORY The three-box model of memory suggests there are three types of memory: sensory memory, short-term memory (STM), and long-term memory (LTM). Sensory memory is a very brief type of memory that lasts less than a second. Sensory memory is important because if information does not get noticed in sensory memory, it cannot be transferred into either short-term or long-term memory. The limits of short-term memory are known. Short-term memory can hold seven (plus or minus two) pieces of information for about 30 seconds or less. A person can extend the amount of time information is held in STM by repeating it over and over (this is called maintenance rehearsal); however, once you stop repeating the information, it is quickly lost. Think of times that you have called information to get the number of the nearest pizza place. You repeat the number over and over and hope your roommate does not come along and ask to borrow your comb, because if your repetition is interrupted, you will forget the number. Many professors believe that most students study in ways that get information into short-term memory, but not in ways that get it into long-term memory.

GETTING INFORMATION INTO LONG-TERM MEMORY Long-term memory can hold an infinite amount of information for an unlimited amount of time. **THAT'S** where you want to store all the information you are studying!! The important question is how to transfer information from short-term memory into long-term memory. The transfer of memory from STM into LTM relies upon the use of elaborative rehearsal. Elaborative rehearsal involves more than the simple repetition of information required by short-term memory; it requires that you make the information meaningful. Making information meaningful requires more than saying "This has deep meaning to me." Meaningfulness can be accomplished by interacting with the material in any **ACTIVE** way. Some examples of ways to make information meaningful include putting it into a story, putting it into a rhyme (i.e. "30 days has September"), forming visual images of the information, forming associations with people or things already familiar to you or associating information to other pieces of information, organizing it into categories, putting it into your own words, explaining it to someone else--almost anything that you do with the information that is **ACTIVE**. Being **ACTIVE** with the information and aiming for **UNDERSTANDING** and not simple repetition of the material are the keys. Almost anything you do with the material that is active will help move it into long-term memory. Passively reading the material will not help the information transfer into long-term memory, but that is the technique most students use.

CRITICAL THINKING AND LONG-TERM MEMORY Critical thinking is emphasized throughout this textbook. Every chapter includes information on how to approach topics critically. Critical thinking requires organizing, analyzing, and evaluating information. This may sound suspiciously like elaborative rehearsal. Critical thinking is important for many reasons. In the context of study skills, critical thinking is important because it involves the same processes that promote the transfer of information into long-term memory.

GETTING MORE INFORMATION INTO SHORT-TERM AND LONG-TERM MEMORY One last piece of information about memory has to do with expanding the amount of information contained in short-term memory. To get information into LTM, it must pass through STM, and we know that STM holds only about seven (plus or minus two) units of information. That does not seem like a practical system, since most textbook chapters seem to contain hundreds of pieces of new information in each chapter! Short-term memory holds **units** or chunks of information, and a strategy to increase the amount of information being held in STM is to include more information in each chunk. For example, you can change 26 separate pieces of information (which far exceeds the capacity of STM) into one piece of information (well within the capacity of STM) by chunking! Whenever you use the word "alphabet" to refer to 26 separate letters, you are chunking. If you organize the information you are studying into categories, or chunks, you will improve your chances of getting more information into LTM in two ways: 1) you will increase the information contained in the units getting into STM, and 2) you will be making the information meaningful by the act of organizing it into the chunks! You can't lose! Making outlines is a good way to chunk information. Outlines naturally organize information into categories (chunks) and subcategories. This study guide presents the information in ways that help you to organize information into chunks, which also helps make the information meaningful.

STUDYING WITH THE SQ3R OR STAYING AWAKE, STAYING ACTIVE, AND OPENING THE DOOR TO LONG-TERM MEMORY

The SQ3R method was developed by Francis Robinson, a psychology professor at Ohio State University. It is a method of reading assignments that implements many techniques that promote the transfer of information into long-term memory. The letters "SQ3R" stand for <u>survey, question, read, receive, review</u>.

SURVEY Before you read a chapter or reading assignment, it is important to survey what is in the chapter and how the information is organized. You can do this by simply looking over the headings or the chapter outlines at the beginning of each chapter. This Study Guide also provides more detailed preview outlines for this purpose. It is important that you survey the information before you read, because surveying turns what otherwise would seem like hundreds of independent facts (which far exceeds the capacity of STM) into a much smaller number (probably five to nine--text book authors know how memory works) of main topics identified in separate headings. Once you have seen the main headings, you have an organizational structure to begin your reading. This helps you organize the information when you begin reading (remember that organizing is one way to make information meaningful, which transfers it into LTM). Surveying a chapter in the text is like going on a trip. Before you arrive at a city you do not know, it is very helpful to look at a map. You quickly can see the location of the airport, your hotel, downtown, the river and the three important sites you want to see. This orients you to your journey. If you do not look at a map before your arrival, you are wandering around without knowing where you are going. You do not want to wander around a 40-page chapter that contains a great deal of information without knowing where you are going.

QUESTION Assume you are taking a college entrance exam that contains a comprehension section. There are several paragraphs for you to read, and then you are to answer five questions about the reading. Would you read the questions before you read the paragraphs, or would you read the paragraphs and then begin to try to answer the questions? Most of you would read the questions first, so that as you read the paragraphs, you could keep the questions in mind and look for the answers while you read. The reasons for formulating questions before you read your text are: 1) to help you read with a purpose, and 2) to help you be more active while you read.

After you have surveyed the chapter, formulate questions by converting the headings, key terms and definitions into questions. For example, "The Major Psychological Perspectives" is a subheading in Chapter 1. "What are the names and key concepts of the major psychological perspectives?" would be an example of changing that subheading into a question. This Study Guide has listed the relevant learning objectives for each. In addition, you should try to formulate additional questions and write them on a separate piece of paper. The intention is that you will write the answers to all these questions while you read the chapter. This helps you read with a purpose: your purpose is to answer the questions. This also helps you to be active while you read. You are being active by looking for the answers to the questions **AND** by writing down the answers as you find them. You will also have answers to all the learning objectives in writing when you go to study for quizzes and exams.

READ   You are now ready to read. You have surveyed the chapter in order to know where you are going and how the chapter is organized. You have formulated your questions in order to know what you are looking for as you read. While reading, you will be organizing the information and answering the questions. These are both ways to increase the transfer of information into long-term memory. As you begin your reading, look at your first question. Open your textbook to the part of the chapter that applies to the question and read in order to answer that question.

RECITE   After you have surveyed the reading assignment to get the general idea of its content, have turned the first heading into a question, and have read that section to answer the question, you are now ready to recite. Reciting helps make information meaningful (did you ever notice that when you speak in class, you tend to remember the information you spoke or asked about?). Also, it is another way that you can be active (which also makes the information meaningful). Reciting requires that you put the information into your own words, and it is an excellent way to identify what you don't yet understand. There are a number of ways to recite.

Using the learning objectives and the questions that you have formulated, recite aloud the answers to the questions (without looking at the answers). You can say definitions or examples of key terms, terms that are listed in bold, or terms that are underlined as a vehicle for reciting information. You can recite responses to learning objectives. Explaining information to other people, either classmates or patient friends who are willing to help, is also a good way to recite the information. Explaining the information to others also allows you to identify areas that you do not understand well. Remember, your recitation of information should be in your own words and should attempt to give examples of the concepts you are describing. If you simply try to memorize definitions given in the text and recite these definitions, you are simply camouflaging maintenance rehearsal.   Remember, getting information into long-term memory involves meaning--so make sure you understand the material and can make it "your own" to get it into long-term memory.

REVIEW   The final step in the SQ3R approach is to review the material again. Frequent reviews, even brief reviews, are among the important keys to learning. After at least one hour, review the material once more. This can be done by going over the main points of the chapter (with your book closed), going over the answers to the questions you have written (without looking at them), and reviewing key terms and concepts. Limit your reviews to about five minutes. Reviews can be used in other ways too. Begin each study session with a five-minute review. Before each class, review notes from the previous class for five minutes. At the end of every class, review your notes for five minutes.

SUMMARY   The SQ3R method incorporates the information that psychologists know about how people learn and remember. The key points to remember include: **BE ACTIVE, MAKE INFORMATION MEANINGFUL, INTERACT WITH THE INFORMATION, AIM FOR UNDERSTANDING NOT JUST REPETITION, THINK CRITICALLY.** All this can be achieved by writing, talking, thinking, making outlines, forming associations, developing questions and examples and putting definitions in your own words. The SQ3R method suggests that these goals can be achieved if you:

1. <u>Survey</u> the information: Use headings and chapter summaries to orient yourself to the information you plan to read. Give the information an organizational structure.
2. <u>Question</u>: Turn the headings, terms, and concepts into questions.
3. <u>Read</u>: Read each section to answer the specific questions that you asked. Write your answers on a separate sheet of paper.
4. <u>Recite</u>: Close your book and rehearse the information contained in the section by answering the relevant questions or giving examples of key terms or concepts.
5. <u>Review</u>: After at least an hour-long break, close your book, turn over your notes and list the main points of the chapter and the answers to your questions.

REMEMBER, this may feel awkward or cumbersome at first, **BUT** the more you use this method, the easier it will become.

WHEN AND WHERE TO STUDY

In many courses, several weeks can pass between tests. You might wonder whether it is better to study intensely the night before the test or to spread out your studying time. Memory research clearly suggests that "cramming" just doesn't work. You may know this from personal experience. Rather than studying for hours and hours just before the test, it is much more effective to study as you go along in the course.

In terms of when to study, the best time to study is immediately after class. **BEFORE** going to class, you should preview the material to be covered, form general questions and read the text. Study the subject that was covered as soon after the lecture as possible. You will find it easier to master the material and will have an opportunity to test your understanding of the lecture if you study right away. The procedure of continuously studying fairly small chunks will also help you to avoid the nightmare of the infrequent studier--the sudden realization that you don't understand any of what you have been covering for the last few weeks. If you study for a short period after each lecture, you will not have to worry about this. You will also find that tomorrow's lecture will be easier to understand if you study today's material and master the essential points covered by your teacher. Most professors structure lectures so that each one builds on earlier lectures and readings. Studying as you go along will guarantee that you are well prepared to get the most out of each new lecture. It is also a good idea to set a specific time to study. Even if it is for a short time, you should study at a regular time every day.

In terms of where to study, many students indicate that they have difficulty concentrating. Upon further examination, it seems that many students study with their TV or CD player on at the same time and place their roommates are having a snack or are on the phone. Some general guidelines about where to study include:
1. Limit the places that you study to one or two special locations. These could be the library, a desk or a designated study area. They are special in the sense that they should be places where the only thing you do there is study. That means you should not study in places where you regularly do something else (such as the dining room table or bed).
2. Make these places free from distractions. Distractions like the TV, telephone or friends can cause studying to be abandoned.

3.   Set a specific time to begin studying and then study in the same place every day. In that way, that place will become a cue to study.

OTHER SKILLS THAT INFLUENCE STUDYING

Many skills influence study habits. The diagnostic checklist at the beginning of this section identifies some of the skills that students must possess to study effectively. Skills that affect studying include the following: time management, note taking, test-preparation, test taking, stress management, using the library, dealing with professors, and classroom participation. All of these abilities are important. In fact, they are so important that entire books have been devoted to helping students develop these skills. Many colleges and universities offer various types of academic assistance, from courses on study skills to individual counseling on study skills. One of the survival skills necessary for college students is to be aware of the services offered by your institution and to make use of them as needed. If you have identified problem areas that influence your performance, you have several choices: find a book on study skills in your library, look for courses at your school that deal with study skills, or identify other campus resources that are available to assist you in developing these abilities.

CHAPTER ONE

What Is Psychology?

LEARNING OBJECTIVES

After studying this chapter, you should be able to do the following:

1.   Define psychology.

2.   Distinguish psychology from pseudoscience and "psychobabble."

3.   Summarize the relationship between the discipline of psychology and public opinion.

4.   Explain eight guidelines for critical thinking.

5.   Summarize the early history and development of psychology and the role of empirical evidence.

6.   Describe the aims and methods of structuralism and functionalism.

7.   Describe the basic ideas of psychoanalysis.

8.   Describe the major principles of the biological, learning, cognitive, psychodynamic, and sociocultural perspectives in psychology.

9.   Discuss humanistic psychology and feminist psychology.

10.   Distinguish between applied and basic psychology.

11.   Discuss and give examples of the concerns of various specialties in psychology.

12.   Distinguish between a psychotherapist, a psychoanalyst, a psychiatrist, a clinical psychologist and other practicing mental health professionals.

13.   Identify basic areas of agreement among psychologists.

BRIEF CHAPTER SUMMARY

Chapter 1 defines psychology and traces the historical and disciplinary roots of the field to its current perspectives, specialties areas and activities. Critical thinking guidelines are described, and students are encouraged to understand and apply these concepts as they read the text. The complexity of human behavior requires that psychology students resist simplistic thinking and the search for simple answers. Five current perspectives and two important movements are identified. The current perspectives include the biological perspective, learning perspective, cognitive perspective, psychodynamic perspective and sociocultural perspective. The two important movements are the feminist and humanistic movements. Each of these approaches reflects a different emphasis and approach to understanding human behavior. Students are encouraged to think about human behavior from each different perspective and use their critical thinking skills to compare and contrast these approaches. A review of the specialty areas within the field helps students appreciate that psychology includes vastly diverse topics and that psychologists are engaged in a wide variety of occupations. Examples include educational psychologists, developmental psychologists, and psychometric psychologists. The practice of psychology, which helps people with mental health problems, is discussed along with a description of types of practitioners within the field of psychology (e.g., counseling psychologists, school psychologists) and those outside of it.

PREVIEW OUTLINE

Before you read the chapter, review the preview outline for each section of the text. After you have read the chapter, close this book and try to <u>re-create</u> the outlines on a blank piece of paper.

I.   **PSYCHOLOGY, PSEUDOSCIENCE, AND POPULAR OPINION**
    A.   **Psychology** - scientific study of behavior and mental processes, and how they are affected by an organism's physical state, mental state and the external environment
    B.   **Psychobabble** - pseudoscience covered by veneer of psychological language
        1. Psychology is based on research evidence, whereas popular opinion is not
        2. Psychobabble confirms existing beliefs; psychology challenges them and deepens our understanding of accepted facts

II. THINKING CRITICALLY AND CREATIVELY ABOUT PSYCHOLOGY
   A. **Critical thinking** - ability and willingness to assess claims and make objective judgments on the basis of well-supported reasons and evidence rather than emotion and anecdote; the basis of all science
   B. **Eight critical-thinking guidelines**
      1. Ask questions; be willing to wonder
      2. Define your terms
      3. Examine the evidence
      4. Analyze assumptions and biases
      5. Avoid emotional reasoning
      6. Don't oversimplify
      7. Consider other interpretations
      8. Tolerate uncertainty

III. PSYCHOLOGY'S PAST: FROM THE ARMCHAIR TO THE LABORATORY
   A. **Early history**
   B. **The birth of modern psychology and Wilhelm Wundt**
   C. **Three early psychologies**
      1. Structuralism and E.B. Titchener
      2. Functionalism and William James
      3. Psychoanalysis and Sigmund Freud

IV. PSYCHOLOGY'S PRESENT: BEHAVIOR, BODY, MIND, AND CULTURE
   A. **The major psychological perspectives**
      1. The biological perspective examines how bodily events interact with the environment to produce perceptions, memories and behavior
      2. The learning perspective examines how the environment and experience affect a person's actions
      3. The cognitive perspective emphasizes what goes on in people's heads; reasoning, remembering, understanding, problem solving
      4. The sociocultural perspective focuses on the social and cultural forces outside the individual that shape every aspect of behavior
      5. The psychodynamic perspective deals with unconscious dynamics within the individual, such as inner forces, conflicts, or instinctual energy
   B. **Two influential movements in psychology**
      1. Humanistic psychology rejects the psychoanalytic perspective as too pessimistic and behaviorism as too mechanistic
      2. Feminist psychology analyzes the influence of social inequities on gender relations and identifies biases in research and psychotherapy

V. WHAT PSYCHOLOGISTS DO
   A. Overview of professional activities
      1. Teach and conduct research in colleges and universities
      2. Provide health or mental health services (psychological practice)
      3. Conduct research or apply its findings in nonacademic settings
   B. Psychological research
      1. Basic psychology - research that seeks knowledge for its own sake
      2. Applied psychology - research concerned with practical uses of knowledge
      3. Some major non-clinical specialties in psychology: experimental psychologists, psychometric psychologists, developmental psychologists, industrial/organizational psychologists, educational psychologists
   C. Psychological practice
      1. Those who try to understand and improve physical and mental health
      2. Practitioners of psychology work in mental or general hospitals, clinics, schools, counseling centers, and private practice
      3. Types of practitioners: counseling psychologists, school psychologists, clinical psychologists; Degrees for practice: Ph.D., Ed.D., Psy.D.
      4. Types of non-clinical psychologist practitioners: psychotherapist, psychoanalyst, psychiatrist, social worker
   D. Psychology in the community

VI. THE MOSAIC OF PSYCHOLOGY
   A. Variety in psychologists' activities, goals, perspectives creates a mosaic
   B. Though there is disagreement about emphasis, psychological scientists and scientist-clinicians agree on basic guidelines
      1. Most believe in importance of empirical evidence
      2. Most reject supernatural explanations of events
      3. Share a fascination with human behavior and mind

PERSPECTIVES TABLE

Complete this table, and then identify similarities and differences between perspectives.

PERSPECTIVE OR MOVEMENT	KEY FIGURES	KEY CONCEPTS AND TERMS	MAJOR INFLUENCES ON BEHAVIOR
BIOLOGICAL PERSPECTIVE			
LEARNING PERSPECTIVE			
COGNITIVE PERSPECTIVE			
PSYCHODYNAMIC PERSPECTIVE			
SOCIOCULTURAL PERSPECTIVE			
HUMANISTIC MOVEMENT			
FEMINIST MOVEMENT			

PRACTICE TEST 1 - Multiple Choice

1.   Psychology is defined as
    A.   the scientific study of behavior and how it is affected by an organism's physical state, mental state and the external environment.
    B.   the scientific study of behavior and mental processes and how they are affected by an organism's physical state, mental state and the external environment.
    C.   the scientific study of mental processes and how they are affected by an organism's physical state, mental state and the external environment.
    D.   the scientific study of groups and institutions in society.

2.   The main difference between psychological knowledge and popular opinion is that
    A.   psychological knowledge is contained in text books, popular opinion is not.
    B.   psychological knowledge is based on research evidence, popular opinion is not.
    C.   findings based on psychological knowledge are often the opposite of popular opinion.
    D.   popular opinion is usually very obvious and psychological knowledge is rarely the expected result.

3.   Unhappy memories are often repressed and then later recalled accurately, most women suffer from emotional symptoms of "PMS," abstinence from alcohol reduce rates of alcoholism are all examples of
    A.   popular opinions that have been supported by research evidence.
    B.   common beliefs that have been contradicted by the evidence.
    C.   scientific research findings.
    D.   ideas that have been rejected by popular opinion.

4.   The ability and willingness to assess claims and make objective judgments on the basis of well-supported reasons and evidence rather than emotion and anecdote defines
    A.   critical thinking.   B.   psychobabble.
    C.   common sense.   D.   psychology.

5.   Which of the following is one of the essential elements of critical thinking?
    A.   Ask questions; be willing to wonder.
    B.   Examine the evidence.
    C.   Avoid emotional reasoning: "If I feel this way, it must be true."
    D.   All of the above are essential elements of critical thinking.

6.   _____ established the first psychology lab in 1879 and is considered the "father of psychology."
    A.   E.B. Titchener   B.   William James
    C.   B.F. Skinner   D.   Wilhelm Wundt

7. An early school of psychology, popularized by E.B. Titchener, attempted to analyze sensations, images and feelings into their most basic elements. This school was called
A. structuralism.
B. introspection.
C. functionalism.
D. behaviorism.

8. A second early school of psychology asked how and why an organism's behavior helps it to adapt to its environment. It was called
A. structuralism.
B. introspection.
C. functionalism.
D. behaviorism.

9. Titchener is to James as
A. trained introspection is to Wundt.
B. functionalism is to structuralism.
C. trained introspection is to functionalism.
D. structuralism is to functionalism.

10. Proponents of the _____ perspective believe that to understand the mind one must study the nervous system, because all actions, feelings and thoughts are associated with bodily events.
A. behavioral
B. psychodynamic
C. cognitive
D. biological

11. You have recently started psychotherapy with a psychologist who believes in the learning perspective. Which of the following statements would she make?
A. "To best address your problem, we must identify the behaviors that are causing problems, the environmental conditions including the rewards and punishments that maintain the behaviors and then we must modify those behaviors."
B. "To help you we must identify your unconscious inner conflicts, memories and emotional traumas from your early childhood."
C. "Your problem has to do with how you are thinking about this situation. You must examine your expectations and try to understand this differently."
D. "We must examine your problem in the context of the broader culture and how cultural expectations and beliefs are affecting your behavior."

12. "To understand a person's actions, we must concentrate on the environmental conditions-the rewards and punishers-that maintain or discourage specific behaviors rather than studying the mind or mental states." This reflects the position of the _____ perspective.
A. learning
B. psychodynamic
C. cognitive
D. biological

13. Which perspective or movement has helped people eliminate unwanted habits?
A. humanism
B. biological
C. learning
D. psychodynamic

14. _____ theorists combine elements of behaviorism with research on thoughts, values, expectations, and intentions.
    A.   Social-cognitive learning   B.   Psychodynamic
    C.   Humanist biological   D.   Biological

15. What goes on in people's heads, including how people reason, remember, understand language, solve problems are some of the topics emphasized by the
    A.   the sociocultural perspective.   B.   humanists.
    C.   social-cognitive theory.   D.   cognitive perspective.

16. "To understand the causes of the high rates of anorexia nervosa among older adolescent women, we must consider the influence of society's norms for female beauty and thinness." This statement reflects which of the following perspectives?
    A.   sociocultural   B.   humanistic
    C.   psychoanalytic   D.   cognitive

17. "The answer to violence and cruelty doesn't reside in instincts, brain circuits or personal dispositions, but in situational, economic and cultural factors." This statement is consistent with the thinking of _____ psychologists.
    A.   cognitive   B.   humanistic
    C.   sociocultural   D.   psychodynamic

18. "Psychological distress is a result of inner forces, specifically unresolved unconscious conflicts from early childhood." This statement reflects the position of the _____ perspective.
    A.   behavioral   B.   psychodynamic
    C.   cognitive   D.   biological

19. Developed in reaction to Freudian pessimism and behavioristic "mindlessness," _____ was based on the notion that human beings had free will.
    A.   feminist psychology   B.   social learning theory
    C.   sociocultural psychology   D.   humanistic psychology

20. Which of the following might be one of the goals of feminist psychology?
    A.   Encourage research on menstruation and motherhood.
    B.   Identify biases in psychological research and psychotherapy.
    C.   Make sure that both male and female subjects are used in research design.
    D.   All of the above.

21. Which of the following best describes the difference between applied and basic research?
    A.   Basic research examines the basic elements of sensations, images and feelings, whereas applied research studies how these processes help a person adapt to the environment.
    B.   Basic psychological research seeks knowledge for its own sake, whereas applied psychological research is concerned with the practical uses of knowledge.
    C.   Applied research seeks knowledge for its own sake, whereas basic research is concerned with the practical uses of knowledge.
    D.   Basic research is based on the psychoanalytic perspective, whereas applied research is based on the humanistic approach.

22. Psychologists who conduct laboratory studies of learning, motivation, emotion, sensation and perception, physiology, and cognition are called _____ psychologists.
    A.   experimental   B.   educational
    C.   developmental   D.   social

23. A developmental psychologist would
    A.   conduct a study on infant attachment behavior.
    B.   conduct research on the role of arousal in the experience of emotions.
    C.   develop a new test to measure personality.
    D.   design and evaluate tests of mental abilities, aptitudes, interests, and personality.

24. A psychometric psychologist
    A.   studies how groups, institutions and the social context influence individuals.
    B.   studies how people change and grow over time physically, mentally and socially.
    C.   designs and evaluates tests of mental abilities, aptitudes, interests and personality.
    D.   studies behavior in the workplace.

25. Psychologists who help people deal with problems of everyday life, such as test anxiety, family or marital problems, or low job motivation, are called _____ psychologists.
    A.   psychometric   B.   clinical
    C.   counseling   D.   school

26. Which of the following is a research area in psychology rather than a practice specialty?
    A.   counseling psychology
    B.   school psychology
    C.   clinical psychology
    D.   educational psychology

27. Which type of psychologist would be most likely to work with highly disturbed people?
    A.   clinical   B.   experimental
    C.   counseling   D.   school

28. A psychotherapist
    A.   has specialized training at a psychoanalytic institute.
    B.   is not required to have any training at all in most states.
    C.   has a medical degree.
    D.   is a psychologist.

29. Dr. Iriko believes that Jon's depression is biochemical and writes him a prescription for antidepressant drugs. She is most likely a
    A.   counseling psychologist.   B.   psychotherapist.
    C.   psychiatrist.   D.   social worker.

30. Though there are many areas of disagreement among psychologists, which of the following describes one of the guidelines on which psychological scientists and scientist-clinicians agree? Most
    A.   agree that psychiatrists are better able to help people than psychologists.
    B.   agree that the behavioral perspective is superior to all other perspectives.
    C.   believe that applied psychology is more important that basic psychology.
    D.   believe in the importance of empirical evidence.

PRACTICE TEST 2 - Short Answer

1.   Psychology is defined as the scientific study of _behavior_ and _mental processes_, and how they are affected by an organism's physical state, mental state and the external environment.

2.   Scientific psychology differs from popular psychology in that it is based on _empirical_ evidence.

3.   _Critical Thinking_ is the ability and willingness to assess claims and make objective judgments on the basis of well-supported reasons and evidence rather than emotion and anecdote.

4.   Two of the eight guidelines for critical thinking are:

   _____

   _____

5.   Early psychologists, like today's psychologists, wanted to describe, _predict_, understand, and _modify_ behavior in order to add to human knowledge and increase human happiness.

6.   William Wundt's favorite research method was _____.

7.   Titchener named this early approach_____.

8.   According to psychoanalysis, distressful symptoms are due to _conflicts and traumas of early childhood_

9.   The _psychodynamic_ perspective is related to Freud's theory of psychoanalysis.

10.   The five major current psychological perspectives are:
   learning, biological, cognative, sociocultural, psychodynamic

11.   The _learning_ perspective is concerned with how the environment and experience affect a person's actions.

12.   Unlike behaviorists and psychoanalysts, humanists believe that human beings have

   _____.

13.   The _cognitive_ is one of the strongest forces in psychology today, and it has inspired an explosion of research on the workings of the mind.

14.   The sociocultural perspective focuses on _social and cultural forces_

15. Within the sociocultural perspective, social psychologists focus on *social rules and roles, groups, and authority and how we are affected or others* while _cultural_ psychologists emphasize how cultural rules and values affect people's development, behavior, and feelings.

16. Psychologists from the _____ movement have noted that many studies used only men as subjects.

17. _Basic_ psychology is the generation of knowledge for its own sake; whereas _applied_ psychology is concerned with the practical uses of such knowledge.

18. _industrial/occupational_ psychologists study behavior in the workplace, whereas _educational_ psychologists study principles that explain learning and look for ways to improve educational systems.

19. Both of the psychological specialties described in question 18 are considered _nonclinical_ specialties.

20. Three examples of practice specialties in psychology are _clinical_, _counseling_, and _school_.

21. In the past, the focus of _developmental_ psychologists was mainly on childhood, but many now study adolescence, young and middle adulthood, or old age.

22. To practice psychology, one must have a _license_, and in almost all states, this requires a _doctorate_ degree.

23. People often confuse clinical psychologists with _psychotherapist_, _psychoanaly_, or _____.

24. _____ have a medical degree and may prescribe medication, whereas _____ are not required to have any degree at all since the term is not legally regulated.

25. Other types of professionals who engage in mental-health fields include _____, _____, and _____.

PRACTICE TEST 3 - Essay

1.   Several activities are described below. For each activity, indicate (a) whether it is an example of applied or basic psychology, (b) the area of specialization most likely to be involved and (c) whether that area of specialization is a clinical or non-clinical area. Explain the reasons for your answers.

   A.   Psychologist David Wechsler designed an intelligence test expressly for use with adults.

   B.   Researchers Hubel and Wiesel (1962, 1968) received a Nobel Prize for their work in the area of vision. They found that special cells in the brain are designed to visually code complex features of an object. Their research involved recording impulses from individual cells in the brains of cats and monkeys.

   C.   Swiss biologist Jean Piaget observed that children of different ages understand concepts and reason differently. Based on his observations, he developed a theory of cognitive development.

   D.   Several researchers have studied work motivation. They have been interested in the conditions that influence productivity and satisfaction in organizations.

   E.   In 1963, Stanley Milgram conducted a classic study on obedience to authority. In subsequent variations of the original study, Milgram and his colleagues investigated the conditions under which people might disobey.

   F.   Strupp conducted research in 1982 to examine the characteristics of effective psychotherapy. He found that the relationship between the therapist and client greatly affects the success of the therapy.

   G.   A national study of 3,000 children in fourth through tenth grades found that over this period of time girls' self-esteem plummeted (American Association of University Women, 1991). As a result of recommendations based on the findings of this and other research, changes in school systems have been suggested.

   H.   Several psychologists have studied the process of career development and use career development theories to assist college students in selecting their careers.

2.   Harold is 17 years old and has been abusing alcohol and marijuana for the past year. He has been missing school and his academic performance is declining. Harold was formerly a "B" student and was involved in sports. He is now getting D's and F's and has dropped out of most extracurricular activities. Answer the following questions: What influences would each of the five perspectives (learning, psychodynamic, biological, cognitive and sociocultural) and two movements in psychology (humanist and feminist) identify as central to the development of Harold's drug problem?

3.   Juanita is suffering from depression and she is interested in seeking professional help for her problem. Briefly describe the general types of treatment that would most likely be utilized by a psychologist, a psychiatrist, a psychoanalyst and a psychotherapist. Indicate the types of training they are likely to have had.

CHAPTER TWO

How Psychologist Do Research

LEARNING OBJECTIVES

After studying this chapter, you should be able to do the following:

1.   List the reasons research methods are important to psychologists.

2.   List and discuss the characteristics of scientific psychological research.

3.   List and discuss the characteristics of descriptive research methods.

4.   Describe and give examples of case studies, naturalistic observation, laboratory observation, tests, and surveys. Discuss the advantages and disadvantages of each.

5.   List and discuss the characteristics and limitations of correlational studies and provide examples of positive and negative correlations.

6.   Distinguish between independent and dependent variables and identify examples of each.

7.   Distinguish between experimental and control groups and discuss the use of placebos.

8.   Describe single- and double-blind studies and explain how they improve experiments.

9.   Discuss the advantages and limitations of experimental research.

10.   List and describe the types of descriptive statistics.

11.   Describe how inferential statistics are used and explain statistical significance.

12.   Compare and contrast cross-sectional and longitudinal studies.

13.   Describe the technique of meta-analysis.

14.   Discuss the principles of the ethical code for conducting research with human beings.

15.   Discuss ethical problems in research, including the use of animals and deception.

16.   Describe some of the reasons for using animals in research.

BRIEF CHAPTER SUMMARY

Chapter 2 discusses the importance of understanding scientific methodology in order to critically evaluate research findings. The text describes the characteristics of scientific research that should be used to evaluate research findings in psychology and in other fields. Three major types of research studies are described: descriptive studies, correlational studies and experimental studies. Descriptive studies include case studies, observational studies, studies based on psychological tests, and studies based on surveys. Correlational studies are a special category of descriptive studies that describe relationships between two variables. Correlational research is very useful in making predictions from one variable to another. Experimental research is the best type to determine cause and effect relationships because it is conducted in a highly controlled fashion. The components of experimental research include independent and dependent variables, random assignment to conditions, and experimental and control conditions. Potential biases in conducting research are discussed, as well as methods to reduce such bias (e.g., single-blind and double-blind studies). The text explains descriptive and inferential statistics and demonstrates how they help to make research findings meaningful. Finally, the ethical concerns revolving around studying human beings and animals are discussed.

PREVIEW OUTLINE

Before you read the chapter, review the preview outline for each section of the text. After you have read the chapter, close this book and try to <u>re-create</u> the outlines on a blank piece of paper.

I. WHAT MAKES PSYCHOLOGICAL RESEARCH SCIENTIFIC?
  A. Why are research methods so important to psychologists?
    1. Helps separate truth from unfounded belief
    2. Helps sort out conflicting views
    3. Helps correct false ideas that may cause people harm
  B. What makes research scientific?
    1. Precision
        a. Start with a theory: organized system of assumptions and principles that purports to explain certain phenomena
        b. From a hunch or theory, derive a specific hypothesis
        c. Operational definitions: terms must be defined in ways that can be observed and measured
    2. Skepticism: accept conclusions with caution but be open to new ideas
    3. Reliance on empirical evidence rather than on personal accounts
    4. Willingness to make "risky predictions" and the principle of falsifiability
    5. Openness in the scientific community so that findings can be replicated

II. DESCRIPTIVE STUDIES: ESTABLISHING THE FACTS

 A. **Case Studies - detailed descriptions of particular individuals**
   1. Advantages include producing detailed picture of one individual
   2. Disadvantages: rely on possibly inaccurate memories, cannot generalize to all human behavior, do not test hypotheses

 B. **Observational Studies – observing, recording behavior without interfering**
   1. Naturalistic observation
   2. Laboratory observation: scientist has greater control but subject might alter his or her behavior

 D. **Tests (assessment instruments) - procedures to measure personality traits, emotional states, aptitudes, interests, abilities and values**
   1. Types of tests
     a. Objective tests - measure states of which person is aware
     b. Projective tests - designed to tap unconscious
   2. Characteristics of a good test
     a. Standardization - uniform procedures for giving, scoring the test
     b. Norms - established standards of performance
     c. Reliability - getting the same results from one time to another
       (1) Test-retest - giving the same test twice
       (2) Alternate-forms - giving different versions of the same test
     d. Validity - a test measures what it set out to measure
       (1) Content validity - test questions ask about a broad array of beliefs and behaviors relevant to what is being measured
       (2) Criterion validity - predicts other measures of the trait

 E. **Surveys**
   1. Gather information by asking people directly
   2. Potential problems with surveys (e.g., bias in question wording, representativeness of sample, lying or forgetting by subjects)

III. CORRELATIONAL STUDIES: LOOKING FOR RELATIONSHIP

 A. **Purpose** – to determine whether two variables are related, and if so, how strongly
 B. **Characteristics of correlations**
   1. Direction of a relationship between variables
     a. Positive correlation - high values of one variable are associated with high values of the other; low values of one variable are associated with low values of the other
     b. Negative correlation - high values of one variable are associated with low values of the other
   2. Correlation coefficient indicates the strength of relationship between the two variables; ranges from -1 (strong negative) to +1 (strong positive)
 C. **Benefits and limitations of correlations**
   1. Benefit - allows someone to predict from one variable to another
   2. Limitation - cannot show causation

IV. EXPERIMENTS: HUNTING FOR CAUSES

A. **Purpose of experimentation** - to look for causes of behavior because the experiment allows the researcher to control the situation being studied

B. **Experimental variables** - the characteristics the researcher is studying
1. Independent variable - the characteristic manipulated by the experimenter
2. Dependent variable - the behavior the researcher tries to predict

C. **Experimental and control conditions**
1. Experimental condition - the condition or group in which subjects receive some amount of the independent variable
2. Control condition - the condition or group in which subjects do not receive any amount of the independent variable
3. Random assignment balances individual differences among subjects between the two groups

D. **Experimenter effects**
1. Single-blind studies - subjects don't know whether they are in the experimental or control group
2. Double-blind studies - neither the experimenter nor the subjects know which subjects are in which group

E. **Advantages and limitations of experiments**
1. Experiments allow conclusions about cause and effect
2. The setting is artificial and subjects' behavior may differ from real life

V. EVALUATING THE FINDINGS

A. **Descriptive statistics: Summarize group data**
1. Arithmetic mean compares group scores between two or more groups
2. Standard deviation shows how clustered or spread out individual scores are around the mean

B. **Inferential statistics: Asking "So What?"**
1. Determines the likelihood that the result of the study occurred by chance
2. Statistical significance - the result is expected to occur by chance fewer than 5 times in 100; it does not necessarily indicate real-world importance
3. Statistically significant results allow general predictions to be made about human behavior, though not about any particular individual

C. **Interpreting the findings: What is the best explanation for the findings?**
1. Researchers must test a hypothesis in different ways several times
   a. Cross-sectional studies - compare groups at one time
   b. Longitudinal studies - study subjects across the life span
2. Researchers must judge the result's importance with procedures like meta-analysis that combine and analyze data from many studies

VI. KEEPING THE ENTERPRISE ETHICAL

A. **The ethics of studying human beings**
  1. American Psychological Association's ethical code
     a. Dignity and welfare of subjects must be respected
     b. People must participate voluntarily and give informed consent
     c. Subjects must be free to withdraw from a study at any time
  2. Use of deception: Researchers are required to consider alternatives to deception, show that a study's potential value justifies the use of deception, and debrief subjects about the study's true purpose afterward

B. **The ethics of studying animals**
  1. Many purposes exist for conducting research using animals (e.g., basic research on a particular species, improve human welfare)
  2. Treatment and regulations have improved due to opposition

RESEARCH METHODS TABLE

Complete this table and compare the differences among the research methods.

RESEARCH METHOD	DEFINITION AND DESCRIPTION	EXAMPLE
CASE HISTORY		
NATURALISTIC OBSERVATION		
LABORATORY OBSERVATION		
TESTS		
SURVEY		
CORRELATIONAL STUDY		
EXPERIMENT		

PRACTICE TEST 1 - Multiple Choice

1. Introductory psychology students study research methodology to
    A. find proof for our existing beliefs so we can argue against those who disagree.
    B. be able to critically evaluate psychological findings.
    C. be able to manipulate statistics to our advantage.
    D. be able to use our own experiences as scientific proofs.

2. Which of the following is <u>NOT</u> a characteristic of scientific research?
    A. reliance on common sense   B. precision
    C. skepticism   D. openness

3. An organized system of assumptions and principles that purports to explain a specified set of phenomena is called a(n)
    A. hypothesis.   B. operational definition.
    C. theory.   D. risky prediction.

4. Which of the following is an example of a hypothesis?
    A. Alcohol decreases reaction time.
    B. Studying improves grades.
    C. Employees perform better in a supportive climate.
    D. All of the above are examples of hypotheses.

5. Defining a term in ways that can be observed and measured is known as
    A. an operational definition.   B. a theory.
    C. common sense.   D. skepticism.

6. Scores on a depression test, changes in time spent sleeping, and food intake might be
    A. hypotheses.   B. theories of depression.
    C. operational definitions of depression.   D. empirical evidence.

7. Which of the following violates the principle of falsifiability?
    A. Lack of evidence for a phenomenon is described as predictable since destroying evidence is an alleged characteristic of the phenomenon under study.
    B. Subjects in a study do not represent the larger population being described.
    C. A study uses only volunteer subjects who differ from non-volunteers.
    D. An experimenter's expectations subtly influence the outcome of a study.

8. Descriptive research methods
    A. explain behavior by identifying the causes of the behavior.
    B. allow the researcher to describe and predict behavior.
    C. include the experimental study.
    D. all of the above.

9. Freud based his theory on studying a small number of particular individuals in great detail. This research method is called a(n)
    A. survey.   B. experiment.
    C. naturalistic observation.   D. case study.

10. One disadvantage of the research method used by Freud is that
    A. it relies on memories, which can be inaccurate.
    B. it is difficult to interpret.
    C. it cannot be used to generalize about human behavior.
    D. all of the above are disadvantages.

11. Naturalistic observations involve
    A. giving subjects a series of psychological tests.
    B. assigning research participants to experimental and control groups.
    C. observing subjects in the natural environment.
    D. asking people a series of questions.

12. In the area of test construction, standardization refers to
    A. the use of uniform procedures in the administration and scoring of a test.
    B. the establishment of standards of performance.
    C. getting the same results over time.
    D. the condition that a test measures what it set out to.

13. _____ validity indicates that the test questions represent fully the trait being measured.
    A. test-retest   B. content
    C. criterion   D. alternate forms

14. Validity is to reliability as
    A. consistency is to accuracy.   B. accuracy is to consistency.
    C. criterion is to content.   D. objective is to projective.

15. You take an intelligence test on Monday and receive a high score. You repeat it on Tuesday and receive a low score. This test apparently lacks
    A. content validity.   B. criterion validity.
    C. test-retest reliability.   D. alternate forms reliability.

16. A problem with surveys is that
    A. their results can by weakened by volunteer bias.
    B. respondents may lie, forget or remember incorrectly.
    C. biases or ambiguities in the wording of questions may exist.
    D. all of the above are potential problems with surveys.

17. To conduct research on attitudes toward abortion, Dr. Kim distributes surveys to people leaving church after a service. One problem with this survey is that
    A. people are likely to lie or forget.
    B. the questions are unclear.
    C. the sample is nonrepresentative.
    D. the procedures are not uniform.

18. Correlations
    A. determine the causes of behavior.
    B. determine whether two or more phenomena are related, and if so, how strongly.
    C. can be expressed on a numeric scale from 1 to 10.
    D. require research participants to be observed in a laboratory.

19. The more Jose studies, the more his test scores improve. This is an example of
    A. a naturalistic observation.   B. a positive correlation.
    C. a negative correlation.   D. proof of causation.

20. Dr. Takahashi is studying the relationship between hair color and shoe size. She is likely to find
    A. a negative correlation.   B. a positive correlation.
    C. zero correlation.   D. it is impossible to say.

21. Based on a correlational study showing that those who exercise regularly experience lower rates of depression, which of the following conclusions can be reached?
    A. Exercise causes a reduction in depression.
    B. People who are depressed stop exercising.
    C. There is a relationship between exercise and depression.
    D. Self-esteem influences both exercise and depression levels.

22. Experimentation is
    A. a type of observational study.
    B. the only research method that looks for the causes of behavior.
    C. one of the descriptive research methods.
    D. more limited in its conclusions than the other types of methodologies.

23. The independent variable is the variable that
    A. is manipulated by the researcher.
    B. the researcher tries to predict.
    C. is defined in a way that can be observed and measured.
    D. cannot be controlled.

24. Dr. Washington is conducting research on the effects of alcohol on reaction time. She assigns students to two groups. One group receives three ounces of alcohol and the other group receives an alcohol-free beverage that looks, smells and tastes like alcohol. Following ingestion of the beverage, the reaction time of subjects in both groups is tested. Which of the variables is the dependent variable?

A. alcohol
B. control group
C. alcohol-free beverage
D. reaction time

25. In the above study, the group of research participants that receives the alcohol-free beverage is called

A. the independent variable.
B. the control group.
C. the experimental group.
D. the random group.

26. In the study described in question 24, neither Dr. Washington nor the research participants knew whether they were in the experimental or control group. This type of study is called a

A. single-blind study.
B. longitudinal study.
C. double-blind study.
D. case study.

27. The purpose of single- and double-blind studies is to

A. control for the effects of volunteer subjects.
B. equate subjects in the experimental and control groups.
C. utilize a placebo.
D. control for the expectations of subjects in a single-blind study and the expectations of both subjects and experimenter in a double-blind study.

28. The arithmetic mean and standard deviation are

A. types of descriptive statistics.
B. inferential statistics.
C. examples of meta-analyses.
D. statistically significant.

29. Inferential statistics

A. summarize individual data into group data.
B. combine data from many studies.
C. study abilities across the life span.
D. tell the researcher the likelihood that the result of the study occurred by chance.

30. In an experiment on teaching methods, subjects in the experimental group received a mean score of 84, and subjects in the control group received a mean score of 77. Before the experimenters can say whether the new technique was superior in this study, they must
   A. calculate the statistical significance of the results to evaluate the probability that this result could have happened by chance.
   B. conduct a meta-analysis.
   C. calculate the statistical significance to determine the real-world importance.
   D. conduct a longitudinal study to see if the improved learning lasts.

31. Cross-sectional studies differ from longitudinal studies in that
   A. cross-sectional studies compare different groups at one time, whereas longitudinal studies examine abilities across the life span.
   B. cross-sectional studies examine groups in the laboratory, whereas longitudinal studies examine behavior in the natural environment.
   C. cross-sectional studies examine abilities across the life span, whereas longitudinal studies compare different groups at one time.
   D. cross-sectional studies cannot establish cause and effect, whereas longitudinal studies can.

32. Meta-analyses are helpful in the interpretation of research findings because they
   A. determine which studies are accurate and which are not.
   B. combine data from many studies.
   C. establish whether the findings have any real-world importance.
   D. establish the statistical significance of studies.

33. For ethical purposes, researchers must show they have considered alternative procedures and that they plan to debrief subjects in order to use
   A. animals.
   B. more than one experimental condition.
   C. an informed consent.
   D. deception.

34. Dr. Milner is conducting a study in which a co-researcher pretends to trip and fall in the presence of research subjects who are taking a reading comprehension test. The subjects have been told the study is on memory, but Dr. Milner is really studying the circumstances under which strangers provide assistance to others. According to ethical principles, Dr. Milner
   A. must demonstrate that his study's potential value justifies the use of deception.
   B. may not continue with this study no matter what he does because it is unethical to be dishonest with the subjects.
   C. never needs to disclose the true purpose of the study to the subjects.
   D. needs only show that no harm will come to the subjects.

35. Psychologists use animals in research
    A. because sometimes practical or ethical considerations prevent the use of human beings as subjects.
    B. to discover practical applications.
    C. to conduct basic research on a particular species.
    D. all of the above are reasons that animals are used in research.

PRACTICE TEST 2 - Short Answer

1. Research methods are important to psychologists because they help separate truth from _____.

2. "Students who spend more time studying perform better in college." This is an example of a _____.

3. Dr. Sanchez is conducting a study on the effects of anxiety on test performance. She is using subjects' scores on a stress test as her _____ definition of anxiety.

4. Any theory that cannot in principle be refuted violates the _____.

5. Scientists must discuss ideas, testing procedures and results so their findings can be _____ to reduce fraud and error.

6. Research methods that allow psychologists to describe and predict behavior but not to explain its causes are _____ methods.

7. A detailed description of particular individuals that is based on careful observation refers to the _____ research method.

8. Often scientists need a good description of behavior as it occurs in the natural environment before they can explain it. This is the primary purpose of _____.

9. _____ tests measure beliefs, behavior, and feelings of which the person is aware, whereas _____ tests are designed to tap the unconscious.

10. To be meaningful, a person's test score should be compared to established standards of performance called _____.

11. At 8:00 a.m. Hank weighs 179 pounds. He moves the scale slightly and decides to weigh himself again. Though it's only a minute later, he now weighs 177. Hank's scale lacks the test characteristic of _____.

12. A test that purports to measure personality, but actually measures verbal abilities lacks _____.

13. If SAT scores are able to accurately predict students' grade point averages, then the SAT is demonstrating that it has _____.

14. A survey on alcohol use among college students reported that alcohol use among students had dramatically decreased. Later the study reported that the subjects were female students from one expensive Ivy League university. This survey did not use a _____ sample of college students.

15. Often one drawback to surveys is that those who agree to participate may differ from those who do not. A psychologist would say these surveys suffer from _____ bias.

16. A _____ is the numerical measure of the strength and direction of the relationship between two _____.

17. Height and weight are _____ correlated, however, this correlation does not show _____ between the two variables.

18. When psychologists want to look for causes of behavior, they must use a more controlled method called the _____.

19. In an experiment on caffeine and alertness, caffeine intake would be the _____ variable and alertness would be the _____ variable.

20. In the study described in question 19, the subjects who receive caffeinated coffee are in the _____ group whereas those who receive decaffeinated coffee are in the _____ group.

21. The decaffeinated coffee is a _____ , which is used for the control group subjects' _____.

22. A study is called _____-blind when the subjects do not know whether they are in the experimental or control group.

23. Numbers summarizing the data we collect from subjects are called _____ statistics.

24. If the result of a study is unlikely to have happened by chance, then we say the result is statistically _____.

25. Research in which groups are all compared at the same time is called _____; in _____ studies, people are followed over a period of time and reassessed at periodic intervals.

PRACTICE TEST 3 - Essay

1.   Determine which research method is best for each situation below and explain why.

   A.   Determine the favorite foods of adolescents.
   B.   Determine whether a person is introverted or extroverted.
   C.   Determine whether or not frustration causes aggression.
   D.   Determine whether level of education is associated with criminal behavior.
   E.   Determine conversational patterns of men and women.
   F.   Determine why a violinist gave up a flourishing career in business to play in the local symphony.
   G.   Determine the parenting patterns used on a child who is having behavior problems and whose parents cannot control him.

2.   In the following experiments identify: 1) a possible hypothesis, 2) the independent and dependent variables, 3) their operational definitions, and 4) experimental and control conditions.

   A.   A study was conducted on the effects of caffeine on studying. Experimental subjects were given 32 ounces of caffeine. Subjects in the control group were given a decaffeinated beverage that looked and tasted like the beverage consumed by the experimental group. After consuming the drinks, all subjects were provided with a chapter of a text to read and then were tested.
   B.   A study was conducted on the effects of types of music on aggressive behavior. There were three experimental groups: one listened to classical music, the second listened to jazz, and the third listened to heavy metal music. Subjects in the control condition were exposed to a white noise machine for the same period of time. Following exposure to the 45-minute music session, all subjects were put in a situation in which they were able to engage in aggressive behavior (punch a punching bag).
   C.   A study was conducted on the effects of exercise on relaxation. There were two experimental groups of subjects. One group engaged in supervised aerobic exercise for 45 minutes. The second experimental group engaged in sit-ups and push-ups for 45 minutes. The control group engaged in a supervised study session. Following the exposure, all subjects were told to wait in a room for the experimenter to return. During this period, they were hooked up to medical equipment monitoring their heart rate, muscle tension, respiration and blood pressure.

3.   Among the following examples, identify which correlations are positive, negative or zero.

        A.   Height and weight
        B.   Smoking and health
        C.   Studying and drop-out rates
        D.   SAT score and grade point average (GPA)
        E.   Education level and height
        F.   Smoking and education level
        G.   Alcohol intake and reaction time
        H.   Alcohol intake and automobile accidents
        I.   Delinquency and education level
        J.   Weight and schizophrenia

4.   After reviewing the ethical guidelines adopted by the American Psychological Association (APA), determine which of the following research practices are ethical or unethical and explain why:

        A.   Require psychology students to participate as subjects in a research study.
        B.   Tell subjects that once they begin a study as a research subject, they must continue until the research is complete.
        C.   Withhold information about the hypothesis and research purposes.
        D.   Deliberately misrepresent research purposes.
        E.   Use animals to check the side-effects of a drug thought to cure depression.
        F.   Carry out a study that causes discomfort in people after securing informed consent that includes full information about possible risks.

6.   Distinguish between independent and dependent variables and identify examples of each.

7.   Distinguish between experimental and control groups and discuss the use of placebos.

8.   Describe single-blind and double-blind studies and explain how they improve experiments.

9.   Discuss the advantages and limitations of experimental research.

CHAPTER THREE

Evolution, Genes, and Behavior

LEARNING OBJECTIVES

1.   Describe two historical positions advanced to explain human similarities and differences.

2.   Distinguish among genes, chromosomes and DNA.

3.   Describe how the basic elements of DNA affect the characteristics of the organism.

4.   Describe one type of research used to search for genes associated with many physical and mental conditions.

5   Explain how natural selection accounts for many similarities among humans.

6.   Explain the assumption that the mind develops as independent "modules."

7.   Describe the approach of evolutionary psychology.

8.   Describe evidence for Chomsky's position on language acquisition as well as the evidence for the role of learning in language acquisition based on artificial neural networks.

9.   Explain sociobiologists' and evolutionary psychologists' views on mating and marriage.

10.   Cite evidence for and against evolutionary approaches to mating and marriage.

11.   Define and discuss the characteristics of heritability and describe how it is studied.

13.   Summarize heritability estimates for intelligence and environmental factors that influence intelligence.

14.   Summarize the debate and research explaining the differences in IQ between blacks and whites, including errors in the interpretation of research findings.

15.   Summarize the prevailing ideas about the role of nature and nurture in explaining similarities and differences among people.

BRIEF CHAPTER SUMMARY

Chapter 3 examines the biological and evolutionary bases of behavior. Evolutionary psychology emphasizes the evolutionary mechanisms that might help explain commonalities in human behavior. Genetic operations and the principle of natural selection contribute to the understanding of commonalities among humans. Language acquisition shares similar features across cultures, suggesting that this is an innate capacity. Evolutionary psychologists (and sociobiologists) argue that certain social behaviors, such as courtship and mating, also have a biological base and serve an evolutionary function. A discussion of heritability helps explain differences among human beings. Heritability is used in an analysis of intelligence. Common misuses of heritability are discussed, along with the difficulties and complexities of behavioral-genetic research. The complexities of human behavior do not allow for simple "either-or" explanations, and the chapter demonstrates the need to be able to tolerate uncertainty in the exploration of the origins of human behavior.

PREVIEW OUTLINE

Before you read the chapter, review the preview outline for each section of the text. After you have read the chapter, close this book and try to re-create the outlines on a blank piece of paper.

I. **UNLOCKING THE SECRETS OF GENES**
   A. **Explaining human similarities and differences**
      1. Two main camps- Those who emphasized genes or nature, and those who focused on experience or nurture
      2. Current position recognizes interaction of heredity and environment
   B. **Definition and characteristics of genes**
      1. Definition - basic units of heredity
      2. Characteristics
         a. Located on chromosomes, each of which contains thousands of genes; all body cells contain 23 chromosome pairs
         b. Chromosomes consist of strands of DNA; genes consist of small segments of this DNA
         c. Some genes are inherited in the same form by everyone; others vary contributing to our individuality
   C. **How elements of DNA affect characteristics of the organism**
      1. Each gene has four basic chemical elements of DNA (A,T,C,G)
      2. The order of arrangement helps determine the synthesis of one of the many proteins that affect every aspect of the body

D. The search for genes that contribute to specific traits
1. It is very difficult to identify a single gene
2. Most traits depend on more than one pair of genes, which makes tracking down the genetic contributions to a trait very difficult
3. Linkage studies - look at genes located close together that may be inherited together across generations
4. Researchers with The Human Genome Project are trying to map the entire human genome, which consists of 3 billion units of DNA
5. Even when a gene is located, its role in physical and psychological functioning is not automatically known

II. THE GENETICS OF SIMILARITY
A. Evolutionary psychologists - apply principles of evolution to human psychological qualities and behavior
B. Evolution and natural selection - general characteristics
1. Definition- A change in the gene frequencies within a population over many generations
2. Why do frequencies change?
   a. Variations arise as genes spontaneously mutate and recombine
   b. Charles Darwin's natural selection: As individuals with a genetically influenced trait become more successful at surviving and reproducing in a particular environment, their genes will become more common and may spread
3. Approach of evolutionary psychology
   a. Asks what challenges humans faced in prehistoric past and draws inferences about behaviors that might have evolved to solve survival problems - evaluates the inferences using research
   b. Assumes the human mind evolved as a collection of specialized modules to handle specific survival problems
C. Innate human characteristics - Common evolutionary history may explain universal abilities such as infant reflexes, attraction to novelty, motive to explore

III. OUR HUMAN HERITAGE: LANGUAGE
A. The nature of language
1. Definition - language is a set of rules for combining elements that are in themselves meaningless into utterances that convey meaning
2. Humans seem to be the only species that acquires language naturally and that can combine sounds to produce original sentences
3. Some non-human animals can be taught aspects of language

B.   The innate capacity for language
1.   Noam Chompsky - changed thinking about how language is acquired
  a.   Language is not learned bit by bit, but with language acquisition device, or "mental module" in the brain
  b.   Children learn surface structure - the way a sentence is spoken - and deep structure - the meaning of a sentence
  c.   Though rules of grammar (syntax) aren't taught to children, they use them to transform surface structures into deep structures
  d.   Psycholinguists' arguments to support Chomsky's position
    (1)   Children in different cultures go through similar stages of language development - born with a universal grammar
    (2)   Children make errors called overregularizations that adults would not, so they are not simply imitating
    (3)   Adults do not consistently correct children's syntax yet children learn to speak correctly
    (4)   Even profoundly retarded children acquire language
    (5)   Infants as young as 7 months can derive simple linguistic rules from a string of sounds
2.   Researchers are trying to identify brain modules and genes involved in language acquisition

C.   Learning and language - experience also plays a role in language
1.   Parents recast or expand on children's sentences, which are then repeated
2.   Biologically determined critical period for learning language

IV.   OUR HUMAN HERITAGE: COURTSHIP AND MATING
A.   Agreement about the role of evolution in simple behaviors, disagreement about complex social behaviors
B.   Evolution and sexual strategies
1.   Sociobiologists believes that gender differences in courtship and mating evolved in response to a species' survival needs
2.   Males and females have faced different survival and mating problems, which has led to differences in behaviors according to sociobiologists
  a.   Males compete for fertile females; females need to "shop" for the male with the best genes since their childbearing is limited
  b.   This may explain why males are more promiscuous than females
C.   Culture and the "genetic leash" – the relative power of biology and culture
1.   Critics of evolutionary approach argue that
  a.   Evolutionary explanations of sexual behaviors are based on stereotypes and actual behaviors often contradict these descriptions
  b.   Among humans, sexual behavior is varied and changeable
2.   Critics worry that evolutionary arguments will be used to justify inequalities and violence

V. THE GENETICS OF DIFFERENCE

A. **The meaning of heritability**- estimates of the proportion of the total variance in a trait that is attributable to genetic variation within a group

B. **Facts about heritability**
1. Heritability estimates apply only to a particular group living in a particular environment, and estimates may differ for different groups
2. Heritability estimates do <u>not</u> apply to individuals, <u>only</u> to variations within a group
3. Even highly heritable traits can be modified by the environment

C. **Computing heritability**
1. Can't estimate heritability directly; must study people whose degree of genetic similarity is known
2. Researchers study those who share either genes or environments; adopted children, identical twins reared apart, and fraternal twins

VI. OUR HUMAN DIVERSITY: ORIGINS OF INTELLIGENCE

A. **Genes and individual differences**
1. Concept of IQ is controversial and IQ tests are criticized
2. Intelligence that produces high IQ scores is highly heritable

B. **The question of group differences**
1. Focus has been on black-white differences in IQ scores and the research has been used for political purposes
2. Between-group studies: problems and conclusions
   a. Heritability estimates based on differences <u>within</u> group cannot be used to compare differences <u>between</u> groups
   b. Black-white IQ differences are influenced by the environment
   c. Sound methodological studies do not reveal genetic differences between blacks and whites

C. **The environment and intelligence**
1. Factors associated with reduced mental ability include poor prenatal care, malnutrition, exposure to toxins, and stressful family circumstances
2. Healthy and stimulating environment can raise mental performance

PRACTICE TEST 1 - Multiple Choice

1.	Historically, those who agree with the nature position and those who believe in the nurture approach
	A.	both agree with sociobiologists.
	B.	are both evolutionary psychologists.
	C.	disagree about the relative importance of nature and nurture in explaining human differences.
	D.	work together to develop the field of behavioral genetics.

2.	Evolutionary psychology and sociobiology
	A.	are branches of behavioral genetics.
	B.	both focus on evolutionary influences on behaviors.
	C.	have very little in common.
	D.	emphasize the role of the environment.

3.	Dr. Ricardo is studying how evolutionary mechanisms might help explain commonalities in language learning, attention, and perception. He is a(n)
	A.	behavioral geneticist.			B.	sociobiologist.
	C.	evolutionary psychologist.			D.	empiricist.

4.	Genes are
	A.	rod-shaped structures found in every cell of the body.
	B.	thread-like strands that make up chromosomes.
	C.	one of the four basic elements of DNA.
	D.	the basic units of heredity.

5.	Chromosomes are
	A.	rod-shaped structures found in every cell of the body.
	B.	located on genes.
	C.	one of the four basic elements of DNA.
	D.	the basic units of heredity.

6.	The full set of genes contained in each cell is the
	A.	DNA.					B.	chromosome.
	C.	genome.					D.	basis.

7.	When a sperm and egg unite at conception, the fertilized egg, and all the body cells that eventually develop from it (except for sperm cells and ova) contain
	A.	46 pairs of chromosomes.			B.	23 chromosomes.
	C.	46 chromosomes in 23 pairs.			D.	23 pairs of genes.

8. Which statement describes the relationship between genes, chromosomes and DNA?
   A. Genes, the basic unit of heredity, are located on chromosomes, which consist of strands of DNA. Genes consist of small segments of DNA molecules.
   B. Genes are composed of chromosomes and DNA.
   C. Chromosomes, the basic unit of heredity, direct the genes and the DNA.
   D. DNA houses both genes and chromosomes in its rod-shaped structures.

9. Most human traits depend on
   A. more than one pair of genes.
   B. a single pair of genes.
   C. one gene.
   D. between 5 and 10 pairs of genes.

10. Dr. Sayeed is trying to track down the genetic contributions to eye color. Which of the following is likely to be true?
   A. Because it is a simple trait, probably a single pair of genes is responsible.
   B. Most human traits, even simple ones, depend on more than one pair of genes.
   C. She can locate the gene or genes through using a high resolution microscope.
   D. She will have to map the entire human genome.

11. In search of a genetic marker for Huntington's disease, researchers studied large families in which this condition was common. This type of study is called a(n)
   A. case study.   B. linkage study.
   C. evolutionary study. D. family research.

12. One reason that new traits keep arising is because of genes' ability to spontaneously.
   A. divide   B. multiply
   C. split   D. mutate

13. Within each gene, elements of DNA are arranged in a particular order, which forms a code that influences the synthesis of particular proteins. This affects every aspect of the body, from its structure to the chemicals that keep it running. This process describes
   A. linkage studies.
   B. how genes affect characteristics of the organism.
   C. how genes mutate.
   D. how natural selection occurs.

14. As gene frequencies change within a population over generations, certain genetically influenced characteristics become more or less common. This refers to
   A. evolution.   B. natural selection.
   C. sociobiology.   D. heritability.

15. A way to explain WHY gene frequencies change is the idea that individuals with traits that are adaptive in an environment will stay alive to reproduce, and over generations their genes will become more common. This describes
   A.   evolution.   B.   natural selection.
   C.   sociobiology.   D.   heritability.

16. Psycholinguists suggest that by applying rules that make up the grammar of language, we are able to understand and produce new sentences correctly. These rules are called
   A.   surface structure.   B.   overregularizations.
   C.   syntax.   D.   mental modules.

17. "Lee gave the ball to Lynne," and "Lynne received the ball from Lee" have
   A.   the same surface structure.
   B.   different deep structures.
   C.   the same surface and deep structures.
   D.   the same deep structure.

18. Though they are learning different languages, Lana from Morocco, Ayse from Turkey and Paulo from Italy are going through similar stages of language development and combine words in ways that adults never would. This supports the conclusion that
   A.   language is learned in bits and pieces.
   B.   the syntax of all languages is remarkably similar.
   C.   the brain contains a language acquisition device that allows children to develop language if they are exposed to an adequate sampling of speech.
   D.   language acquisition is primarily the result of imitation of speech.

19. Chomsky's contribution to the understanding of language acquisition was the idea that
   A.   language is learned bit by bit, as one might learn a list of U.S. presidents.
   B.   there is a critical period for learning language.
   C.   children go through different stages of language development.
   D.   language is too complex to learn bit by bit, so there must be a "mental module" in the brain that allows young children to develop language.

20. Which of the following supports Chomsky's position on language acquisition?
   A.   Children everywhere go through similar stages of linguistic development.
   B.   Children combine words in ways adults never would, which rules out imitation.
   C.   Even children who are profoundly retarded acquire language.
   D.   All of the above support Chomsky's position on language acquisition.

21. Which of the following reflects the sociobiological view on mating and marriage?
   A.   Marriage and mating behaviors have been learned through reinforcements.
   B.   Males and females have faced different kinds of survival and mating problems and have evolved differently in aggressiveness and sexual strategies.
   C.   Socialization accounts for differences in mating behaviors.
   D.   None of the above reflects the sociobiological position.

22. "It pays for males to compete for access to fertile females and to try to inseminate as many females as possible; because females can conceive and bear only a limited number of offspring, it pays for them to be selective and look for the best mate." This reflects the position of
    A. outdated psychologists.
    B. an empiricist.
    C. sociobiology.
    D. Chomsky.

23. Critics of the evolutionary approach cite which of the following positions to support their view?
    A. Though humans and animals may engage in similar behaviors, the motives or origins of the behaviors differ.
    B. Not all animal and human behavior conforms to the sexual stereotypes.
    C. Among human beings, sexual behavior is extremely varied and changeable.
    D. All of the above are arguments used by critics of the evolutionary approach.

24. Heritability
    A. estimates the proportion of difference in a trait that is attributable to genetic variation within a group.
    B. is equivalent in meaning to the term genetic.
    C. estimates the proportion of a trait that is attributable to genes in an individual.
    D. estimates the proportion of difference in a trait that is attributable to genetic variation between groups.

25. Heritability can be used to estimate
    A. IQ differences between whites and Asians.
    B. IQ differences among Harvard graduates.
    C. how much of an individual's IQ is determined by heredity.
    D. exactly which genes are responsible for intelligence.

26. To study the heritability of a particular trait, which groups of people are studied?
    A. adopted children and twins   B. unrelated people
    C. biological mothers and daughters   D. husbands and wives

27. Heritability estimates of intelligence for children and adolescents
    A. are very low since IQ is shaped primarily by environmental influences.
    B. vary widely, but they have an average of .50.
    C. have an average of .90
    D. have an average of .10

28. Pete is adopting a child whose biological parents have low IQs. Pete asks whether this child is also likely to have a low IQ. Which of the following is the best response?
    A. The child is also quite likely to have a low IQ, since heritability of IQ is high.

B. The IQs of the child's biological parents are irrelevant, since environmental influences outweigh heritability.

C. While IQ is at least in part heritable, environmental influences can have a great impact; however, it is impossible to make predictions about any individual.

D. Nothing is known about the heritability of IQ.

29. Which of the following is a flaw in genetic theories of black-white differences in IQ?
A. Blacks and whites do not grow up, on average, in the same kind of environment.
B. Because of racial discrimination and de facto segregation, black children receive less encouragement and fewer opportunities than whites.
C. Heritability estimates based on one group (whites) are used to estimate the role heredity plays in differences between groups.
D. All of the above are flaws.

30. Children fathered by black and white American soldiers in Germany after World War II, and reared in similar German communities by similar families, did not differ significantly in IQ. This study
A. supports genetic theories explaining black-white IQ differences.
B. refutes genetic theories explaining black-white IQ differences.
C. has been criticized for methodological errors.
D. demonstrates the IQ superiority of blacks over whites.

31. Two pots of tomatoes were planted with seeds of identical quality. One pot used enriched soil and one pot used impoverished soil. A comparison of the plants from each of these pots is analogous to
A. comparing the IQs of two Asian-Americans from similar socioeconomic backgrounds, communities and school systems.
B. looking for a genetic explanation of IQ differences between blacks and whites.
C. comparing the IQs of two siblings.
D. None of the above

32. Which of the following is an environmental influence on IQ that can have a negative impact on mental ability?
A. poor prenatal care   B. malnutrition
C. exposure to toxins   D. all of the above

PRACTICE TEST 2 - Short Answer

1. _____ are the basic units of heredity, and they are located on _____.

2. Collectively, the 100,000 or so human genes are referred to as the human _____.

3. To find the gene responsible for Huntington's disease, researchers studied large families in which this condition was common. This approach is called a _____ study.

4. _____ psychologists try to explain commonalities in language learning, perception memory, sexuality, and many other aspects of behavior.

5. As genes become more common or less common in the population, so do the characteristics they influence. This is referred to as _____.

6. Gene frequencies in a population change because genes spontaneously _____.

7. The principle of _____ says that individuals with a particular genetically influenced trait tend to be more successful at staying alive long enough to produce offspring; their genes will become more and more common in the population.

8. Evolutionary psychologists believe that the human mind developed as a collection of specialized and independent _____ to handle specific survival problems.

9. Evolutionary psychologists believe that certain abilities, tendencies, and characteristics evolved because they were useful to our ancestors. Two of these abilities or tendencies include _____ and _____.

10. Language is a set of _____ for combining meaningless _____ into utterances that convey meaning.

11. "Mary kissed John" and "John was kissed by Mary" have the same _____ structure but a different _____ structure.

12. _____ said that language was far too complex to be learned bit by bit. Therefore, there must be an innate mental module for learning language called a language _____ device.

13. One piece of evidence that children have an innate mental module for language is that children in different cultures go through _____ of linguistic development.

14. The fact that children who are not exposed to language until late childhood rarely speak normally supports the idea that there is a _____ in language development during the first few years of life.

15. _____ believe that human gender differences in courtship and mating evolved in response to our species' survival needs.

16. Evolutionary psychologists differ from sociobiologists in that they tend to argue less by _____ and focus on the _____ in human mating and dating practices around the world.

17. Critics of evolutionary approaches to infidelity and monogamy argue that these explanations are based on _____ of gender differences.

18. The proportion of the total variance in a trait that is attributable to genetic variation within a group is called _____.

19. Heritability estimates do not apply to _____.

20. To estimate the heritability of a trait, researchers study _____ children and _____ twins.

21. For children and adolescents, heritability estimates of intelligence average around _____ and the estimates for adults are in the _____ range.

22. Genetic explanations for differences in intelligence between blacks and whites are flawed because they use estimates based on a white sample to estimate the role of heredity in _____ differences.

23. Negative environmental influences on mental ability include poor _____ care and _____.

PRACTICE TEST 3 - Essay

1. A. You are working in a drug treatment program. You hear many clients in this program describe their alcoholic family backgrounds and state their belief that their alcoholism is genetic. Using information about genes, chromosomes and DNA, give a general description of how this might be possible.
    B. You attend a lecture in which an author of a self-help book on alcoholism says that alcoholism is fifty percent inherited and, therefore, if you have an alcoholic parent, you have a fifty percent chance of becoming an alcoholic. Discuss the problems with these statements using the facts about heritability.
    C. If you wanted to search for the genes associated with alcoholism, describe the type of study you would conduct and how you would go about collecting your data.

2. Using the approach of evolutionary psychology, expand on the idea that the following characteristics were inherited because they were useful during the history of our species (i.e., they had an evolutionary function).
    A. the feeling of disgust
    B. intuition
    C. self-concept
    D. kinship
    E. male promiscuity
    F. female selectivity

3. Compare Chomsky's position with an earlier position on the acquisition of language and use arguments to support this view.

4. A. Describe a study that you would design to evaluate the heritability of intelligence. Describe your conclusions about both hereditary and environmental influences on intelligence. What cautionary statements would you make about the heritability estimate?
    B. Based on your research findings, you are to make recommendations to a federal panel convened to develop a parental training program for low-income families to help them promote intellectual development in their children. Discuss the recommendations you would make to the panel.

CHAPTER FOUR

Neurons, Hormones, and the Brain

LEARNING OBJECTIVES

1.   List and describe the features and functions of the central and peripheral nervous systems.

2.   Distinguish between the somatic and autonomic nervous systems.

3.   Distinguish between the sympathetic and parasympathetic nervous systems.

4.   Describe the structure of a neuron and explain how impulses are transmitted from one neuron to another.

5.   Describe recent research on stem cells and neurogenesis.

6.   Describe the roles of neurotransmitters and endorphins.

7.   Describe the functioning of hormones, specifically those in which psychologists are especially interested.

8.   List and describe techniques psychologists use to study brain functions.

9.   List and describe the location and function of each of the major portions of the brain.

10.   Summarize the functions of the brain's two hemispheres and explain their relationship.

11.   Describe the general position taken by neuroscientists on the self, and discuss two specific approaches advanced by scientists to explain the sense of a unified self.

12.   Summarize the evidence on whether there are sex differences in the brain and how any differences might affect behavior.

13.   Describe the effect of experience on brain development.

BRIEF CHAPTER SUMMARY

Chapter 4 reviews the brain and nervous system. The central nervous system is composed of the brain and spinal cord. It receives incoming messages from the senses, processes that information, and sends output to the muscles and organs. The nerves in the rest of the body are part of the peripheral nervous system, which is composed of the somatic nervous system, which permits sensation and voluntary actions, and the autonomic nervous system, which regulates glands, internal organs, and blood vessels. The autonomic nervous system is composed of the sympathetic nervous system, which mobilizes the body for action, and the parasympathetic nervous system, which conserves energy. The nervous system is made up of nerve cells or neurons. A neuron's key components are dendrites, the cell body, and an axon, which ends in axon terminals. A neural message goes from dendrites to axon via an electrical impulse. Neurons communicate with other neurons through chemicals called neurotransmitters. They are released by one neuron and temporarily received by another at the synapse, a tiny space between two neurons. A variety of methods for mapping the brain, such as EEG, TMS, PET scans, and MRI, are discussed. Different brain structures and their functions are explained, along with general issues about how the brain processes information. Research on split-brain patients, who have had the corpus callosum cut, is discussed, along with the insights into hemispheric specialization.

PREVIEW OUTLINE

Before you read the chapter, review the preview outline for each section of the text. After you have read the chapter, close this book and try to <u>re-create</u> the outlines on a blank piece of paper.

I. **THE NERVOUS SYSTEM: A BASIC BLUEPRINT**
    A.   **The central nervous system (CNS)**
        1.   Functions - receives, processes, interprets and stores incoming information; sends out messages to muscles, glands, internal organs
        2.   Parts - brain and spinal cord (an extension of the brain which can produce automatic reflexes without the help of the brain)
    B.   **The peripheral nervous system (PNS)** - handles the input and output of the CNS
        1.   Functions
            a.   Sensory neurons - bring input to CNS from skin, muscles, organs
            b.   Motor neurons - carry output to muscles, glands and organs
        2.   Divisions
            a.   Somatic system (also called skeletal nervous system)
            b.   Autonomic system - regulates blood vessels, glands, organs
                (1)   Sympathetic nervous system - mobilizes body for action
                (2)   Parasympathetic nervous system - slows action

II. COMMUNICATION IN THE NERVOUS SYSTEM

    A.   **Components of the nervous system** – include both neurons and glial cells

    B.   **The structure of the neuron**

         1.   Dendrites - receive messages from other neurons, transmit to cell body

         2.   Cell body - keeps the neuron alive, determines whether to fire

         3.   Axon - transmit messages from cell body to neurons, muscles or glands

         4.   Nerves - bundles of nerve fibers in the PNS

    C.   **How neurons communicate**

         1.   Synapse - axon terminal, synaptic cleft, membrane of receiving dendrite

         2.   Neural impulses - how neurons communicate

             a.   Electrical impulse, or action potential

             b.   Synaptic vesicles release chemical neurotransmitters

             c.   They excite or inhibit the firing of the receiving neuron

             d.   Neurons either fire or do not fire (all or none)

    D.   **Chemical messengers in the nervous system**

         1.   Neurotransmitters- Versatile couriers

             a.   Each binds only to certain types of receptor sites

             b.   Some better understood neurotransmitters and some of their effects

                 (1)   Serotonin - sleep, mood, and other behaviors

                 (2)   Dopamine - movement, learning, memory, emotion

                 (3)   Acetylcholine - muscle action, memory, emotion, cognition

                 (4)   Norepinephrine - heart rate, learning, memory, emotion

                 (5)   GABA - inhibitory neurotransmitter

         2.   Endorphins- The brain's natural opiates (endogenous opioid peptides) reduce pain, promote pleasure as well as other behaviors

         3.   Hormones- Long-distance messengers

             a.   Produced in endocrine glands and released into the bloodstream

             b.   Some may also be classified as neurotransmitters

             c.   Hormones of interest to psychologists include melatonin (regulates biological rhythms), adrenal hormones (related to emotion and stress), and sex hormones (androgens, estrogens, progesterone)

III. MAPPING THE BRAIN - methods for studying the brain
    A.   **Lesion method** - damaging or removing section of brain in animals
    B.   **Electrode methods - detect electrical activity of the neurons**
        1.   Electroencephalogram (EEG)
        2.   Needle electrodes and microelectrodes
    C.   **Positron-Emission Tomography - PET scan**
        1.   Records biochemical changes in the brain as they occur
        2.   Utilizes a radioactive substance to indicate brain activity
    D.   **Magnetic Resonance Imaging (MRI)**
        1.   Uses magnetic fields and radio frequencies
        2.   New "functional MRI" captures brain changes very quickly
    E.   **Cautions about brain research**
        1.   Findings are difficult to interpret
        2.   Results don't tell us what is happening inside the person's head

IV. A TOUR THROUGH THE BRAIN
    A.   **Localization of function** - different brain parts perform different tasks
    B.   **The brain stem** - rises out of spinal cord
        1.   Medulla - regulates automatic functions; breathing and heart rate
        2.   Pons - regulates sleeping, waking, and dreaming
        3.   Reticular activating system - network of neurons, extends upward and connects with higher brain areas; screens information, alertness
    C.   **The cerebellum** – atop brain stem; regulates balance and coordination of muscle movement; may play a role in remembering skills, analyzing sensory information
    D.   **The thalamus** - relays motor impulses out of brain, directs incoming sensory messages to higher centers
    E.   **The hypothalamus and pituitary gland**
        1.   Hypothalamus - associated with survival drives, such as hunger, thirst, emotion, sex and reproduction, body temperature
        2.   Pituitary gland - "master gland" governed by hypothalamus
    F.   **Limbic system** - loosely interconnected structures involved in emotions
        1.   Amygdala - evaluates sensory information to determine its importance
        2.   Hippocampus - allows formation and storage of new memories
    G.   **Cerebrum** - site of higher forms of thinking
        1.   Divided into two halves or cerebral hemispheres that are connected by a band of fibers called the corpus callosum
            a.   Each hemisphere controls opposite side of the body
            b.   Each hemisphere has somewhat different talents (lateralization)
        2.   Cerebral cortex - layers of densely packed cells covering the cerebrum
            a.   Occipital lobes - contain the visual cortex
            b.   Parietal lobes - contain somatosensory cortex
            c.   Temporal lobes - involved in memory, perception and emotion
            d.   Frontal lobes - contain the motor cortex; responsible for making plans and thinking creatively, Broca's area (speech production)

V. THE TWO HEMISPHERES OF THE BRAIN

A. **Split brains: A house divided**
1. Normal brain - the two hemispheres communicate via the corpus callosum
2. Split brain refers to surgery in which the corpus callosum is severed
3. Daily lives of split-brain patients were not much affected, but effects on perception and memory are observable under experimental conditions

B. **A question of dominance**
1. Many researchers believe the left side is dominant because cognitive skills, including language, rational and analytic abilities, originate here
2. Others point to abilities of the right hemisphere: superior spatial-visual abilities, facial recognition, nonverbal sounds, music appreciation
3. Differences are relative; in real life, the hemispheres cooperate

VI. TWO STUBBORN ISSUES IN BRAIN RESEARCH

A. **Where is the self?**
1. Most neuroscientists believe that the mind can be explained in physical terms as a product of the cerebral cortex
2. One theorist suggests the brain consists of independent parts that deal with different aspects of thought; another suggests that a unified self is an illusion and that the brain is independent modules working in parallel

B. **Are there "his" and "hers" brains?**
1. Efforts to identify male-female differences have reflected biases
2. Some evidence that male and female brains are physically different, but many conclusions can be drawn and findings often have changed
3. Problems exist with conclusions drawn by popular writers about sex differences in the brain

Complete this chart by identifying the function that corresponds to the brain structure listed in the left column.

BRAIN STRUCTURE	FUNCTION
BRAIN STEM	
Medulla	
Pons	
Reticular Activating System	
CEREBELLUM	
THALAMUS	
Olfactory Bulb	
HYPOTHALAMUS	
PITUITARY GLAND	
LIMBIC SYSTEM	
Amygdala	
Hippocampus	
CEREBRUM	
Left Cerebral Hemisphere	
Right Cerebral Hemisphere	
Corpus Callosum	
Cerebral Cortex	
Occipital Lobes	
Temporal Lobes	
Parietal Lobes	
Frontal Lobes	
Association Areas	

PRACTICE TEST 1 - Multiple Choice

1. The function of the central nervous system is
   A. to receive, process and interpret incoming information.
   B. to send out messages to muscles.
   C. to send out messages to glands and organs.
   D. all of the above.

2. The peripheral nervous system
   A. is made up of the brain and spinal cord.
   B. handles the central nervous system's input and output.
   C. depends exclusively on sensory neurons.
   D. depends exclusively on motor neurons.

3. The _____ receives, processes, interprets and stores incoming information from the senses and sends out messages destined for the muscles, glands, and internal organs. The _____ handles its input and output.
   A. central nervous system; peripheral nervous system
   B. peripheral nervous system; autonomic nervous system
   C. sympathetic nervous system; parasympathetic nervous system
   D. peripheral nervous system; central nervous system

4. The _____ nervous system is part of the peripheral nervous system.
   A. somatic   B. sympathetic
   C. autonomic   D. all of the above

5. One function of the somatic nervous system is to
   A. carry information from the senses to the CNS and from the CNS to the skeletal muscles.
   B. carry information to the glands and organs.
   C. control the sympathetic and parasympathetic nervous systems.
   D. process information in the brain.

6. The autonomic nervous system is involved with
   A. voluntary responses.
   B. the nerves connected to the senses and skeletal muscles.
   C. involuntary responses such as the regulation of blood vessels and glands.
   D. only sensory nerves.

7. The sympathetic nervous system governs _____ responses, whereas the parasympathetic nervous system governs _____ responses.
   A. voluntary; involuntary   B. involuntary; voluntary
   C. arousal; relaxing   D. sensory; motor

8.   Neurons
      A.   are the basic units of the nervous system.
      B.   are held in place by glial cells.
      C.   transmit electrical messages throughout the nervous system.
      D.   are characterized by all of the above.

9.   The three main parts of the neuron are the
      A.   dendrites, cell body and axon.
      B.   axon, dendrites and synapse.
      C.   synapse, impulse and cleft.
      D.   myelin sheath, dendrites and synapse.

10.   The _____ receive messages from other neurons, whereas the _____ carry
      messages on to other neurons or to muscle or gland cells.
      A.   cell bodies; dendrites
      B.   dendrites; axons
      C.   axons; dendrites
      D.   myelin sheaths; cell bodies

11.   Neurons are like catchers and batters. The _____ are like catchers because they
      receive information; the _____ are like batters because they send on the message.
      A.   dendrites; axons   B.   cell bodies; axons
      C.   axons; dendrites   D.   dendrites; glials

12.   The cell body
      A.   determines whether the neuron should fire.
      B.   receives incoming impulses from other neurons.
      C.   speeds the conduction of the neural impulse.
      D.   connects with the synapse.

13.   When a neural impulse reaches the tip of the axon terminal,
      A.   the neuron fires.
      B.   synaptic vesicles in the synaptic end bulb release neurotransmitters that cross the
            synaptic cleft and lock into receptor sites on the post-synaptic neuron.
      C.   the synaptic end bulb sends an electrical current into the dendrites of the next
            neuron.
      D.   the synaptic end bulb locks into the receptor sites on the post-synaptic dendrites.

14.   During Dr. Wisch's hospital rounds, he meets with patients who are suffering with
      Alzheimer's disease, Parkinson's disease and severe depression. To understand these
      disorders better, he looks to the role of
      A.   hormones.   B.   endorphins.
      C.   neurotransmitters.   D.   melatonin.

51

15. How do neurotransmitters affect the post-synaptic neuron?
    A. They cause a change in the electrical potential, exciting the neuron and causing it to fire.
    B. They cause a change in the electrical potential, either exciting or inhibiting the next neuron.
    C. They cause a change in the electrical potential, inhibiting the neuron and stopping it from firing.
    D. They do not make contact with the next neuron; they stay in the synapse.

16. Serotonin, dopamine, acetylcholine and norepinephrine are
    A. adrenal hormones.   B. endorphins.
    C. sex hormones.   D. neurotransmitters.

17. Mood, memory, well-being, Alzheimer's disease, depression, sleep, appetite, pain and temperature regulation are all influenced by
    A. dopamine.   B. neurotransmitters.
    C. endorphins.   D. all of the above.

18. During a dangerous situation, pain sensations are reduced. This reduction of pain is due to an increase in
    A. testosterone levels.
    B. endorphin levels.
    C. androgen levels.
    D. insulin levels.

19. _____ are chemicals that are released directly into the bloodstream, which then carries them to organs and cells that may be far from their point of origin.
    A. Neurotransmitters   B. Endorphins
    C. Hormones   D. Neuromodulators

20. Androgen, estrogen and progesterone are three types of
    A. sex hormones.   B. neurotransmitters.
    C. neurons.   D. neuromodulators.

21. The _____ is a method for analyzing biochemical activity in the brain that uses injections containing a harmless radioactive element.
    A. MRI (magnetic resonance imaging)
    B. PET scan (positron-emission tomography)
    C. EEG (electroencephalogram)
    D. EP (evoked potentials)

22. Brain stem is to _____ as cerebrum is to _____.
    A. emotions; vital functions
    B. vital functions; emotions
    C. higher forms of thinking; vital functions
    D. vital functions; higher forms of thinking

23. The limbic system includes the
    A. cortex and corpus callosum.
    B. spinal cord and brain.
    C. cerebellum and brain stem.
    D. amygdala and hippocampus.

24. The _____ has deep crevasses and wrinkles that enable it to contain billions of neurons without requiring people to have the heads of giants.
    A. corpus callosum   B. cerebral cortex
    C. cerebellum   D. hypothalamus

25. The four distinct lobes of the cortex are the
    A. occipital, parietal, temporal and frontal lobes.
    B. sensory, auditory, visual and motor lobes.
    C. hind, mid, fore and association lobes.
    D. front, back, side and top lobes.

26. Which of the following summarizes the different hemispheric functions?
    A. The left brain is more active in logic and the right brain is associated with visual-spatial abilities.
    B. The left brain is more active in artistic and intuitive tasks, and the right brain is more involved in emotional and expressive abilities.
    C. The left brain has visual-spatial abilities, while the right brain is more involved in artistic and creative activities.
    D. The right brain is more dominant and the left brain is more subordinate.

27. If Lucy is like most people, her _____ is most involved when she calculates a math problem and her _____ is most active when she reads a map.
    A. right brain; left brain   B. left brain; right brain
    C. corpus callosum; cerebellum   D. amygdala; thalamus

28. Localization of function refers to the fact that
    A. personality traits are reflected in different areas of the brain.
    B. information is distributed across large areas of the brain.
    C. different brain parts perform different jobs and store different sorts of information.
    D. brain processes are like holography.

29. The issue of whether there are sex differences in the brain is controversial because
    A. evidence of anatomical sex differences in humans is contradictory.
    B. findings have flip-flopped as a result of the biases of the observers.
    C. even if anatomical differences exist, we do not know what they mean.
    D. all of the above reasons.

30. Throughout life, new learning results in the establishment of new synaptic connections in the brain, with stimulating environments producing the greatest changes. Conversely, some unused synaptic connections are lost as cells or their branches die and are not replaced. This indicates that the brain
    A. is more lateralized than scientists once thought.
    B. continues to develop and change in response to the environment.
    C. develops new brain cells on a regular and ongoing basis.
    D. is more holistic than scientists once thought.

PRACTICE TEST 2 - Short Answer

1. The nervous system is divided into two main parts: the ___central___ nervous system, which receives, processes, interprets, and stores incoming information, and the ___peripheral___ nervous system, which contains all parts of the nervous system outside the brain and spinal cord.

2. The peripheral nervous system is divided into the ___somatic___ nervous system, which controls the skeletal muscles and permits voluntary action, and the ___autonomic___ nervous system, which regulates blood vessels, glands, and internal organs and works more or less without a person's conscious control.

3. The autonomic nervous system is divided into the ___sympathetic___ nervous system, which mobilizes the body for action and increases energy, and the ___parasympathetic___ nervous system, which conserves and stores energy.

4. Neurons have three main parts. The ___cell body___ contains the biochemical machinery for keeping the neuron alive.

5. The ___dendrites___ of a neuron receive messages from other nerve cells and transmit them toward the cell body. The ___axons___ transmits messages away from the cell body to other cells.

6. Most neurons are insulated by a layer of fatty tissue called the ___Myelin Sheath___ that prevents signals from adjacent cells from interfering with each other and speeds up the conduction of neural impulses.

7. Individual neurons are separated by tiny gaps called the ___synaptic cleft___

8. When an electrical impulse reaches the ___axon terminal___ of a neuron, chemical substances called ___neurotransmitter___ are released into the synapse. Once across the synapse, the molecules fit into sites on the receiving neuron, changing the membrane of the receiving cell.

9. What any given neuron does at any given moment depends on the net effect of all the messages being received from other neurons. The message that reaches a final destination depends on the rate at which individual neurons are firing, how many are firing, what types are firing and where they are located. It does NOT depend on how strongly neurons are firing because the firing of a neuron is an _____ event.

10. _Endorphines_ are chemical messengers that reduce pain and promote pleasure. Dopamine, serotonin, and norepinephrine are examples of another type of chemical messenger called _neurotransmitters_

11. Hormones originate primarily in the _Endocrine_ glands, which deposit them into the bloodstream where they are carried to organs and cells.

12. Neurotransmitters affect a variety of behaviors. Low levels of _____ and _____ may be implicated in severe depression; _____ affects memory and loss of cells producing this neurotransmitter may help account for some of the symptoms of Alzheimer's disease.

13. The three main types of sex hormones that occur in both sexes (though in differing amounts) are _testosterone_, _progesterone_, and _estrogen_.

14. Living brains can be studied by probing them with electrodes. The procedure for obtaining brain wave recordings is called a(n) _electroncephalogram_

15. Other methods of investigating living brains are PET scans, which record biochemical changes in the brain as they are happening, and _____ which utilize magnetic fields and radio frequencies to explore the "inner space" of the brain.

16. This dense network of neurons, which extends above the brain stem into the center of the brain and has connections with higher areas, screens incoming information and arouses the higher centers when something happens that demands their attention. Without the _____ system, we could not be alert or perhaps even conscious.

17. The structures of the brain stem include the __pons__ that is responsible for sleeping, waking, and dreaming, and the _medulla_, that is responsible for bodily functions like breathing and heart rate. Standing atop the brain stem, the _cerebellum_ contributes to a sense of balance and muscle coordination.

18. The _Thalamus_ is a busy traffic officer that directs sensory messages from the spinal cord to higher brain centers.

19. The _Hypothalamus_ sits beneath the thalamus and is involved with drives vital for survival, such as hunger, thirst, emotion, sex, and reproduction.

20. The _____ system is heavily involved in emotions.

21. Case histories of brain-damaged people such as H.M. indicate that the _hippocampus_ enables us to store new information for future use.

22. The cerebral cortex, the layer of cells that covers the cerebrum, is divided into four distinct lobes. The _occipital_ lobes contain the visual cortex, the _parietal_ lobes contain the somatosensory cortex, the _temporal_ contain the auditory cortex, and the _frontal_ lobes contain the motor cortex.

23. A large bundle of nerve fibers called the _corpus callosum_ connects the two cerebral hemispheres. The left and right sides of the brain seem to have somewhat different tasks and talents, a phenomenon known as _lateralization of hemispheres_

24. There are two main language areas in the brain. _Wernicke's_ area is involved in language comprehension and is located in the _temporal_ lobe, and _Broca's_ area is involved in speech production and is located in the _frontal_ lobe.

25. To examine the issue of sex differences, we need to ask two separate questions: Do physical differences actually exist in male and female brains, and if so, what do they have to do with _____?

PRACTICE TEST 3 - Essay

1. You are sitting at your desk trying to study for a test you are very nervous about, and all you can focus on is the stereo playing in the other room. You get up, go to the other room and turn down the stereo. Beginning with the external stimuli (the sound) and ending with your movement to the other room, describe:
   A. from the standpoint of a single neuron
   B. the brain structures that are involved, in sequence
   C. the nervous system involvement

2. For each scenario, indicate the brain structure(s) most likely to be involved in the behavior that is described.
   A. Dr. Smith inserts an electrode into a structure within the brain. As this electrode is activated, the person sweats and shivers, feels hungry and thirsty, and sometimes even seems angry and sexually aroused.
   B. A computer-enhanced image has enabled a research team to observe the flow of information within the nervous system. While watching this flow, the researchers notice that incoming sensory messages are relayed through this center before finally reaching their destination in the cerebral hemispheres.
   C. As a result of a serious automobile accident, Fred's ability to make plans and show initiative were seriously impaired.
   D. Bjorn's great grandmother has had a serious stroke. As a result, she is unable to speak, though she appears to understand and respond non-verbally to what is being said.
   E. Tiffany's elderly neighbor is showing signs of memory loss.
   F. Mary has been unable to continue as a gymnast since the lower rear area of her brain was damaged in a car accident. All tasks requiring balance or coordinated movements are beyond Mary's capacities.

3. As a result of mixing tranquilizers and alcohol, Helen has become what is called "brain dead," and though she does not respond to people, she continues to live without any life-sustaining equipment. Which parts of her brain have been damaged and which parts continue to function?

4.   In the descriptions that follow, cortical functions are disrupted in various ways. From the descriptions identify the cortical structures and state their functions.

   A.   Removing a tumor from an area just behind her forehead has dramatically altered Denise's personality. Previously outgoing and warm, she is now hostile and needs prodding to get anything done.

   B.   Lately Ralph has been experiencing tingling sensations in various body parts and he sometimes "forgets" where his hands and fingers are. Tests reveal a growth near the surface of the brain just under the center of his head.

   C.   Hazan has a large blind spot in his visual field and doctors have eliminated the possibility of eye and optic nerve problems.

5.   In the examples below, identify whether the phenomena are primarily related to the functioning of the right hemisphere, the left hemisphere, or both.

   A.   Ken is being tested for school placement. Part of the test involves putting puzzle pieces together so they form geometric shapes. Ken performs well.

   B.   Another portion of the test involves reading simple sentences aloud. Ken garbles the words and says them in an improper sequence.

   C.   A third portion of the test requires Ken to respond to sets of photographs, each set containing five pictures of a person posed identically except for facial expression.

   D.   The last portion of the test assesses manual dexterity in the non-dominant arm and hand. Because Ken is left-handed, he is required to perform all sorts of mechanical tasks with his right hand. He fails this part of the test.

   E.   What overall conclusion might be reached about Ken's hemispheric functioning?

CHAPTER FIVE

Body Rhythms and Mental States

LEARNING OBJECTIVES

1. Define consciousness and the biological rhythms often associated with states of consciousness.

2. Describe circadian rhythms, including how they are studied and how they may be desynchronized.

3. Discuss examples of ultradian and infradian rhythms and distinguish endogenous rhythms from those caused by external factors.

4. Summarize the research evidence on "PMS" and discuss whether emotional symptoms associated with "PMS" are tied to the menstrual cycle.

5. Summarize theories about the biological functions of sleep.

6. Distinguish between rapid eye movement (REM) and non-REM periods in sleep and describe the four stages of non-REM sleep.

7. Summarize the principles of the psychoanalytic, problem-solving, mental housekeeping and activation-synthesis theories of dreaming.

8. List the types of psychoactive drugs that can alter states of consciousness and describe their physical and behavioral effects.

9. List and explain the factors that influence the effects of psychoactive drugs.

10. Define hypnosis and summarize its characteristics.

11. Describe the dissociation and sociocognitive theories of hypnosis.

BRIEF CHAPTER SUMMARY

Chapter 5 examines biological rhythms and states of consciousness. There are three types of endogenous rhythms: circadian (occurs once a day), ultradian (occurs more than once a day), and infraradian (occurs less than once a day). During the sleep cycle, four stages of non-rapid eye movement (NREM) sleep alternate with rapid eye movement sleep (REM) approximately every ninety minutes during the night. Dreaming is more likely to happen during REM sleep. Although the purpose of dreams is not conclusively known, psychologists have proposed several explanations, such as dreams as the "royal road to the unconscious" (Freud), the problem-focused explanation, dreams as the by-product of mental housekeeping, and the activation synthesis theory. Classes of consciousness-altering drugs include stimulants, depressants, opiates, and psychedelics. The characteristics of hypnosis are discussed, as are the two principal theories of hypnosis: the dissociative theories (and the hidden observer) and the sociocognitive approach.

PREVIEW OUTLINE

Before you read the chapter, review the preview outline for each section of the text. After you have read the chapter, close this book and try to re-create the outlines on a blank piece of paper.

I. **Biological rhythms: The tides of experience**
    A.   **Definitions**
         1.   Consciousness - awareness of oneself and the environment
         2.   Biological rhythms - regular fluctuations in biological systems
              a.   Entrainment - synchronization of rhythms with external events
              b.   Endogenous rhythms - occur in absence of external cues - 3 types
                   (1)   Circadian rhythms - occur every 24 hours
                   (2)   Infradian rhythms - occur less often than once a day
                   (3)   Ultradian rhythms - occur more often than once a day
    B.   **Circadian rhythms** - exist in plants, animals, insects, and humans
         1.   The body's clock
              a.   Controlled by the suprachiasmatic nucleus (SCN)
              b.   SCN regulates neurotransmitters and hormones (e.g., melatonin)
         2.   When the clock is out of sync
              a.   Change in routine may cause internal desynchronization
              b.   Cycles are affected by environmental and individual factors

C.   Mood and long-term rhythms - infradian rhythms
1.   Does the season affect moods? Seasonal affective disorder (SAD)
2.   Does the menstrual cycle affect moods?
    a.   Clear support for emotional symptoms of premenstrual syndrome (PMS) is lacking
    b.   Research on hormonal influences on men is lacking
    c.   Conclusion - few people of either sex are likely to undergo personality shifts because of hormones

D.   The rhythms of sleep - ultradian rhythms
1.   Why we sleep? Some theories
    a.   Sleep is recuperative for the body
    b.   Sleep is necessary for normal mental functioning
2.   The realms of sleep - sleep is not an unbroken state of rest
    a.   Ultradian cycle occurs, on average, every 90 minutes
       (1)   4 Non-REM stages, each deeper than the previous
          1 - small, irregular brain waves; light sleep
          2 - high-peaking waves called sleep spindles
          3 - delta waves begin; slow with high peaks
          4 - mostly delta waves and deep sleep
       (2)   REM sleep (also called paradoxical sleep) is characterized by active brain waves, increased heart rate and blood pressure, limp muscles, and dreaming

II. EXPLORING THE DREAM WORLD

A.   Characteristics of dreams – inward focus of attention, lucid dreams
B.   Theories of dreams - every culture has its theories about dreams
1.   Dreams as unconscious wishes (Freud)
    a.   Manifest content - what we experience and remember
    b.   Latent content - hidden, symbolic; unconscious wishes
2.   Dreams as reflections of current concerns
    a.   Reflect ongoing, conscious concerns of waking life
    b.   Some believe dreams provide an opportunity for resolving problems
3.   Dreams as a by-product of mental housekeeping
    a.   Physiological information-processing approach; unnecessary neural connections are eliminated, important ones are strengthened
    b.   Dreams are the remains of the sorting, scanning and sifting process
4.   Dreams as interpreted brain activity: Activation-synthesis theory
    a.   Dreams are the result of neurons firing spontaneously in the lower brain (in the pons) that are sent to the cortex
    b.   Signals from pons have no meaning, but the cortex tries to make sense of, or synthesize, them

III. CONSCIOUSNESS-ALTERING DRUGS

A. **Altering mood and consciousness**
1. Efforts to alter mood and consciousness appear to be universal
2. During the 1960s, people sought to produce altered states of consciousness

B. **Classifying drugs**
1. Psychoactive drug - substance affecting perception, mood, thinking, memory or behavior by changing the body's biochemistry
2. Classified according to the drug's effects on central nervous system
   a. Stimulants - speed up activity in central nervous system; include cocaine, amphetamines, nicotine, caffeine
   b. Depressants (sedatives) - slow down activity in central nervous system; include alcohol, tranquilizers, barbiturates
   c. Opiates - mimic endorphins; include opium, morphine, heroine, methadone
   d. Psychedelics - alter normal thought and sometimes produce hallucinations; include LSD, mescaline, psilocybin
   e. Anabolic steroids and Marijuana - don't fit other classifications

C. **The physiology of drug effects**
1. Effects produced by acting on neurotransmitters in a variety of ways
2. Some drugs lead to tolerance and withdrawal

D. **The psychology of drug effects** - effects depend on a person's physical condition, experience with the drug, and environmental setting

IV. THE RIDDLE OF HYPNOSIS

A. **Definition - procedure in which the practitioner suggests changes in the sensations, perceptions, thoughts, feelings, or behavior of the subject**

B. **The nature of hypnosis** - researchers agree on the following:
1. Responsiveness depends more on person being hypnotized than hypnotist's skill
2. Participants cannot be forced to do things against their will; Hypnotic inductions increase suggestibility but only to a modest degree
3. Hypnosis does not increase the accuracy of memory; it can increase amount of information remembered, but it also increases errors
4. Does not produce a literal re-experiencing of long-ago events
5. Hypnosis has been effective for medical and psychological purposes

C. **Theories of hypnosis** - two competing theories predominate
1. Dissociation theories - a split in consciousness in which one part of the mind operates independently of the rest of consciousness; hidden observer
2. The sociocognitive approach
   a. The effects are a result of the interaction between the hypnotist and the abilities, beliefs, and expectations of the subject
   b. People are playing the role of a hypnotized person without faking

PRACTICE TEST 1 - Multiple Choice

1. Jim likes to get drunk and smoke marijuana because this enables him to see himself and the world differently. This motive is consistent with which of the following statements about consciousness?
   A. Consciousness is awareness of one's bodily changes or rhythms.
   B. Consciousness is awareness of oneself and the environment.
   C. Consciousness is directly related to changes in brain wave patterns.
   D. Consciousness is a philosophical issue that cannot be defined.

2. As part of a research study, Bob is living in a comfortable room with a VCR and stereo, but there are no windows, clocks or sounds coming in from outside. He is told to eat, sleep and work whenever he feels like doing so. This type of study is used to
   A. examine sensory deprivation.
   B. examine the affect of daylight on depression.
   C. explore endogenous circadian rhythms.
   D. attempt to modify infradian rhythms.

3. Geraldo goes to sleep by 11:00 p.m. and awakens at 7:00 a.m. This cycle is a(n)
   A. infradian rhythm.   B. circadian rhythm.
   C. nocturnal rhythm.   D. ultradian rhythm.

4. The seasonal migration of birds is an example of
   A. a circadian rhythm.   B. an infradian rhythm.
   C. an ultradian rhythm.   D. a diurnal rhythm.

5. Which of the following is an example of an ultradian rhythm?
   A. stomach contractions   B. hormone level fluctuations
   C. appetite for food   D. all of the above

6. Periods of dreaming and non-dreaming occur during the night in
   A. a circadian rhythm.   B. an infradian rhythm.
   C. an ultradian rhythm.   D. a diurnal rhythm.

7. Which of the following can desynchronize circadian rhythms?
   A. an overseas trip   B. switching shifts at work
   C. going on daylight savings time   D. all of the above

8. Menstrual cycle research on hormones and mood shifts suggests that
   A. for most people, hormones are reliably and strongly correlated with mood.
   B. hormonal shifts cause mood shifts.
   C. mood changes cause hormonal shifts.
   D. no causal relationship has been established between hormonal shifts and moods.

9.   Which of the following conclusions reflects the findings on premenstrual symptoms?
      A.   The idea of mood swings as a premenstrual symptom has been questioned since men and women don't differ in the number of mood swings they experience in a month.
      B.   For most women, the relationship between cycle stage and symptoms is weak.
      C.   There is no reliable relationship between cycle stage and work efficiency.
      D.   All of the above have been found.

10.   Sleep is necessary
      A.   because of its recuperative properties.
      B.   because the brain requires sleep.
      C.   to repair cells and remove waste products from the muscles.
      D.   for all of the above reasons.

11.   The brain waves that occur when you first go to bed and relax are called
      A.   alpha waves.   B.   delta waves.
      C.   beta waves.   D.   gamma waves.

12.   Joe is a subject in a sleep study. When his brain emits occasional short bursts of rapid, high-peaking waves called sleep spindles, he is in which stage of sleep?
      A.   stage 1   B.   stage 3
      C.   stage 2   D.   stage 4

13.   REM sleep is called paradoxical sleep because
      A.   dreams are often paradoxical and they occur most often in REM sleep.
      B.   the brain is extremely active but the body is devoid of muscle tone.
      C.   people are easily awakened, even though it is a deep sleep.
      D.   the brain is very calm and inactive, but the body is quite active.

14.   After the first 30 to 45 minutes of sleep, you have progressed from stage 1 sleep to stage 4 sleep. After this, you
      A.   go into a prolonged non-REM period.
      B.   enter REM sleep.
      C.   progress back up the ladder from stage 4 to stage 3 to stage 2 to stage 1.
      D.   go back to stage 1 and continue through the four stages all night.

15.   The most vivid dreams occur during
      A.   the menstrual cycle.   B.   REM sleep.
      C.   stage 1 sleep.   D.   non-REM sleep.

16.   When Ruth dreams, she is in the dream, but also observing the dream and controlling what happens in it. Ruth is experiencing
      A.   nightmares.   B.   manifest dreams.
      C.   lucid dreams.   D.   REM dreams.

17. According to the _____ hypothesis, dreams express our unconscious desires.
    A. information-processing hypothesis   B. psychoanalytic hypothesis
    C. activation-synthesis hypothesis   D. problem-solving hypothesis

18. Which hypothesis suggests that dreams result from cortical attempts to interpret spontaneous neural activity?
    A. mental housekeeping   B. psychoanalytic
    C. activation-synthesis   D. problem solving

19. Psychoactive drugs work primarily by affecting
    A. brain structures.   B. bodily rhythms.
    C. neurotransmitters.   D. blood flow to the brain.

20. Which of the following are psychoactive drugs?
    A. tobacco   B. opium
    C. caffeine   D. all of the above

21. Though cocaine is a(n) _____, heroin is a(n) _____, and marijuana is a(n) _____, they can all produce euphoria.
    A. stimulant; psychedelic; depressant
    B. amphetamine; opiate; psychedelic
    C. psychedelic; stimulant; unclear category
    D. stimulant; opiate; unclear category

22 Alcohol, tranquilizers and sedatives are examples of
    A. opiates.   B. depressants.
    C. psychedelics.   D. stimulants.

23. When Micky began using drugs, he used only a small amount. After six months, he required more and more to achieve the same effect. Micky experienced
    A. withdrawal.   B. brain damage.
    C. tolerance.   D. mental set.

24. Hank and Bill both used the same amount of cocaine, but they each had different reactions. Which of the following differences between them might account for this?
    A. physical condition   B. expectations for the drug
    C. prior experience with cocaine   D. all of the above

25. Which of the following statements describes the effect of hypnosis on memory?
    A. "age regression" allows one to remember childhood experiences accurately.
    B. under hypnosis, people can accurately recall events from earlier lives.
    C. memories recalled under hypnosis are often vivid but inaccurate.
    D. memory errors decrease under hypnosis.

26. Which evidence argues against the credibility of age regression?
    A. Subjects who were age regressed as part of a study could not accurately recall their favorite comforting object from age three.
    B. Subjects in a study did not know basic facts about the time period in which they were supposed to have lived in a previous life.
    C. When people are regressed to an earlier age, brain wave patterns do not resemble those of children.
    D. all of the above

27. Those who believe that hypnotic state differs from normal consciousness believe
    A. that hypnosis involves dissociation.
    B. the powers of hypnosis are exaggerated.
    C. that suggestion alone can produce the same results.
    D. all of the above.

28. Those who say hypnosis is a(n) _____ believe that hypnosis involves role-playing.
    A. altered state   B. deliberate deception
    C. sociocognitive process   D. none of the above

29. Susan, who is normally very modest, is removing some of her clothes under hypnosis. How might this be explained, according the theory that hypnosis is a social-cognitive process?
    A. She is in an altered state.
    B. She has dissociated.
    C. She is playing the role of a hypnotized person.
    D. She has relinquished control to the hypnotist.

PRACTICE TEST 2 - Short Answer

1. _____ is defined as the awareness of oneself and the environment.

2. The sleep cycle is an example of a(n) _____ rhythm.

3. Circadian rhythms are controlled by a biological clock called the _____.

4. An example of an ultradian rhythm is _____. An example of an infradian rhythm is _____.

5. Internal _____ occurs when your normal routine changes, such as when you must take a long airplane flight over many time zones.

6. Few people of either sex are likely to undergo personality shifts solely as a result of _____.

7. The majority of vivid dreams occurs during _____.

8. The short bursts of rapid, high-peaking waves that occur during Stage 2 sleep are known as sleep _____.

9. REM sleep is called paradoxical sleep because the body is _____ while the brain is _____.

10. _____ dreaming occurs when people are aware that they are dreaming.

11. Psychoanalytic theory suggests that we must distinguish the obvious, or _____, content of a dream from the hidden, or _____, content that reveals the true meaning of the dream.

12. The theory of dreaming that suggests dreams are the remains of a sorting, scanning, and sifting process is called the _____ view.

13. The _____ hypothesis suggests that dreams are the result of spontaneous neural firing.

14. _____ drugs affect perception, mood, thinking, memory or behavior.

15. Drugs are classified according to their effects on the _____.

16.   Amphetamines, cocaine, caffeine, and nicotine are all examples of _____.

17.   Some drugs, such as heroine and tranquilizers can lead to _____, a state in which larger and larger doses are needed to produce the same effect.

18.   The psychoactive drugs exert effects by influencing _____ levels.

19.   Several factors influence the way a particular individual reacts to the use of a drug. Two of those factors are _____ and _____.

20.   Some research shows that alcohol can provide an excuse for violent behavior. This is called the _____ phenomenon.

21.   Hilgard suggests that only one part of consciousness goes along with hypnotic suggestions. The other part is like a _____, watching but not participating.

22.   Some people report that hypnosis has helped them recall long-ago events. These memories are likely to be _____.

23.   The _____ explanation of hypnosis suggests that during hypnosis a split in consciousness occurs.

24.   Hypnosis has been used effectively for _____ purposes.

25.   The _____ explanation regards hypnosis as a form of role playing.

PRACTICE TEST 3 - Essay

1. Identify which type of rhythm each example represents and explain why.
    A. hunger
    B. mating behavior in dogs and cats
    C. fatigue
    D. sexual behavior in human beings
    E. concentration
    F. full moons

2. Dr. Irving is conducting a survey on premenstrual syndrome (PMS). Of the 100 subjects who responded to the survey, 70% indicated that they experience PMS on a regular basis. Compare these findings to the research in the text that argues against PMS and answer the following questions:
    A. How was PMS defined? What symptoms were included and why is this important?
    B. What are some of the problems with the self-reporting of PMS symptoms?
    C. Describe possible influences of expectations and attitudes toward menstruation on the results of the survey.
    D. Describe the results of research findings from studies that did not reveal their true purpose.

3. For the ninth grade science project, Megan kept a detailed diary of her sleep experiences during a one-month interval. The information obtained and her conclusions are submitted below. Using actual evidence related to sleep, comment on each of these claims:

    A. During the period of the study, I awakened myself once during each night at different times. Each time I woke myself up, I felt the same as when I wake up in the morning. This indicates that sleep actually is the same kind of thing all through the night.
    B. I was allowed to stay up all night twice. It was really hard to keep my eyes open at around 4:00 a.m., but by 6:00 a.m. I felt wide awake. This suggests that the loss of sleep is invigorating.
    C. After missing sleep two nights in a row, I felt like going to bed extra early the next day. This indicates that we need to catch up on our rest.
    D. Even though I felt O.K. after missing sleep for two nights, I got a "D" on an exam at school. This suggests that maybe sleep loss has more effects than I thought!
    E. During the time of the study, I had two dreams and my sister had five. This indicates that we only dream several times a month.

4. Gretchen had a dream that she and her husband had gone horseback riding. He was far ahead of her and, though she was riding as fast as she could, she was unable to catch up. Eventually she lost her way and was unsure where she was going. She dismounted her horse and found that she was in a beautiful valley, and she stopped there and felt very peaceful. Identify which theory would give each of the following interpretations of this dream:

    A. This dream has little significance or meaning. It represents the attempt of the cortex to make sense of random neuronal firing in the brainstem.
    B. This dream has little significance. It represents the brain's mental housekeeping. It is sorting, scanning and sifting new information into "wanted" and "unwanted" categories.
    C. The dream has great significance. It is likely to be a dream about Gretchen's unresolved relationship with her father. She has always felt abandoned by him and could never win his attention or affection, which she has always deeply desired.
    D. The dream has to do with Gretchen's concern that she cannot keep up with her husband's pace. He always has more energy than she does and although she tries, what she would most like to do is "get off the merry-go-round," relax, and take life easier.

5. For each type of drug listed below, indicate the following: 1) the type of drug, 2) the common effects of the drug, and 3) the result of abusing the drug.

    A. alcohol
    B. tranquilizers
    C. morphine
    D. amphetamines
    E. cocaine
    F. LSD
    G. marijuana

CHAPTER SIX

Sensation and Perception

LEARNING OBJECTIVES

1.   Distinguish between sensation and perception.

2.   Distinguish between anatomical and functional codes in the nervous system.

3.   Define psychophysics, absolute and difference thresholds and signal detection theory.

4.   Explain sensory adaptation, sensory deprivation, sensory overload and selective attention.

5.   List the characteristics of light waves and their correspondence to the visual experience.

6.   Identify the parts of the eye and describe how they convert light to vision.

7.   Discuss two theories of color vision and their connection to stages of processing.

8.   Explain how form, distance and depth perception occur.

9.   List and explain visual constancies and distinguish them from visual illusions.

10.   Describe how sound wave characteristics correspond to loudness, pitch, and timbre.

11.   Identify the parts of the ear, describe how they convert sound to hearing, and discuss the role of perceptual processes in making sound meaningful.

12.   List and explain the factors that affect gustation (taste) and olfaction (smell).

13.   List the four skin senses.

14.   Describe the gate-control theory of pain and the updated version of this theory.

15.   Describe the internal senses of kinesthesis and equilibrium.

16.   Summarize the evidence for innate abilities in perception and describe the psychological and cultural influences on perception.

17.   Discuss the evidence on the effectiveness of "subliminal perception" tapes and the existence of ESP.

BRIEF CHAPTER SUMMARY

Chapter 6 examines the processes of sensation and perception and the relationship between them. Receptors in the senses change physical energy into neural energy. The physical characteristics of the stimuli correspond to psychological dimensions of our sensory experience. Psychophysics (how the physical properties of stimuli are linked to psychological experiences), signal detection theory, sensory adaptation and sensory overload are discussed. The general processes of vision, hearing, taste, smell, pain, equilibrium and kinesthesis are reviewed. For each of these senses, the chapter examines the relevant biological structures processes (e.g., rods and cones) as well as the relevant theories that explain perception (e.g., trichromatic theory and opponent-process theory to explain how we see color). Once sensation has occurred, the process of organizing and interpreting the sensory information, or perception, begins. Perceptual strategies, including depth and distance strategies, visual constancies and form perception strategies, are described. Some perceptual abilities appear to be inborn, whereas others are influenced by psychological, environmental and cultural factors. The gate control theory of pain and a newer, modified version of the theory are reviewed. Conscious and nonconscious processes are examined, and extrasensory perception (ESP) is critically evaluated.

PREVIEW OUTLINE AND REVIEW QUESTIONS

Before you read the chapter, review the preview outline for each section of the text. After you have read the chapter, close this book and try to <u>re-create</u> the outlines on a blank piece of paper.

I. **OUR SENSATIONAL SENSES**
    A.   **Definitions**
        1.   Sensation - the detection of physical energy emitted or reflected by physical objects by cells (receptors)
        2.   Perception - organizing sensory impulses into meaningful patterns
    B.   **The riddle of separate sensations** - how we can explain separate sensations?
        1.   There are five widely known senses and other lesser-known senses; all of them evolved to help us survive
        2.   Sense receptors (cells in sense organs) detect a stimulus and convert the energy into electrical impulses that travel along nerves to the brain
        3.   The nervous system encodes the neural messages using anatomical codes and functional codes (Doctrine of specific nerve energies)
    C.   **Measuring the senses**
        1.   Psychophysics - how the physical properties of stimuli are related to our psychological experience of them
        2.   Absolute threshold – the smallest amount of energy a person can detect reliably (50 percent of the time)

3.   Difference thresholds - the smallest difference in stimulation that a person can detect reliably; also called just noticeable difference (j.n.d.)

4.   Signal detection theory
        a.   Accounts for response bias (tendency to say yes or no to a signal)
        b.   Separates sensory processes (the intensity of the stimulus) from the decision process (influenced by observer's response bias)

D.   **Sensory adaptation**
1.   Senses designed to respond to change and contrast in the environment
2.   Decline in sensory responsiveness occurs when a stimulus is unchanging; nerve cells temporarily get "tired" and fire less frequently
3.   Sensory deprivation studies - subjects became edgy, disoriented, confused

E.   **Sensory overload**
1.   "Cocktail party phenomenon" - blocking out unimportant sensations
2.   Selective attention - protects us from being overwhelmed with sensations

II. VISION
A.   **What we see**
1.   Psychological dimensions of visual world - hue, brightness, saturation
2.   Physical properties of light - wavelength, intensity, complexity

B.   **An eye on the world - parts of the eye**
1.   Parts of the eye include cornea, lens (focuses light), iris (controls amount of light that gets into eye) and pupil (dilates to let light in)
2.   Retina - in the back of the eye where the visual receptors are located
        a.   Rods - sensitive to light, not to color
        b.   Cones - see color, but need more light to respond

C.   **Why the visual system is not a camera**
1.   Eyes are not a passive recorder of external world; neurons build picture
2.   Visual system cells have response specialties (feature detectors in animals)
3.   Controversy over specialized "face modules" in the brain

D.   **How we see colors**
1.   Trichromatic theory – first level of processing – three types of cones
2.   Opponent-process theory – second stage of processing (ganglion cells)

E.   **Constructing the visual world**
1.   Visual perception - the mind interprets the retinal image and constructs the world using information from the senses
2.   Form perception - Gestalt descriptions of how we build perceptual units include: figure/ground, proximity, closure, similarity, continuity
3.   Depth and distance perception - binocular cues and monocular cues
4.   Visual constancies - when seeing is believing
        a.   Perceptual constancy - perception of objects as unchanging though the sensory patterns they produce are constantly shifting
        b.   Shape, location, brightness, color and size constancies

III. HEARING
   A.   **What we hear**
      1.   Stimulus for sound is a wave of pressure created when an object vibrates, which causes molecules in a transmitting substance (usually air) to move
      2.   Characteristics of sound
         a.   Loudness - intensity (amplitude) of a wave's pressure; decibels
         b.   Pitch - frequency (and intensity) of wave; measured in hertz
         c.   Timbre - complexity of wave; the distinguishing quality of a sound
      3.   Psychological properties of sound - loudness, pitch, timbre
   B.   **An ear on the world - the process of hearing**
      1.   Sound wave passes into the outer ear through a canal to strike the eardrum
      2.   Eardrum vibrates at the same frequency and amplitude as the wave
      3.   The wave vibrates three small bones, then to the cochlea
      4.   Organ of Corti in the cochlea contains the receptor cells called cilia, or hair cells, which are imbedded in the basilar membrane
      5.   The hair cells initiate a signal to the auditory nerve, which carries the message to the brain
   C.   **Constructing the auditory world**
      1.   Perception is used to organize patterns of sounds to construct meaning
      2.   Strategies include figure/ground, proximity, continuity, similarity, closure
      3.   Loudness is a distance cue; using both ears helps estimate direction

IV. OTHER SENSES
   A.   **Taste: Savory sensations**
      1.   Chemicals stimulate receptors on tongue, throat and roof of mouth
         a.   Papillae - bumps on tongue - contain taste buds
         b.   Replaced every 10 days - number declines with age
      2.   Four basic tastes: salty, sour, bitter, sweet – and a new one (umami)
         a.   Each taste produced by a different type of chemical
         b.   Flavors are a combination of the four, but unclear how this occurs
         c.   Taste is heavily influenced by smell, temperature and texture of food, culture, and individual differences
   B.   **Smell: The sense of scents**
      1.   Receptors are specialized neurons (5 million) in a mucous membrane in upper part of nasal passage that respond to chemical molecules in the air
      2.   Signals travel from receptors to the brain's olfactory bulb by the olfactory nerve to the higher regions of the brain
      3.   The psychological impact of odors may be because olfactory centers in the brain are linked to areas that process memories and emotions
   C.   **Senses of the skin**
      1.   Skin protects the innards, it helps identify objects, it is involved in intimacy, and it serves as a boundary
      2.   Skin senses include - touch, warmth, cold and pain

D. **The mystery of pain**
1. Pain differs from other senses in that the removal of the stimulus doesn't always terminate the sensation
2. Gate-control theory of pain - for years, the leading explanation
   a. To experience pain sensation, impulses must pass a "gate" of neural activity that sometimes blocks pain messages
   b. The theory correctly predicts that thoughts and feelings can influence pain perception
   c. Limitations of gate-control theory - cannot explain pain that occurs without injury or disease or phantom limb pain
3. Updating the gate-control theory
   a. The brain not only responds to incoming pain signals, but it is also capable of generating pain on its own
   b. An extensive matrix of neurons in the brain may have an abnormal pattern of activity, resulting in the experience of pain

E. **The environment within**
1. Kinesthesis - tells us about location and movement of body parts using pain and pressure receptors in muscles, joints, and tendons
2. Equilibrium - gives information about body as a whole
3. Normally, kinesthesis and equilibrium work together

V. PERCEPTUAL POWERS: ORIGINS AND INFLUENCES
A. **Inborn abilities and perceptual lessons**
1. Studies show that experience during a critical period may ensure survival and the development of skills already present at birth
2. Research concludes that infants are born with many perceptual abilities

B. **Critical periods – research on visual acuity of kittens**
C. **Psychological and cultural influences on perception**
1. Perceptions affected by needs, beliefs, emotions, expectations
2. Culture and experience also influence perception

VI. PUZZLES OF PERCEPTION
A. **Subliminal perception - perceiving without awareness**
1. Evidence exists that simple visual images can affect your behavior even when you are unaware that you saw it
2. Nonconscious processes in memory, thinking, decision making
3. However, there is no evidence for subliminal <u>persuasion</u>

B. **Extrasensory perception: Reality or illusion?**
1. Most reports come from anecdotal accounts
2. Some studies under controlled conditions found positive results, but methodological problems existed and results were not replicated
3. Conclusion is that there is no supporting scientific evidence

C. **Lessons from a magician** - we can be easily tricked by our senses

PRACTICE TEST 1 - Multiple Choice

1.   When energy in the environment stimulates receptors in the sense organs, we experience
        A.   perception.   B.   sensory overload.
        C.   sensation.   D.   sensory adaptation.

2.   The eyes, ears, tongue, nose, skin and internal body tissues all contain
        A.   anatomical codes.   B.   functional codes.
        C.   sense receptors.   D.   sense organs.

3.   Perception differs from sensation in that
        A.   perception allows us to organize and interpret sensations.
        B.   perception is the raw data coming in from the senses.
        C.   sensation is an organizing and interpretive process; perception is not.
        D.   perception can be measured; sensations cannot.

4.   Which theory argues that light and sound produce different sensations because they stimulate different brain parts?
        A.   signal detection theory   B.   trichromatic theory
        C.   doctrine of specific nerve energies   D.   opponent-process theory

5.   Which of the following best accounts for the fact that light and sound produce different sensations due to the specific cells that are firing, how many are firing, the rate at which they are firing and the patterning of each cell's firing?
        A.   anatomical codes   B.   functional codes
        C.   doctrine of specific nerve energies   D.   feature detectors

6.   _____ stimulate different nerve pathways, which go to different places in the brain, whereas focusing on the number, rate and pattern of the firing of particular cells in response to certain stimuli describes _____.
        A.   anatomical codes; functional codes   B.   neural codes; cellular codes
        C.   functional codes; anatomical codes   D.   psychophysics; transduction

7.   Signal detection theory takes into account
        A.   observers' response tendencies.
        B.   sensory differences among species.
        C.   the role of feature detectors.
        D.   which cells are firing, how many cells are firing and the rate at which they fire.

8.   As a research participant, Betsy is asked to compare lights within several pairs of lights and indicate whether one is brighter than the other. Betsy is being asked to detect
        A.   the absolute threshold.   B.   the j.d.n.
        C.   the difference threshold.   D.   Weber's Law.

9.   Researchers have found that sensory deprivation may
     A.   lead to confusion and grouchiness.
     B.   produce a restless, disoriented feeling.
     C.   cause hallucinations.
     D.   cause all of the above.

10. Maria enjoys the wonderful smells from the kitchen when she first arrives at her mother's house, but she no longer notices them after a while. What accounts for this?
     A.   sensory adaptation   B.   selective attention
     C.   absolute thresholds   D.   difference thresholds

11. In class, Jonah is completely focused on the professor's words, though there are noises and distractions all around him. This is best explained by
     A.   sensory adaptation.   B.   selective attention.
     C.   sensory deprivation.   D.   sensory overload.

12. Humans experience the wavelength of light as
     A.   hue or color.   B.   brightness.
     C.   saturation or colorfulness.   D.   wave complexity.

13. The fovea contains
     A.   only rods.   B.   only cones.
     C.   an equal number of rods and cones.   D.   more rods than cones.

14. Rods are to cones as
     A.   bright light is to dim light.   B.   the iris is to the pupil.
     C.   black and white vision is to color vision.   D.   none of the above.

15. The visual receptors are located in the
     A.   cornea.   B.   pupil.
     C.   lens.   D.   retina.

16. The optic nerve connects
     A.   rods and cones.   B.   the cornea with the brain.
     C.   the pupil and the lens.   D.   the retina with the brain.

17. Which theory of color vision suggests that one type of cone responds to blue, another type of cone to green, and a third to red?
     A.   doctrine of specific nerve energies   B.   opponent-process theory
     C.   trichromatic theory   D.   feature detector theory

18. Which theory of color vision best explains negative afterimages?
     A.   trichromatic theory   B.   opponent-process theory
     C.   doctrine of specific nerve energies   D.   Weber's Law

19. Which Gestalt strategy would explain why you see $$$AAA### as three groups of figures instead of nine separate figures?
    A. closure
    B. figure-ground
    C. continuity
    D. similarity

20. The slight difference in sideways separation between two objects as seen by the left eye and the right eye is called
    A. a binocular cue.
    B. a depth cue.
    C. retinal disparity.
    D. all of the above.

21. As you watch a door opening, its image changes from rectangular to trapezoidal, yet you continue to think of the door as rectangular. What explains this phenomenon?
    A. perceptual constancy
    B. retinal disparity
    C. monocular depth cues
    D. selective attention

22. Pitch is the dimension of sound related to the
    A. amplitude of a pressure wave.
    B. frequency of a pressure wave.
    C. distinguishing quality of a sound.
    D. complexity of a pressure wave.

23. The part of the ear that plays the same role in hearing as the retina plays in vision is called the
    A. cochlea.
    B. eardrum.
    C. organ of Corti.
    D. auditory nerve.

24. Rods and cones are to vision as the _____ is/are to hearing.
    A. cilia or hair cells
    B. eardrum
    C. basilar membrane
    D. cochlea

25. The cilia are imbedded in the _____ of the _____.
    A. cochlea; auditory nerve
    B. basilar membrane; cochlea
    C. eardrum; cochlea
    D. cochlea; basilar membrane

26. When you bite into a piece of bread or an orange, the taste is a result of
    A. a combination of the four basic tastes: salty, sour, bitter and sweet.
    B. a combination of the four basic tastes: salty, smooth, pungent and sweet.
    C. the activation of specific taste receptors.
    D. the taste receptors located in a specific part of the tongue.

27. How does the sense of smell differ from the sense of vision and taste?
   A. Smell does not have receptor cells.
   B. Although vision and taste have limited numbers of basic cell types, smell may have as many as a thousand.
   C. Smell uses anatomical coding and not functional coding, whereas vision and taste use both.
   D. There are fewer basic smells than basic tastes or colors.

28. The skin senses are
   A. tickle, temperature, touch and pain.
   B. tickle, itch, tingle and burn.
   C. touch, warmth, cold and pain.
   D. warmth, heat, cool and cold.

29. Phantom pain
   A. does not exist.
   B. is strictly psychological.
   C. may occur because a matrix of neurons in the brain is generating pain signals.
   D. is a result of the increase in pain fibers.

30. Calan is trying to balance on her left leg while holding her right foot with her left hand. Her ability to balance relies on the sense of _____, and her ability to grab her foot relies on the sense of _____.
   A. equilibrium; kinesthesis
   B. kinesthesis; equilibrium
   C. touch; equilibrium
   D. coordination: touch

31. Malga can touch her finger to her nose with her eyes shut. What allows her to do this?
   A. the olfactory sense   B. kinesthesis
   C. equilibrium   D. ESP

32. Which group is studied to evaluate whether perceptual abilities are inborn?
   A. cats
   B. people who first gained sensation as an adult
   C. babies and infants
   D. all of the above

PRACTICE TEST 2 - Short Answer

1.   _perception_ is the process by which sensory impulses are organized and interpreted.

2.   The two basic kinds of code used by the nervous system to convey sensations are
     _____ and _____ codes.

3.   Researchers in the field of _____ study the relationships between physical
     properties of stimuli and our psychological experience of them.

4.   The smallest amount of energy that a person can detect reliably is known as the
     absolute threshold.

5.   The smallest difference between two stimuli that a person can reliably detect is the
     JND .

6.   Signal-detection theory holds that responses in a detection task consist of both a
     _____ process and a _____ process.

7.   When a stimulus is unchanging or repetitious, receptors may stop firing so that we no
     longer notice it. This process is referred to as sensory _adaptation_ .

8.   The amount or intensity of light emitted or reflected by an object determines its
     Brightness

9.   Although located in the eye, the structure known as the _____ is actually part of the
     brain.

10. The visual receptors sensitive to low levels of light are called _rods_ ; receptors
     sensitive to color are called _cones_ .

11. _____ cells are responsive to specific patterns, such as horizontal versus
     vertical lines.

12. Humans almost always organize the visual field into figure and _ground_ .

13. The Gestalt principle of _closure_ suggests that the brain tends to fill in gaps in order
     to perceive complete forms.

14. Our tendency to perceive objects as stable and unchanging even when the sensory
     patterns they produce are changing is referred to as perceptual _consistancy_ .

15. An opponent-process cell that fired in response to red would turn _____ in response to green.

16. The receptors for hearing are hair cells embedded in the _____, in the interior of the _____.

17. The physical properties that correspond to the loudness of a sound is the _____of the pressure waves in the air.

18. The four basic tastes are _____, _____, _____, and _____. A possible fifth basic taste is _____.

19. People's responses to particular odors are affected by both _____ and individual differences.

20. The skin senses include _pressure_, _warmth_, _cold_, and _pain_.

21. The _Gate_ theory of pain holds that pain depends on whether neural impulses get past a point in the spinal cord and reach the brain.

22. _____ tells us where our body parts are located, and _____ tells us the orientation of the body as a whole.

23. A widely used procedure for studying depth perception in children is the _____ procedure.

24. Certain psychological influences affect perception. These include needs, beliefs, _____, and _____.

25. _____ refers to telepathy, clairvoyance, precognition, and out-of-body experiences.

PRACTICE TEST 3 - Essay

1. Explain the phenomena listed below in terms of the concept listed after it.

    A. Roberta is shopping at a flea market and has just refused to buy a scarf because the salesperson is charging $10 and she saw it at another stall for $8.00. Later that week, she is shopping for a new car and does not think anything about spending an extra $2.00 for a car. Discuss this as an analogy of Weber's Law.

    B. A nurse notices that patients perform more poorly on auditory tests - tests of auditory thresholds - when they are tired as a result of losing sleep. Analyze the effects of their performance using signal detection theory.

    C. John is looking all over for his glasses when his wife points them out at the top of his head. Explain this behavior using principles of sensory adaptation.

    D. Malcolm is studying for a test in psychology while the TV is blaring and his roommate is on the phone in the same room. Discuss this in relation to sensory overload.

2. Starting with a light wave, describe what happens to that wave from the environment to the brain, including all relevant structures.

3   Assume that you are developing a color-generating device that will reproduce the colors in the human color spectrum. Explain which colors you need and why, according to the two theories of color vision listed below.

    A. Trichromatic theory
    B. Opponent-process theory

4. You are watching a monitor that depicts sound waves. Describe what changes in the sound would accompany the modifications indicated below.

    A. The sound waves remain constant except for their height, which is increasing.
    B. The wave frequency is changing.
    C. Waves of different types are being increasingly mixed together.

5.   In each of the examples below, identify and describe the Gestalt principle involved.

    A.   People scattered on a beach appear to be in clusters.
    B.   A sequence of dots on a canvas appears to form a face.
    C.   People crowded on a soccer field appear to be two different teams and referees.
    D.   A wall seems to be continuous even though vines block sections from view.

6.   Psychological factors can influence what we perceive and how we perceive it. Identify the psychological factors that could influence the following perceptions.

    A.   You had an argument with your sister. As you are walking home from school, she drives past you. You saw her look at you but figured that she did not stop because she is angry with you.
    B.   You think that your neighbor is an unethical character. One day you see him entering his house during the day and you are certain that he is sneaking around so that no one will see him.
    C.   You are expecting your best friend to come visit you and you are very excited. Every time you hear something, you run to the door, certain that there was a knock.

CHAPTER SEVEN

Learning and Conditioning

LEARNING OBJECTIVES

1. Identify the two types of conditioning shown by behaviorists to explain human behavior.

2. List and explain the four components of classical conditioning.

3. List and explain the four principles of classical conditioning.

4. Compare the traditional and recent views of how associations are formed between unconditioned and conditioned stimuli.

5. Describe both the impact of classical conditioning on everyday life and the therapeutic technique of counterconditioning.

6. Compare and contrast the principles of operant and classical conditioning.

7. List and explain the three types of consequences a response can lead to and distinguish between positive and negative reinforcement and primary and secondary reinforcement.

8. Describe shaping, extinction, stimulus generalization and stimulus discrimination in operant conditioning.

9. Distinguish between continuous and intermittent schedules of reinforcement and describe the four types of intermittent reinforcement schedules.

10. Describe how superstitions might be learned according to operant conditioning.

11. List and discuss six limitations of punishment as a way of controlling behavior and state a more effective strategy.

12. Distinguish between intrinsic and extrinsic reinforcers, and discuss the effects of extrinsic reinforcers on motivation. Describe how extrinsic reinforcers should be used.

13. Explain social-cognitive theories and compare them to conditioning models of learning.

14. Compare and contrast cognitive approaches and behavioral approaches.

BRIEF CHAPTER SUMMARY

Chapter 7 explores how we learn to make permanent changes in our behaviors due to experience. Two broad types of learning are explored: conditioning models and social-cognitive models. Both conditioning models suggest that learning is acquired through simple stimulus-response associations without the involvement of mental processes. Classical conditioning explains how we learn involuntary behaviors, such as fears and preferences. Operant conditioning explains how we learn complex behaviors as a result of favorable or unfavorable consequences of our actions. These consequences can take the form of positive reinforcement, negative reinforcement, or punishment. In addition, when reinforcement is not continuous (intermittent), the schedules of reinforcement may vary (i.e., fixed ratio, variable ratio, fixed interval, variable interval). Biological limitations to conditioning also are discussed. Social-cognitive theories expand behavioral principles to recognize the role that mental processes play in the acquisition of new behaviors. Observational learning and latent learning are two social-cognitive theories of learning.

PREVIEW OUTLINE

Before you read the chapter, review the preview outline for each section of the text. After you have read the chapter, close this book and try to <u>re-create</u> the outlines on a blank piece of paper.

I. **INTRODUCTION TO LEARNING**
    A.   **Definitions**
        1.   Learning - any relatively permanent change in behavior that occurs because of experience
        2.   Behaviorism - the school of psychology that accounts for behavior in terms of observable events, without reference to mental entities
        3.   Conditioning - a basic kind of learning that involves associations between environmental stimuli and responses
    B.   **Two types of conditioning: classical and operant**
    C.   **Other approaches to learning**
        1.   Social-cognitive learning theories hold that mental processes must be included in theories of human learning
        2.   Learning is not so much a change in behavior, but a change in knowledge that has the potential for affecting behavior

II. CLASSICAL CONDITIONING - began with the research of Ivan Pavlov
A. **New Reflexes from old - terminology**
1. Unconditioned stimulus (US) - thing that elicits an automatic response
2. Unconditioned response (UR) - response that is automatically produced
3. Conditioned stimulus (CS) - when an initially neutral stimulus comes to elicit a conditioned response after being paired with a US
4. Conditioned response (CR) - response that is elicited by a CS
5. Classical conditioning - procedure by which a neutral stimulus is regularly paired with a US and the neutral stimulus becomes a CS, which elicits a CR that is similar to the original, unlearned one

B. **Principles of classical conditioning**
1. Extinction - repeating the conditioned stimulus without the stimulus, and the conditioned response disappears
2. Spontaneous recovery
3. Higher-order conditioning - a neutral stimulus can become a conditioned stimulus by being paired with an already established conditioned stimulus
4. Stimulus generalization - after a stimulus becomes a conditioned stimulus for some response, other, similar stimuli may produce the same reaction
5. Stimulus discrimination - different responses are triggered by stimuli that resemble the conditioned stimulus in some way

C. **What is actually learned in classical conditioning?**
1. The stimulus to be conditioned should precede the unconditioned stimulus because the CS serves as a signal for the US
2. Many psychologists say that the learner learns information that is more than an association between two stimuli; that the CS predicts the US
3. Rescorla introduced cognitive concepts; organism as information seeker to form a representation of the world

III. CLASSICAL CONDITIONING IN REAL LIFE - recognized early by John B. Watson
A. Learning to like - conditioning positive emotions (e.g., used in advertising)
B. Learning to fear - conditioning negative emotions
1. Humans biologically primed to learn some fears and tastes more easily than others
2. Phobias (irrational fears) can be learned through conditioning (e.g., Little Albert) and unlearned through counterconditioning
C. Reacting to medical treatments may generalize to a range of other stimuli

IV. OPERANT CONDITIONING
A. **Introduction to operant conditioning**
1. Behavior becomes more or less likely, depending on its consequences; emphasis is on environmental consequences
2. Whereas classical conditioning involves reflexive responses, operant conditioning shapes complex, voluntary responses
B. **The birth of radical behaviorism – Thorndike and Skinner**

C.   The consequences of behavior
1.   The sooner a consequence follows a response, the greater its effect
2.   Primary and secondary reinforcers and punishers - can be very powerful
    a.   Primary reinforcers satisfy physiological needs
    b.   Primary punishers are inherently unpleasant
    c.   Secondary reinforcers (and punishers) are reinforcing (and punishing) through association with other (primary) reinforcers
3.   Positive and negative reinforcers and punishers
    a.   Positive reinforcement - something pleasant follows a response; negative reinforcement - something unpleasant is removed
    b.   Positive punishment - something unpleasant occurs; negative punishment - something pleasant is removed

D.   Principles of operant conditioning
1.   Extinction - learned response weakens when the reinforcer is removed
2.   Spontaneous recovery - the return of a response that has been extinguished
3.   Stimulus generalization - a response occurs to stimuli that resemble the stimuli present during the original learning
4.   Stimulus discrimination - the ability to distinguish between similar stimuli and responding only to the one that results in the reinforcer
5.   Discriminative stimulus signals whether a response will pay off
6.   Learning on Schedule - the pattern of delivery of reinforcements
    a.   Partial or intermittent schedules - reinforcing only some responses which can result in learning superstitious behaviors
        (1)   Fixed-ratio schedules
        (2)   Variable-ratio schedules
        (3)   Fixed-interval schedules
        (4)   Variable-interval schedules
    b.   For a response to persist, it should be reinforced intermittently, which will make the response more difficult to extinguish
7.   Shaping - gradually reinforcing responses that are more similar to the desired response (successive approximations to the desired response)
8.   Biological limits on learning - limitations of genetic predispositions and physical characteristics, instinctive drift

E.   Skinner: The man and the myth
1.   Did not deny the existence of consciousness; said that it cannot explain behavior, and that aspects of consciousness are learned behaviors
2.   Controversial idea that free will is an illusion (determinism)

V. OPERANT CONDITIONING IN REAL LIFE

A. **General problems** - if reinforcers, punishers, and discriminative stimuli in life remain the same, it is difficult to change behaviors

B. **Behavior modification** - operant conditioning programs used in real life

C. **The pros and cons of punishment**
   1. When punishment works - for behaviors that can't be ignored or rewarded; with some criminals (consistency matters more than severity)
   2. When punishment fails
      a. Punishment is often administered inappropriately or mindlessly
      b. The recipient often responds with anxiety, fear or rage
      c. Effects can be temporary; may depend on punisher being present
      d. Most misbehavior is hard to punish immediately
      e. Punishment conveys little information about desired behavior
      f. A punishment may be reinforcing because it brings attention
   3. Alternatives to punishment - avoid abuse, give information about desirable behavior, try extinction, and reinforce the alternate behaviors

D. **The problem with reward**
   1. Misuses of reward - rewards must be tied to the desired behavior
   2. Why rewards can backfire - people work for intrinsic as well as extrinsic reinforce and extrinsic reinforcers can interfere with intrinsic motivation

VI. LEARNING AND THE MIND

A. **Latent learning**
   1. Tolman and Honzik's experiment with latent learning
   2. Learning can occur even when there is no immediate response and when there is no obvious reinforcement

B. **Introduction to social-cognitive theories**
   1. Added higher-level cognitive processes to the idea of how people learn
   2. Humans have attitudes, beliefs, and expectations that affect how they acquire information, make decisions, and reason

C. **Learning by observing** - called observational learning
   1. Vicarious conditioning occurs from observing a model
   2. Supported by Bandura's studies with children learning social behaviors
   3. The case of media violence

LEARNING THEORIES

Complete the following chart by providing responses under each model of learning.

	OPERANT CONDITIONING	CLASSICAL CONDITIONING	SOCIAL-COGNITIVE THEORIES
INDICATE WHAT IS LEARNED			
EXAMPLES			
IDENTIFY KEY FIGURES			
LIST KEY TERMS			
LIST PRINCIPLES			

PRACTICE TEST 1 - Multiple Choice

1.   Learning is
      A.   memorization of information.
      B.   acquisition of practical skills.
      C.   any relatively permanent change in behavior that occurs because of experience.
      D.   any relatively permanent change in behavior.

2.   A neutral stimulus becomes a conditioned stimulus by
      A.   preceding it with an unconditioned stimulus.
      B.   following it with an unconditioned stimulus.
      C.   pairing it with a conditioned response.
      D.   reinforcing it.

3.   Once a neutral stimulus becomes a conditioned stimulus, it
      A.   can elicit a conditioned response.
      B.   can elicit an unconditioned response.
      C.   elicits a voluntary response.
      D.   elicits none of the above.

4.   A loud, sudden clap behind a child causes the child to cry. The child's tears are called the
      A.   conditioned stimulus.   B.   unconditioned stimulus.
      C.   conditioned response.   D.   unconditioned response.

5.   Every time I open any can of food, my cat Luna, comes running. The food is
      A.   an unconditioned stimulus.   B.   an unconditioned response.
      C.   a conditioned stimulus.   D.   a conditioned response.

6.   In the above question, the can opener is
      A.   an unconditioned stimulus.   B.   an unconditioned response.
      C.   a conditioned stimulus.   D.   a conditioned response.

7.   When Olympia threw tantrums, her father ignored this behavior and eventually it lessened. Ignoring her behavior is an example of
      A.   extinction.   B.   stimulus generalization.
      C.   stimulus discrimination.   D.   spontaneous recovery.

8.   If the CS is repeatedly presented without the US, what will happen?
      A.   extinction   B.   stimulus discrimination
      C.   stimulus generalization   D.   higher-order conditioning

9. If a stimulus similar to the conditioned stimulus is repeatedly presented without being followed by the unconditioned stimulus, it will stop evoking the conditioned response. The differential responses to the conditioned stimulus and the similar stimulus demonstrate
    A. extinction.
    B. stimulus discrimination.
    C. stimulus generalization.
    D. higher-order conditioning.

10. _____ views state that a CR is learned simply because the CS and US occur close together in time, whereas _____ views suggest that information is conveyed by one stimulus about another.
    A. Recent; traditional
    B. Social learning; traditional
    C. Traditional; recent
    D. Classical; operant

11. Tastes and fears are examples of behaviors learned through
    A. operant conditioning.
    B. social learning.
    C. imitation.
    D. classical conditioning.

12. Peter was afraid of rabbits. John Watson and Mary Cover Jones presented a rabbit to Peter along with milk and crackers and eventually Peter could play with the rabbit. This technique is called
    A. operant conditioning.
    B. counterconditioning.
    C. spontaneous recovery.
    D. higher-order conditioning.

13. Classical is to operant as
    A. learning is to instinct.
    B. voluntary is to involuntary.
    C. involuntary is to voluntary.
    D. unlearned is to instinct.

14. A difference between classical and operant conditioning is that
    A. classical conditioning does not involve consequences.
    B. classical conditioning involves reflexive responses.
    C. operant conditioning involves more complex responses than classical conditioning.
    D. all of the above are differences.

15. In operant conditioning, a response may lead to one of three types of consequences. One consequence strengthens or increases the probability of the response that it follows. This consequence is known as
    A. neutral.
    B. reinforcement.
    C. punishment.
    D. higher-order conditioning.

16. "Because you took out the garbage, you don't have to do the dishes." Which learning principle does this represent?
    A. positive reinforcement
    B. punishment
    C. negative reinforcement
    D. primary reinforcement

17   "Because you got all 'A's, you get to go on vacation." This represents
      A.   positive reinforcement.   B.   punishment.
      C.   negative reinforcement.   D.   primary reinforcement.

18.   When a stimulus or event that follows a response weakens it or makes it less likely to
      recur, it is called
      A.   negative reinforcement.   B.   positive reinforcement.
      C.   punishment.   D.   secondary reinforcement.

19.   _____ is a primary reinforcement, whereas _____ is/are a secondary reinforcement.
      A.   Food; money   B.   Food; water
      C.   Money; grades   D.   Applause; food

20.   Cindy's teacher tells her parents, "Cindy's misbehavior is just for attention. You should
      just ignore her and it should stop." Cindy's teacher is using what principle?
      A.   primary reinforcement   B.   extinction
      C.   stimulus generalization   D.   stimulus discrimination

21.   Extinction, stimulus generalization and stimulus discrimination are principles of
      A.   classical conditioning only.   B.   operant conditioning only.
      C.   classical and operant conditioning. D.   counter-conditioning.

22.   When Tyra throws a tantrum in the supermarket, her father tries to talk to her calmly or to
      ignore her behavior. Sometimes, he does not have the patience to be calm and he just
      gives her a cookie to quiet her down. He has put her on
      A.   a partial reinforcement schedule.   B.   a variable schedule.
      C.   an intermittent reinforcement schedule. D.   all of the above.

23.   One time Hiro got an extra $20 from a money machine. Though it has never happened
      since, Hiro keeps going to that machine whenever possible just in case the error is
      repeated. He is on a
      A.   continuous reinforcement schedule. B.   variable-interval schedule.
      C.   variable-ratio schedule.   D.   fixed-ratio schedule.

24.   Receiving your pay check every Friday represents what type of reinforcement schedule?
      A.   fixed-interval   B.   fixed-ratio
      C.   variable-interval   D.   variable-ratio

25.   You take a quiz on every chapter in psychology. Some chapters are covered in one class
      and some chapters require two classes. This is a _____ reinforcement schedule?
      A.   fixed-interval   B.   fixed-ratio
      C.   variable-interval   D.   variable-ratio

26. You wear your "lucky sweater" whenever you have a test because you got an A on two tests while wearing that sweater. This is an example of
   A. a fixed-interval schedule.   B. stimulus generalization.
   C. a learned superstition.   D. none of the above.

27. A prison has instituted a program to teach inmates problem-solving skills, life-coping skills and career training. This program addresses which problem related to punishment?
   A. The effects of punishment may depend on the presence of the punisher.
   B. Punishment may be reinforcing misbehavior because of the attention received.
   C. Punishment conveys little information about how to behave differently.
   D. Those who are punished often respond with anxiety, fear or rage.

28. One disadvantage of punishment is
   A. the effects of punishment are enduring.
   B. punishment conveys a great deal of information, sometimes too much to absorb.
   C. most behavior is too difficult to punish immediately.
   D. all of the above.

29. Nick is a struggling artist who loves his work. He becomes well-known and people are now commissioning him to paint. He finds that his passion for his work has decreased. What has happened?
   A. Intrinsic reinforcers have interfered with extrinsic reinforcers.
   B. He has been put on a token economy and does not like it.
   C. Extrinsic reinforcers have interfered with intrinsic motivation.
   D. His love for his work has been extinguished through the absence of reinforcers.

30. Tolman's experiments demonstrating latent learning showed that
   A. learning can occur even though it may not be immediately expressed.
   B. rats are capable of insight.
   C. extrinsic reinforcement can reduce intrinsic motivation.
   D. personality characteristics interact with environmental influences.

31. Social-cognitive theories differ from conditioning models of learning in that
   A. proponents study higher-level cognitive processes as well as environmental influences.
   B. social learning theories do not utilize discrimination and generalization.
   C. they are more scientific than conditioning models of learning.
   D. they focus almost exclusively on the use of primary reinforcers.

32. Maggie is 16 years old and learning to drive. Though she has never driven before, she is able to put the key in the ignition, turn the starter and put the car into gear. Which of the following best explains these abilities?
   A.   Maggie's intelligence
   B.   observational learning
   C.   cognitive maps
   D.   the ABCs of learning

33. Bandura's study with children who watched the short film of two men playing with toys demonstrated which of the following?
   A.   Children must be rewarded to imitate models.
   B.   Children were likely to imitate the aggressive behaviors of adults in the film.
   C.   Children will only imitate other children, not adults.
   D.   Aggression cannot be learned through imitation.

PRACTICE TEST 2 - Short Answer

1. Any relatively permanent change in behavior that occurs because of experience is
    _____.

2. When a neutral stimulus is paired with an unconditioned stimulus that elicits some
    reflexive unconditioned response, the neutral stimulus comes to elicit a similar or related
    response. The neutral stimulus is then called a _____.

3. If a conditioned stimulus is repeatedly presented without the unconditioned stimulus, the
    conditioned response eventually disappears. This is called _____.

4. The process by which a neutral stimulus becomes a conditioned stimulus by being paired
    with an already established conditioned stimulus is known as _____ conditioning.

5. Julia developed a conditioned fear response to the cocker spaniel that bit her. She is now
    afraid of all dogs. This is called stimulus _____.

6. In stimulus _____, different responses are made to stimuli that resemble the
    conditioned stimulus in some way.

7. Many theorists believe that the conditioned stimulus (CS) elicits a conditioned response
    (CR) because the CS _____ the US, not simply because they are associated with
    one another.

8. Responses such as fear are often acquired through conditioning, and can be extinguished
    in the same way. One method for eliminating such fear responses is _____, which
    pairs a feared object with another object that elicits responses incompatible with fear.

9. In _____ conditioning, behavior becomes more or less likely to occur depending on
    its _____.

10. A response may be strengthened or may be more likely to occur again as a result of a
    stimulus known as a _____.

11. In classical conditioning, _____ responses are learned whereas in operant
    conditioning, more _____ responses are likely to be learned.

12. Pain, cold, and food are considered _____ reinforcers, whereas money, praise, and smiles are considered _____ reinforcers.

13. In _____ reinforcement or punishment, something is given following a desired or undesired response; in _____ reinforcement or punishment, something is taken away or withdrawn following a desired or undesired behavior.

14. Frequently, people confuse _____ reinforcement with _____ because both involve unpleasant stimuli.

15. Punishment _____ the likelihood of a response, whereas negative reinforcement _____ the likelihood of a response.

16. Responses are more resistant to extinction when they are not always followed by a reinforcer. Such schedules are called _____ schedules of reinforcement.

17. Real estate agents are paid when they sell a home, regardless of how long it takes for them to sell one. This is a _____ schedule of reinforcement.

18. In many occupations, employees are paid every two weeks. This is a _____ schedule of reinforcement.

19. In _____, you initially reinforce a tendency in the right direction, then gradually require responses that are more and more similar to the final, desired response.

20. An alternative to punishment is a combination of _____ and _____.

21. _____ reinforcers are not inherently related to the activity being reinforced but _____ are.

22. Regardless of the strength of the reinforcer, human beings cannot be taught to live underwater without a life support system. This fact demonstrates the _____ limits on learning.

23. Learning that is not immediately displayed in an overt response is called _____.

24. In _____ learning, the learner observes a model making certain responses and experiencing the consequences.

25. The _____ theories focus on the role played by beliefs, interpretations of events, and other cognitions.

PRACTICE TEST 3 - Essay

1.   In the following examples, identify the unconditioned stimulus, unconditioned response, conditioned stimulus and conditioned response.

    A.   When your father is angry with you, he calls you by both your first and middle names. Every time you hear him call you that way, you become anxious.

    B.   You keep your dog's leash in the front closet. Every time you go to get something out of the closet, Fido comes running excitedly and waits to go out.

    C.   Your true love wears a certain perfume. Every time you smell that perfume, you feel happy inside.

    D.   You had a terrifying car accident at the corner of Park Place and Main Street. Now every time you approach that corner, you feel anxious.

2.   In the following examples identify the principles of classical conditioning, such as stimulus discrimination, stimulus generalization, extinction, etc.

    A.   While caring for your friend's dog, you notice that it displays a cowering posture as you roll up a newspaper. You try this several more times with magazines or stacks of notebook paper and the dog displays the same behavior. You become convinced that this dog is generally afraid of rolled-up paper.

    B.   Joan, a dog breeder, has been phobic about Doberman pinschers since one attacked her. After the attack, she felt tense and apprehensive whenever she walked by a Doberman, even if the dog was in a cage or on a leash, though she was never uncomfortable with any other type of dog. Recently she has been experiencing a change in her feelings toward Dobermans. She was given four Doberman puppies to sell and since being around them for several months, she is no longer fearful of Dobermans.

    C.   At a red light, Bob and Fred automatically tensed and felt chills when they heard the screech of tires behind them. Later, while watching a car race, Bob remarked that the screeching of tires was having little effect on them then.

    D.   After Bill got food poisoning from roast chicken, he vowed he would never return to that restaurant nor would he ever eat chicken again. All he wanted was to go home and eat his mother's cooking. As he entered the kitchen, he became nauseated when he saw the turkey sitting on the table.

3. Identify whether the consequences in the following examples are positive or negative reinforcement, or positive or negative punishment. Indicate the probable effects of the consequences, according to operant theories of learning.

    A. A buzzer sound continues until a seat belt is fastened.
    B. Whenever Joe picks up a cigarette, his roommate complains and insults him.
    C. Whenever Warren does the dishes, his girlfriend compliments and kisses him.
    D. Whenever Fred skis down the most difficult slopes, he always has a bad fall.

4. Identify the problem or problems in the following examples and, using principles of learning theories, suggest the changes needed.

    A. Ten-year-old Sara is expected to keep her room clean. Her parents check her room weekly and in the past year, her room was clean on 20 occasions. Sara's parents praised her lavishly on 10 of those occasions that her room was clean and on the other 10 occasions, Sara received no reinforcement. This technique has not been working well since on any given day, the room is likely to be a mess.
    B. Baby Ari is not yet sleeping through the night. Every time the baby cries, one of his parents picks him up. His parents decide that after checking to make sure the baby is O.K., they will just let him cry. Ari cries and cries for five nights in a row. On the first four nights, his parents kept to their agreement, but on the fifth night, they couldn't stand it any longer and picked him up. Now Ari is crying more than ever.
    C. Sue is always in trouble in class. Her teacher has tried everything he knows to make her behave: talking to her privately, having her stay after class, and scolding her in public. Regardless of what he does, her misbehavior continues.

5. Below is an application of punishment. Identify the problems demonstrated in this example and suggest a more effective approach.

A parent discovers crayon marks and scribbling on a recently painted wall. Tommy, 18-months-old, is angrily pulled from the playpen, brought before the wall, and harshly told, "No! No! No!", and given a sharp slap on the back of his hand. He is still crying when placed in the crib for a nap. Things become quiet for a time, and then the sound of movement is heard. A quick check shows Tommy is not in his crib. A search locates Tommy in the office room. He has doodled in various places with pens and pencils from the desk.

6.   Identify the schedule of reinforcement that is being used in each example.

    A.   Pop quizzes
    B.   Quizzes after every chapter
    C.   Quizzes every Monday
    D. $10 for every A

7.   Describe similarities and differences between social-cognitive and behavioral models of learning.

CHAPTER EIGHT

Behavior in Social and Cultural Context

LEARNING OBJECTIVES

1.   Discuss the focus of the field of social psychology and cultural psychology.

2.   Describe two controversial studies (Milgram study, prison study) and discuss how they illustrate the influence of roles on behavior.

3.   List and explain the reasons why people obey authority and when they may disobey.

4.   Summarize the principles and components of attribution theory.

5.   Describe the relationship between attitudes and behavior.

6.   Define attitudes and identify important influences on attitudes.

7.   List and explain persuasive and manipulative techniques of attitude change.

8.   Discuss some reasons for conforming to social pressure in a group.

9.   Define diffusion of responsibility, groupthink, social loafing, and deindividuation. Discuss the conditions under which each of these is most likely to occur and the consequences of each process.

10.   Discuss the steps involved in disobedience, dissent, and altruistic action.

11.   Define ethnocentrism and explain its consequences.

12.   Describe some of the effects of competition.

13.   Describe ways that stereotypes are useful and three ways which they distort reality.

14.   Define prejudice and the psychological, social, and financial functions that perpetuate it.

15.   Discuss approaches for reducing prejudice and conflict between groups.

BRIEF CHAPTER SUMMARY

Chapter 8 examines some of the main topic areas in the fields of social psychology and cultural psychology, which study the individual in the social and cultural context. The influence of the social context begins with norms or rules that people are expected to follow. Each of us fills many social roles that are governed by norms about how a person in that position should behave. The roles we fill and the rules that govern those roles heavily influence our behavior, as demonstrated by two classic studies (Milgram's investigation of obedience and the prison study). These studies show how roles can override our own beliefs and values. The social context also influences our thought processes. Attempts to change our attitudes are all around us. To resist unwanted persuasion, one must think critically about information from all sources. Attributions—the way we explain why events happen—influence our responses to the world. Certain types of attributional errors and tendencies can occur that may cause misinterpretations of events (e.g., fundamental attribution error, self-serving bias). Behaviors such as groupthink, conformity, deindividuation, and social loafing can occur as a result of the presence and influence of other group members. The chapter examines the factors that influence independent action, particularly altruism and dissent. The importance of group identity and interactions among groups are discussed. Stereotypes help us organize new information, but they also distort reality (e.g, the tendency to exaggerate differences between groups). The origins of prejudice and efforts to reduce prejudice are discussed. Finally, the chapter raises the question of human nature and its influence on behavior. Studying individuals in a social context helps to identify the normal social influences that contribute to behaviors we often think result from individual or personality factors.

PREVIEW OUTLINE

Before you read the chapter, review the preview outline for each section of the text. After you have read the chapter, close this book and try to re-create the outlines on a blank piece of paper.

I. **ROLES AND RULES**
    A. **Definitions**
        1. Social psychology and cultural psychology - fields that examine the influence of social and cultural environment on individuals and groups
        2. Norms – unspoken rules about how we are supposed to act
        3. Roles - positions in society that are regulated by norms about how people in those positions should behave
    B. **The obedience study by Milgram**
        1. Subjects thought they were in an experiment about learning and were instructed to shock another subject when an error was made
        2. All participants gave some shock; two-thirds obeyed the experimenter and gave all the shocks despite cries of pain

3.   Subsequent studies found disobedience occurs when the experimenter left the room, the victim was right there in the room, etc.

4.   Conclusion - Obedience is a function of the situation, not of personalities

5.   Evaluating the obedience study: some considered the study unethical, but the Milgram study highlighted the danger of unquestioning obedience

C.   The prison study by Zimbardo

1.   When college students were randomly assigned to be prisoners or guards, prisoners became passive and panicky, while some guards became abusive

2.   Behavior depends on social roles, which can overrule personality, values

D.   The power of roles

1.   People obey because they believe in the authority's legitimacy and to avoid negative outcomes and gain positive ones

2.   Why do people obey when it's not in their interest or violates their values?

a.   Investing the authority, not themselves, with responsibility

b.   Routinization - defining the activity as routine; normalizing it

c.   Rules of good manners - people lack the words to disobey

d.   Entrapment - commitment to course of action is escalated

II. SOCIAL INFLUENCES ON BELIEFS

A.   Social cognition - how the social environment influences thoughts, beliefs, etc.

B.   Attributions - explanations we make for behavior

1.   Types of attributions and biases

a.   Situational attributions - identify the cause of an action as something in the environment or situation

b.   Dispositional attributions - identify the cause of an action as something in the person, such as a trait or motive

c.   Fundamental attribution error - tendency to overestimate dispositional factors and underestimate the influence of the situation when explaining someone else's behavior

d.   Self-serving bias – tendency to take credit for good actions and rationalize mistakes when explaining one's own behavior

e.   Just-world hypothesis - the need to believe the world is fair and that good people are rewarded and bad people are punished

C.   Attitudes – beliefs that may be explicit or implicit

1.   Not always based on reason; can be based on conformity, habit, rationalization, economic self-interest, generational events

2.   Attitudes can change to achieve consistency; to reduce cognitive dissonance (when two attitudes or an attitude and a behavior conflict)

3.   Attitudes are also influenced by other people trying to persuade us

a.   Friendly persuasion – enhanced by repetition (validity effect), argument by admired person, linking message to good feelings

b.   Coercive persuasion (brainwashing) suppresses ability to reason, to think critically, and to make good choices; person's access to information is severely controlled, often by a powerful leader

III. INDIVIDUALS IN GROUPS

A.   Conformity

1.   Asch's conformity study – comparing line segments

2.   People conform for a variety of reasons including identification with group members, popularity, self-interest, and to avoid punishment

3.   Conformity has good and bad sides, but it can suppress critical thinking

B.   Groupthink - the tendency for all members of the group to think alike and suppress disagreement; often results in faulty or even disastrous decisions

1.   Occurs when a group's need for total agreement overwhelms its need to make the wisest decision

2.   Groupthink more likely when group has illusion of invulnerability, self-censors, and the group pressures dissenters to conform

3.   Groupthink can be counteracted if doubt and dissent are encouraged and if decisions are made by a majority rather than by unanimity

C.   The anonymous crowd

1.   Diffusion of responsibility

    a.   The more people who are around when a problem occurs, the less likely one of them will offer assistance

    b.   Individuals fail to act because they believe someone else will do so

    c.   May explain why crowds of people fail to respond to an emergency

2.   Social loafing - diffusion of responsibility in work groups; individuals work less and let others work harder

    a.   More likely to occur when members not accountable, when workers feel that others are getting a "free ride," when the work itself is uninteresting, and when working harder duplicates efforts

    c.   Social loafing declines when the challenge of a job is increased and when each member has a different job

3.   Deindividuation - losing all awareness of individuality and sense of self; people more likely to conform to the norms of the specific group situation

    a.   Increases willingness to do harm, break the law (e.g., riots)

    b.   Can also increase friendliness and self-disclosure

D.   Disobedience and dissent

1.   Altruism - the willingness to take selfless or dangerous action for others

2.   Reasons for altruistic action include a combination of personal convictions and situational influences

3.   Steps involved in disobedience, dissent, and altruism

    a.   The individual perceives the need for intervention or help

    b.   The individual decides to take responsibility; depends on risks

    c.   The costs of doing nothing outweigh the costs of getting involved

    d.   The individual has an ally

    e.   The individual becomes entrapped; once initial steps have been taken, most people will increase their commitment

IV. GROUP CONFLICT AND PREJUDICE

A. Group identity: us versus them

1. Ethnocentrism - the belief that one's own culture is superior to others
2. Personal identities are based on particular traits and unique history; social identities are based on the groups we belong to
3. Influence of social identities
    a. Social identities create "us" or ingroup, versus "them" categories
    b. Us-them identities are strengthened when the groups compete
    c. Competition can have positive results (e.g., better inventions) and negative results (e.g., reduced motivation)
    d. Interdependence in reaching mutual goals (cooperation) can reduce competitiveness and hostility

B. Stereotypes

1. Summary impression of a group in which all members of that group are viewed as sharing common traits that may be positive, negative, or neutral
2. Stereotypes help us process new information, retrieve memories, organize experience, make sense of differences, and predict how people will behave
3. Stereotypes can distort reality (e.g., exaggerate differences <u>between</u> groups, underestimate differences <u>within</u> other groups)

C. Prejudice - a negative stereotype and a strong, unreasonable dislike or hatred of a group or its individual members

1. Resists rational argument and evidence; resistant to change
2. Prejudice may serve psychological, social, cultural, & economic functions
3. Though studies show prejudice in North America is decreasing, there is disagreement about how to accurately measure prejudice
4. Implicit or unconscious prejudice may be more pervasive than explicit prejudice; it can be measured via symbolic measures of racism, behavioral measures, or measures of unconscious associations with the target group
5. Conditions that must be met in order to reduce prejudice or group conflict
    a. Both sides must have equal legal status, economic opportunities, and power
    b. The larger culture must endorse egalitarian norms and provide moral support and legitimacy for both sides
    c. Both sides must have opportunities to work and socialize together, formally and informally
    c. Both sides must cooperate; work together for common goal

PRACTICE TEST 1 - Multiple choice

1. Rules that regulate "correct" behaviors for a manager or an employee are called
    A. norms.   B. occupational roles.
    C. social rules.   D. depersonalization.

2. In the obedience experiments, Milgram found that people were more likely to disobey the experimenter and refuse to administer shock when
    A. the experimenter stayed in the room.
    B. the subject administered shocks directly to the victim in the same room.
    C. authority figures, rather than "ordinary" people, ordered subjects to continue.
    D. the subject worked with a peer who also administered shocks.

3. In Milgram's obedience studies, the person most likely to disobey would be a subject who
    A. felt very upset about administering shocks to another person.
    B. worked with peers who refused to go further.
    C. had strong moral and religious principles.
    D. had a very passive personality.

4. In the obedience experiments, what percentage of the subjects administered the maximum amount of shock to the victim?
    A. only 1 to 2 percent   B. approximately two-thirds
    C. 30 percent   D. all of the subjects

5. The major point of the prison study was
    A. to demonstrate that certain personality types should not be in positions of authority.
    B. that people's behavior depends largely on the roles they are asked to play.
    C. that students are very suggestible and are not good research subjects.
    D. how quickly people are corrupted by power.

6. Which conclusion is shared by the prison study and the obedience study?
    A. The roles people played influenced their behavior more than their personalities.
    B. What people did depended on the role they were assigned.
    C. Social roles and obligations have a powerful influence on behavior.
    D. All of the above

7. Which of the following causes people to obey when they really would rather not?
    A. entrapment   B. good manners
    C. routinization   D. all of the above

8. When Ashley's husband forgot to run an errand, she attributed his forgetting to his selfishness. When Andy's wife forgot to run an errand, he attributed her forgetting to her being preoccupied with problems at work. Ashley made a(n) _____ attribution, whereas Andy made a(n) _____ attribution.
   A. dispositional; situational
   B. situational; dispositional
   C. self-serving; external
   D. internal; dispositional

9. "Sally rides her bike to school because she is athletic" is an example of
   A. a dispositional attribution.
   B. the self-serving bias.
   C. the fundamental attribution error.
   D. situational attribution.

10. "Jennifer rides her bike to school because she can't get a ride" is an example of
    A. a dispositional attribution.
    B. the self-serving bias.
    C. the fundamental attribution error.
    D. situational attribution.

11. In attributing causes to other people's behaviors, the tendency to overestimate the effects of personality factors and underestimate the effects of situational factors is called
    A. a dispositional attribution.
    B. the just-world hypothesis.
    C. the fundamental attribution error.
    D. the self-serving bias.

12. I believe that I got an A in geometry because I'm a hard worker, but I got a D in biology because the teacher doesn't like me. This demonstrates
    A. the just-world hypothesis.
    B. the self-serving bias.
    C. the fundamental attribution error.
    D. blaming the victim.

13. "People get what they deserve" is an example of
    A. the just-world hypothesis.
    B. situational attribution.
    C. the fundamental attribution error.
    D. the self-serving bias.

14. When Hortense was diagnosed with cancer, she believed that she must have done something wrong to have deserved such an illness. Her belief is an example of
    A. a situational attribution.
    B. guilt.
    C. the just-world hypothesis.
    D. an internal attribution.

15. Attitudes are affected by
    A. thinking.
    B. conformity.
    C. habit.
    D. all of the above.

16. Students were asked to publicly advocate the importance of safe sex, and then list the reasons for their own past failure to use condoms. Afterwards, they experienced
    A. friendly persuasion.
    B. cognitive dissonance.
    C. coercive persuasion.
    D. insight.

17. Following their confrontation with the discrepancy between their attitudes and their behaviors, what would the students in the previous question be most likely to do?
    A. increase their use of condoms
    B. make no change in their behavior
    C. decrease their use of condoms
    D. none of the above

18. That repetition increases the perception that familiar statements are true demonstrates
    A. cognitive dissonance.
    B. generational identity.
    C. the validity effect.
    D. coercive persuasion.

19. One of the techniques that facilitates coercive persuasion is
    A. repeating a piece of information over and over.
    B. exposing people to arguments from someone they admire.
    C. defining a person's problems in simplistic terms, and offering simple answers.
    D. offering people food while listening to an argument.

20. People are likely to conform
    A. in order to keep their jobs, win promotions or win votes.
    B. if they wish to be liked.
    C. if they want to avoid being unpopular.
    D. for all the reasons listed above.

21. In close-knit groups, members tend to think alike and suppress dissent. This is called
    A. group polarization.
    B. risky shift.
    C. diffusion of responsibility.
    D. groupthink.

22. Geraldo's boss always likes to be right and to be the "expert" on any topic. Whenever their work team meets, he becomes irritated with whoever disagrees with him. If anyone tries to speak up to him, others in the group quickly change the subject to be sure no one challenges him. What is occurring in this situation?
    A. groupthink
    B. diffusion of responsibility
    C. social loafing
    D. deindividuation

23. A woman was stabbed and none of the numerous onlookers called for help. What accounts for this?
    A. social loafing
    B. conformity
    C. diffusion of responsibility
    D. deindividuation

24. The willingness to take selfless or dangerous action on behalf of others is called
    A. interdependence.
    B. individuation.
    C. altruism.
    D. all of the above.

25. Which of the following is <u>NOT</u> one of the factors that predicts altruism?
   A. an altruistic personality
   C. perceiving the need for help

   B. an ally
   D. entrapment

26. The belief that one's own culture or ethnic group is superior to all others is called
   A. ethnic separatism.
   B. social norms.

   B. prejudice.
   D. ethnocentrism.

27. A stereotype
   A. may be positive.
   C. helps us to organize the world.

   B. may be negative or neutral.
   D. includes all of the above.

28. Stereotypes can be helpful because they help us
   A. increase the accuracy of our opinions about particular individuals.
   B. see the differences between groups.
   C. rapidly process new information and organize experience.
   D. do all of the above.

29. Students are shown a slide of a white male committing a crime against a black male. Later, when they are asked what they saw, most reported seeing a black male committing a crime against a white male. This error is a result of the fact that stereotypes
   A. produce selective perception.
   B. accentuate differences between groups.
   C. underestimate differences within other groups.
   D. help us process new information.

30. Stereotypes distort reality by
   A. accentuating differences between groups.
   B. producing selective perceptions.
   C. underestimating differences within other groups.
   D. propagating all of the above.

31. An unreasonable negative feeling toward a category of people is called
   A. ethnocentrism.
   B. prejudice.

   B. a stereotype.
   D. social identity.

32. Which characteristic is most likely to lead to evil actions?
   A. adherence to roles, obedience to authority, conformity, entrapment
   B. lack of developed conscience
   C. mental illness
   D. an evil nature

109

PRACTICE TEST 2 - Short Answer

1.   _____ are positions in society regulated by norms that describe how people in those positions should behave.

2.   In the obedience study by Milgram, psychologists were surprised to find that _____ of the subjects gave all the shocks.

3.   In the prison study, the "prisoners" became panicky and helpless and some of the guards became tyrannical and cruel. Their behavior probably depended on the _____they were asked to play.

4.   The obedience studies and the prison study demonstrate the power of social roles to influence behavior. Some of the reasons that people obey authority, even when it's not in their own interest or may violate their own values, are the rules of good _____ and _____, which occurs when commitment to a course of action is escalated.

5.   How the social environment influences thoughts, beliefs, and memories and how people's perceptions of themselves and others affect their relationships is the subject matter of social _____.

6.   A _____ attribution identifies the cause of an action as something in the environment.

7.   The tendency to overestimate _____ factors and underestimate the influence of the _____ when explaining someone else's behavior describes the _____ attribution error.

8.   The _____ occurs when people take credit for positive actions and attribute the bad ones to the situation.

9.   The need to believe that the world is fair, and that good people are rewarded and bad people are punished, is called the _____.

10.   A relatively stable opinion is a(n) _____.

11.   The more a statement is repeated, the more people will believe that it is true. This is known as the _____ effect.

12.   _____ persuasion techniques suppress people's ability to reason, to think critically, and to make good choices.

13.   _____ refers to a behavior performed when carrying out an order from someone in authority. In contrast, _____ refers to behavior or attitudes that occur as a result of real or imagined group pressure.

14.   Certain historical decisions have been made by strong leaders who discouraged disagreement, preferred unanimous decisions, and did not get opinions from people outside the group. These decisions were a result of _____.

15.   Rather than bystander apathy, _____ may account for why individuals in crowds fail to respond to an emergency.

16.   One reason for social loafing in a work group may be that the work is _____.

17.   _____ increases a person's willingness to do harm to someone else, to cheat and to break the law. It may also be a primary reason for mob violence.

18.   _____, or the willingness to take risks or dangerous action for others, may be a result of a combination of both conscience and situational influences.

19.   People have _____ identities based on their nationality, ethnic heritage, occupation, and social roles.

20.   "We" are good, noble, and humane; "they" are bad, stupid, and cruel. Such beliefs reflect _____.

21.   Believing that all "Wispians" are good in math, is a(n) _____. Disliking and refusing to live next to a Wispian is an example of _____.

22.   One way stereotypes distort reality is that they _____ differences between groups and _____ differences within other groups.

23.   The "cycle of _____" can result from unfamiliarity or discomfort with a group.

24.   Social and cultural psychologists suggest that human behavior depends more on _____ organization than on human nature.

PRACTICE TEST 3 - Essay

1.   Identify the influences and effects of roles and norms in the prison study and the obedience study.

2.   A group of students were asked to explain the source of a person's grades. They provided the explanations below. Examine each explanation and identify the explanatory device it relies upon.

   A.   Grades result from a person's intelligence and self-discipline. When these are high, grades are good and vice versa.
   B.   Grades depend on doing the right things. A person should earn good grades for reading instructions, meeting deadlines, and turning in assignments. If a person does not do these things, he or she deserves bad grades.
   C.   Grades depend on quality teaching and educational materials. If the teacher is good, students should be motivated and do well.
   D.   Grades depend on luck. Sometimes it doesn't matter whether a person has studied or not if the test is tricky.

3.   You need to get a B in all of your classes to get the scholarship you need. You are right on the border between a B and a C in your Spanish class. Using information on persuasion, discuss how you might approach your Spanish teacher to attempt to persuade him to give you the benefit of the doubt.

4.   Dr. Wong requires a group project in her sociology class. She wants each group to design a federally funded project to reduce the number of homeless and provide appropriate services for those who remain homeless. She is aware of all the principles of group behavior and she wants to reduce the likelihood of social loafing, diffusion of responsibility, groupthink, deindividuation, group polarization and competition. She wants to increase cooperation and independent action. Develop a set of instructions she should use to meet all of her goals for this assignment.

5.   Jan and her sister are having a debate about the Agyflops, people from a country located in the Pacific Ocean. Jan's sister does not like the Agyflops and is explaining why to Jan. Most of her reasons are based on stereotypes. For each statement Jan's sister makes, indicate which problem with stereotypes it exemplifies.

A.   "When I visited Agyflopia, everyone was so unfriendly. No one smiled."

B.   "They are so different from us. Americans are so direct, but you never know what the Agyflops are thinking."

C.   "I guess that there are many Agyflops in school with us, but they never seem to speak correctly and they always seem so stupid."

6.   Why is prejudice so hard to eliminate? You are the principal of a school with students from many different backgrounds. Design a program that attempts to improve relationships and reduce prejudice.

CHAPTER NINE

Thinking and Intelligence

LEARNING OBJECTIVES

1.   Define thinking.

2.   Define and distinguish among concepts (including basic concepts and prototypes), propositions and cognitive schemas.

3.   Distinguish among subconscious processes, nonconscious processes and mindless conscious processing.

4.   Distinguish between an algorithm and a heuristic.

5.   Distinguish among reflective judgment, inductive, deductive, and dialectical reasoning, and between informal and formal reasoning.

6.   List and describe the stages of reflective judgment, according to studies by King and Kitchener.

7.   Discuss six types of cognitive bias that can influence reasoning.

8.   Describe the conditions under which people are most likely to try to reduce dissonance.

9.   Define and explain the g factor in intelligence.

10.   Distinguish between the psychometric approach and cognitive approaches to intelligence.

11.   Discuss the objectives, uses, and criticisms of IQ tests.

12.   Describe the components of Sternberg's theory of intelligence and discuss whether these components are measured on most intelligence tests.

13.   Describe factors other than intelligence that contribute to achievement.

14.   Discuss the cognitive abilities found in nonhuman animals.

BRIEF CHAPTER SUMMARY

Chapter 9 examines the elements and processes of thinking. Concepts, propositions, schemas, and images are all elements of thought. Deductive and inductive reasoning are types of formal reasoning that are useful for well-specified problems that have a single correct answer. Dialectical reasoning and reflective judgment are types of informal reasoning that are useful for more complex problems that require critical thinking. Several cognitive biases affect rational thinking and cause cognitive errors and distortions. Intelligence is a characteristic that is difficult to define but is related to one's ability to think. Theorists examine intelligence using two approaches: the psychometric approach, which attempts to measure intelligence through tests, and the cognitive approach, which examines the aspects or domains of intelligence. Sternberg's triarchic theory is described. Intellectual achievement as measured by test scores is heavily influenced by such factors as motivation and attitude. Finally, psychologists also are interested in the cognitive abilities of nonhumans. Whether animals have the cognitive capacity for language has been studied and debated.

PREVIEW OUTLINE

Before you read the chapter, review the preview outline for each section of the text. After you have read the chapter, close this book and try to <u>re-create</u> the outlines on a blank piece of paper.

I. **THOUGHT: USING WHAT WE KNOW**
- A. **The elements of cognition**
  1. Thinking - mental manipulation of internal representations of objects, activities and situations
  2. Concepts - a mental category that groups objects, relations, activities, abstractions or qualities having common properties
     - a. Basic concepts - those with a moderate number of instances
     - b. Prototype - most representative example of a concept
  3. Proposition - units of meaning made of concepts that express unitary idea
  4. Cognitive schemas - mental network of knowledge, beliefs, expectations
  5. Mental images - mental representations, often visual
- B. **How conscious is thought?**
  1. Subconscious processes - outside of awareness but can be made conscious
  2. Nonconscious processes - remain outside of awareness
  3. Mindlessness - acting, speaking, making decisions out of habit

II. REASONING RATIONALLY

A. **Reasoning** - mental activity that involves operating on information in order to reach conclusions; drawing inferences from observations or facts

B. **Formal reasoning: algorithms and logic**
1. Algorithms - procedures guaranteed to produce a solution (a recipe)
2. Deductive reasoning - if the premises are true, the conclusion must be true
3. Inductive reasoning - the conclusion probably follows from the premises, but could conceivably be false

C. **Informal reasoning: heuristics and dialectical thinking**
1. Heuristics - rules of thumb that don't guarantee an optimal solution
2. Dialectical reasoning - comparing different views to resolve differences

D. **Reflective judgment** - critical thinking; the ability to evaluate and integrate evidence, relate evidence to theory or opinion, and reach conclusions

III. BARRIERS TO REASONING RATIONALLY

A. **Availability heuristic -** judging the probability of an event by how easy it is to think of examples

B. **Avoiding loss** - making decisions based on avoiding loss

C. **Mental sets** - trying to solve problems by using rules that worked in the past

D. **Hindsight bias** - believing that an outcome was known all along

E. **Confirmation bias** - paying attention to what confirms our beliefs

F. **Cognitive consistency** - motivation to reduce cognitive dissonance that occurs when a person simultaneously holds two cognitions that are inconsistent or holds a belief that is inconsistent with the person's behavior

IV. MEASURING INTELLIGENCE: THE PSYCHOMETRIC APPROACH

A. **g factor** - Many believe in a general ability that underlies all other abilities

B. **The psychometric approach** - traditional approach that focuses on how well people perform on standardized mental tests
1. Achievement tests - measure knowledge that has been taught
2. Aptitude tests - measure ability to acquire skills and knowledge

C. **The invention of IQ Tests**
1. Binet measured children's mental age (MA) - intellectual development relative to other children's
2. Wechsler developed test for adults (WAIS) and children (WISC)
3. Culture-free tests (non-verbal tests) and culture-fair tests (used items common to many cultures) are unable to eliminate bias
4. Scores are influenced by expectations which shape stereotypes, which can affect scores by creating doubt, called stereotype threat
5. Tests have value (they do predict school performance), but educators must recognize the limits of the tests and use them better

V. DISSECTING INTELLIGENCE: THE COGNITIVE APPROACH

A. **The triarchic theory of intelligence** - Robert Sternberg identifies three aspects
1. Componential intelligence – includes metacognition
2. Experiential intelligence – includes creativity in new situations
3. Contextual intelligence – includes tacit knowledge (practical knowledge)

B. **The theory of multiple intelligences**
1. Gardner's theory of multiple intelligences
2. Emotional intelligence – understanding your own and others' emotions

C. **Thinking critically about intelligence(s)**
1. There is disagreement about the idea of new intelligences
2. Some say some of Gardner's domains are personality traits or talents

D. **Motivation and intellectual success**
1. Terman study showed motivation was determining factor in life success
2. Stevenson study found that Asian students far outperformed American students on math tests and the gap is increasing
   a. Differences could not be accounted for by educational resources or intellectual abilities
   b. American parents had lower standards for their children's performance and were more likely than Asian parents to believe math ability was innate
   c. American students did not value education as much

VI. ANIMAL MINDS

A. **Animal intelligence** - subject of study in cognitive ethology
1. Cognitive ethologists say animals anticipate future events, make plans, coordinate their activities with others of their species
2. Even complex actions may involve pre-wired behavior, not cognition
3. Some behaviors do demonstrate cognitive abilities

B. **Animals and language**
1. Primary ingredient in human cognition is language
2. Criteria for language
   a. Meaningfulness - adequate ability to refer to things, ideas, feelings
   b. Displacement - permits communication about objects not present
   c. Productivity - ability to produce and comprehend new utterances
3. By these criteria, animals communicate but do not have language
4. Early efforts to teach language had success which was followed by skepticism and recognition of methodological problems in the research
5. Newer research better controlled; has found that with training animals can use symbols, signs, understand some words, learn without formal training
6. Some evidence non-primates can acquire aspects of language

PRACTICE TEST 1 - Multiple Choice

1. The ability to think
    A. is defined as the physical manipulation of the environment.
    B. confines us to the immediate present.
    C. allows for the mental manipulation of internal representations of objects, activities and situations.
    D. incorporates all of the above.

2. A mental category that groups things that have common properties is called a
    A. concept.   B. symbol.
    C. proposition.   D. schema.

3. Relationships between concepts are expressed by
    A. super concepts.   B. symbols.
    C. propositions.   D. schemas.

4. Propositions are
    A. complicated networks of knowledge.   B. prototypes.
    C. units of meaning made up of concepts. D. composed of schemas.

5. Processes that are automated, such as typing or driving, are called _____, whereas making decisions without stopping to analyze what we are doing makes use of

    _____.
    A. subconscious processes; nonconscious processes
    B. mindlessness; subconscious processes
    C. nonconscious processes; mindlessness
    D. subconscious processes; mindlessness

6. Nonconscious processes refer to
    A. processes that can be brought into consciousness when necessary.
    B. decisions that are made without thinking very hard.
    C. processes that are outside awareness but affect behavior.
    D. the practice of operating on information in order to reach conclusions.

7. "All cats have fur. This animal is a cat. Therefore, it has fur." This is an example of
    A. deductive reasoning.   B. dialectical reasoning.
    C. inductive reasoning.   D. divergent thinking.

8. Inductive reasoning
   A. is used when the premises provide support for the conclusion, but the conclusion still could be false.
   B. is often used in scientific thinking.
   C. allows for a specific conclusion.
   D. incorporates all of the above.

9. When information is incomplete or many viewpoints compete, it is necessary to use
   A. informal reasoning.
   B. formal reasoning.
   C. inductive reasoning.
   D. deductive reasoning.

10. For complicated problems in real life, it is best to use
    A. dialectical reasoning.
    B. informal reasoning.
    C. reflective judgment.
    D. all of the above.

11. When asked about his views on abortion, Carl responds, "That's what I was brought up to believe." According to Kitchener and King, he is in the _____ stage of reflective thought.
    A. quasi-reflective
    B. prereflective
    C. reflective judgment
    D. none of the above

12. People are more likely to take risks
    A. for a potentially more rewarding solution than for a smaller sure gain.
    B. if the risks are perceived as a way to avoid loss.
    C. when the results are explained in terms of lives saved not lives lost.
    D. none of the above.

13. Which of the following helps to explain the popularity of lotteries and why people buy earthquake insurance?
    A. confirmation bias
    B. loss aversion
    C. availability heuristic
    D. hindsight bias

14. Unless your coursework is totally determined for you, you probably use _____ to decide what courses to take.
    A. an algorithm
    B. a heuristic
    C. deductive reasoning
    D. hindsight

15. Though Allison lives comfortably in a city with a high crime rate, she is afraid to visit California because of a potential earthquake. Which cognitive bias does this represent?
    A. loss aversion
    B. availability heuristic
    C. cognitive dissonance
    D. confirmation bias

16. Harry and Larry are in a very boring class. It is a required course for Harry, but Larry chose to take this course, and it is too late to withdraw. What is likely to happen?
   A. Harry is likely to try to reduce dissonance by saying he likes the class.
   B. Larry is likely to try to reduce dissonance by saying he likes the class.
   C. Larry is not likely to experience any dissonance.
   D. Both are likely to experience dissonance.

17. The g factor refers to
   A. a general ability that underlies all specific abilities.
   B. a technique using factor analysis.
   C. the psychometric approach to intelligence.
   D. all of the above.

18. The psychometric approach to intelligence focuses on
   A. culture-free and culture-fair tests.
   B. how well people perform on standardized mental tests.
   C. those with learning disabilities.
   D. strategies people use when problem solving.

19. Dr. Bell is more interested in how students arrive at their answers on IQ tests than in their scores. This represents
   A. the psychometric approach to intelligence.   B. the triarchic theory.
   C. the cognitive approach to intelligence.   D. practical intelligence.

20. Componential, experiential, and contextual refer to
   A. Gardner's domains of intelligence.   B. aspects of metacognition.
   C. the triarchic theory of intelligence.   D. divergent thinking.

21. Though Emily has never travelled overseas before, she is coping well with and adapting well to new situations on her trip to Europe. Which type of intelligence is involved?
   A. componential   B. contextual
   C. experiential   D. metacognitive

22. Which of the following are measured on most intelligence tests?
   A. experiential intelligence   B. componential intelligence
   C. contextual intelligence   D. all of the above

23. Based on the studies comparing Asian and American school children, which of the following contributes to achievement?
   A. whether skills are seen as innate or learned
   B. standards for performance
   C. expectation for involvement in outside activities
   D. all of the above

24. Jacob's IQ score is in the upper one percent of the distribution, yet he continues to get Cs in school. What might explain this?

A. low contextual intelligence B. poor practical intelligence
C. low motivation D. mild brain damage

25. Cognitive ethology refers to the study of cognitive processes in
    A. humans.
    B. children.
    C. the elderly.
    D. nonhumans.

26. Which of the following summarizes the current thinking on language ability in nonhumans?
    A. Nonhumans are able to use the basics of language.
    B. Though animals have greater cognitive abilities than is often thought, scientists are divided on this issue.
    C. Animals do not demonstrate any of the aspects of human language.
    D. Only primates (chimpanzees and gorillas) have shown any type of language abilities.

27. Kanzi can use a sign to represent food that is not present in the room. This represents which feature of language?
    A. meaningfulness B. productivity
    C. displacement D. creativity

PRACTICE TEST 2 - Short Answer

1. Thinking can be defined most simply as the _____ manipulation of information.

2. One unit of thought is the _____, a mental category grouping objects, relations, activities, abstractions, or qualities that share certain properties.

3. Horse, shoe, chair are all examples of _____ concepts that have a moderate number of instances.

4. "Psychology is interesting" is an example of a(n) _____, while "Psychology is an interesting subject and it is one of the most popular majors. Psychologists work with people, but they also conduct research and engage in consultation" is an example of a(n) _____.

5. While nonconscious processes remain outside of awareness, _____ processes can be brought into consciousness when necessary.

6. "Intuition" and "insight" are thought to be a result of _____ processes.

7. In deductive reasoning, if the premises are true, the conclusion _____ be true, in inductive reasoning, if the premises are true, the conclusion _____ be true.

8. Inductive reasoning and deductive reasoning are types of _____ reasoning. Problems requiring this type of reasoning can be solved by applying an _____, a set of procedures guaranteed to produce a solution.

9. Juries must weigh opposing viewpoints. They would be most likely to use _____ to reach a verdict in a case.

10. Critical thinking requires that people ask questions, analyze assumptions, tolerate uncertainty and resist oversimplification. These abilities require _____ judgment.

11. The idea that any judgment is as good as any other and is purely subjective would be most likely to occur in the _____ stage of reflective judgment.

12. One kind of rigidity that can hamper problem solving is biases due to _____, a tendency to approach problems in a particular way due to prior experience with similar problems.

13.   That a person might be more afraid of an airplane crash than something much more likely to occur, like a car accident, may be a result of the _____.

14.   Cognitive _____ occurs when a person simultaneously holds two cognitions that are psychologically inconsistent or holds a belief that is inconsistent with the person's behavior.

15.   _____ tests measure skills and knowledge that have been taught, whereas _____ tests measure ability to acquire skills and knowledge.

16.   The _____ focuses on how well people perform on standardized mental tests while the _____ emphasizes the strategies people use to solve problems.

17.   IQ tests have been criticized for being _____ in favor of certain groups. In an attempt to address this problem, psychologists developed tests that were intended to be _____ free and fair.

18.   Some people believe that a _____ ability underlies the many specific abilities tapped by intelligence tests, whereas others believe that there are _____ and independent intelligences.

19.   According to Sternberg's _____ theory, a person who easily adapts to the demands of new environments exhibits _____ intelligence.

20.   Sternberg has identified three facets of intelligence: _____, _____, and _____.

21.   Intellectual achievement also depends on _____ and _____.

22.   The cross-cultural study by Stevenson found that American parents had _____ standards for their children's performance and for schools than Asian parents.

23.   The three criteria for language are meaningfulness, _____, and _____.

24.   Attributing human emotions to certain animal behavior is an example of _____.

PRACTICE TEST 3 - Essay

1. List a prototype for each of the concepts listed below.
    A. clothing
    B. animal
    C. pet
    D. relative

2. In each of the following examples, indicate what type of reasoning is most suitable for each problem and explain why.

    A. A navigator must determine the ship's position from the knowledge of a standard formula and the position of the North Star.
    B. A psychologist must determine if nonconformity facilitates creativity.
    C. A scientist must decide whether to pursue a career in teaching or research.
    D. A couple must decide if they are going to have a child.

3. Identify the cognitive biases in each of the following situations.
    A. Richard would rather drive 1,000 miles than fly because it is safer.
    B. Not only did you choose to go to this party 45 minutes away, but you convinced three other friends to go along. Even though no one is enjoying the party, you say you are having a good time.
    C. Jane doesn't want to get married and John does. When discussing the issue, Jane brings up only troubled relationships she knows of and cannot think of any of the happy relationships.

4. In the following examples identify what type of intelligence is being described, according to Sternberg's theory.
    A. Dr. Morris can go into a big organization and quickly identify the problem and select effective strategies for its solution.
    B. Dr. Mira works with people in psychotherapy and knows which strategies are working and when she needs to try something different.
    C. Regardless of what group of people Nicholas finds himself with, he is able to quickly adjust to the situation, handle himself appropriately and feel comfortable with himself.

5. Do animals have cognitive abilities? Make a case for and against this question.

CHAPTER TEN

Memory

LEARNING OBJECTIVES

1. Discuss the reconstructive nature of memory and the implications for legal cases.

2. Compare recognition, recall, priming, relearning, and explicit and implicit memory.

3. Describe the "three-box model" of memory and explain its components.

4. Describe the parallel distributed processing model of memory.

5. Discuss the role of sensory memory.

6. Describe the processes and limitations of short-term memory (STM).

7. Describe the characteristics of long-term memory (LTM), and explain how information is organized.

8. Distinguish among procedural, declarative, semantic, and episodic memories.

9. Explain the limitations of the three-box model in accounting for the serial position effect.

10. Describe techniques for keeping information in short-term memory and for transferring information to long-term memory.

11. Summarize current findings about the physiological processes involved in memory.

12. List and discuss theories of why forgetting occurs, including childhood amnesia.

13. Describe the relationship between a person's "life story" and actual memories.

BRIEF CHAPTER SUMMARY

Chapter 10 examines the nature of memory. Memory does not record events like a video camera to be replayed at a later time. Rather, our memories incorporate outside information into our recollections so that what we recall is a reconstruction of events and not necessarily a memory of them. Memory is tested using recall, retrieval, and relearning methods. There are two prominent models of memory: the information-processing model, which compares memory processes to computer processes, and the parallel-distributed processing model, which states that knowledge is represented as connections among thousands of processing units operating in parallel. The three-box model, an information-processing model, suggests that there are three types of memory: sensory memory, short-term memory, and long-term memory. Psychologists are interested in knowing what kinds of brain changes take place when we store information. Research examines memory and its relationship to neurons, brain structures, and hormones. There are several different theories that explain why we forget. They include decay theory, replacement theory, interference theory, repression, cue-dependent forgetting, and theories about childhood amnesia.

PREVIEW OUTLINE

Before you read the chapter, review the preview outline for each section of the text. After you have read the chapter, close this book and try to <u>re-create</u> the outlines on a blank piece of paper.

I. **RECONSTRUCTING THE PAST**
   A.   **Memory** is the capacity to retain and retrieve information
   B.   **Reconstructing the past** - memory is a reconstructive process
   C.   **The fading flashbulb** - memories of dramatic (even positive) events can be inaccurate over time
   D.   **The conditions of confabulation**
      1.   The person has thought about the imagined event many times
      2.   The image of the event contains a lot of details
      3.   The event is easy to imagine
      4.   The person focuses on his or her emotional reactions to the event

II. **MEMORY AND THE POWER OF SUGGESTION**
   A.   **The eyewitness on trial**
      1.   People fill in missing pieces from memories, which can lead to errors
      2.   Errors especially likely when ethnicity of suspect differs from witness
      3.   The power of suggestion - way a question is asked or the more often a story is told can influence what and how much is recalled
   B.   **Children's testimony** – children are most suggestible when there's pressure to conform to expectations, and when they want to please the interviewer

III. **IN PURSUIT OF MEMORY**
   A.   **Measuring memory**

      1.   Explicit memory is conscious recollection

      2.   Two ways of measuring explicit memory: recall and recognition

      3.   Implicit memory is unconscious retention in memory

B.   Models of memory

      1.   Three-box model (information-processing)

         a.   Sensory memory - retains information for a second or two

         b.   Short-term memory (STM) - holds limited amount for 30 seconds

         c.   Long-term memory (LTM) - accounts for longer storage

      2.   Parallel distributed processing (connectionist) model

         a.   Information is processed simultaneously, or in parallel

         b.   Considers knowledge to be connections among thousands of units

IV. THE THREE-BOX MODEL

A.   Sensory memory: fleeting impressions

      1.   Includes separate memory subsystems for each of the senses

      2.   Pattern recognition compares a stimulus to information already contained in long-term memory; it then goes to short-term-memory or it vanishes

B.   Short-term memory: memory's scratch pad

      1.   Holds information up to about 30 seconds as an encoded representation

      2.   Working memory - holds information retrieved from long term memory for temporary use

      3.   The leaky bucket - holds seven (plus or minus two) chunks of information

C.   Long-term memory: final destination - capacity is unlimited

      1.   Organization in long-term memory

         a.   Information is organized by semantic categories

         b.   Network models - contents is a network of interrelated concepts

      2.   The contents of long-term memory

         a.   Procedural memories - knowing how

         b.   Declarative memories - knowing that

      3.   From short-term to long-term memory - three-box model has been used to explain the serial position effect

V. THE BIOLOGY OF MEMORY

A.   Changes in neurons and synapses

      1.   In STM, changes within neurons temporarily alter neurotransmitter release

      2.   LTM changes involve permanent structural changes in the brain

B.   Locating memories

      1.   Areas in frontal lobes very active during short-term memory tasks

      2.   Formation of declarative memories involve hippocampus

      3.   Procedural memories involve the cerebellum

      4.   Different brain involvement for implicit and explicit memory tasks

      5.   A memory is a cluster of information distributed across areas of the brain

C.   Hormones and memory

      1.   The adrenalin connection - hormones released during stress enhance memory, but high levels interfere with ordinary learning

2.   Sweet memories - the effect of these hormones may be due to glucose

VI. HOW WE REMEMBER
A.   **Effective encoding**
  1.   Some encoding is effortless; some is effortful
  2.   Rehearsal - review or practice of material while you are learning it
     a.   Maintenance rehearsal - maintains information in STM only
     b.   Elaborative rehearsal - associating new information with stored knowledge
  3.   Deep processing - processing of meaning
B.   **Mnemonics** - strategies for encoding, storing and retaining information

VII.   WHY WE FORGET
A.   **The decay theory** - memories fade with time; doesn't apply well to LTM
B.   **Replacement** - new information wipes out old information
C.   **Interference -** retroactive interference (new information interferes with old) or proactive interference (old information interferes with new)
D.   **Cue-dependent forgetting** - forgetting due to lack of retrieval cues
E.   **Repression** - Freud said painful memories are blocked from consciousness (also called psychogenic amnesia)

VIII.   AUTOBIOGRAPHICAL MEMORIES: THE WAY WE WERE
A.   **Childhood amnesia: the missing years**
  1.   May occur because brain areas involved in formation or storage of events are not well developed until a few years after birth
  2.   Cognitive explanations have also been offered - lack of a sense of self, differences between early and later cognitive schemas, impoverished encoding, a focus on routine
B.   **Memory and narrative: the stories of our lives**
  1.   Narratives are a unifying theme to organize the events of our lives
  2.   Themes serve as a cognitive schema that guides what we remember
  3.   Reminiscence bump - tendency to recall certain periods and not others

IX. MEMORY AND MYTH
A.   Unreliable memories are those from the first years of life, those that become increasingly unlikely, and those that result from suggestive techniques
B.   Memories are considered most reliable when there is corroborating evidence, other signs of trauma, and they are recalled without pressure from others

PRACTICE TEST 1 - Multiple Choice

1. The reconstructive nature of memory refers to
    A.   the alteration of remembered information to help make sense of it.
    B.   the capacity to retain and retrieve information.
    C.   the ability to retrieve from memory previously encountered material.
    D.   vivid, detailed recollections of circumstances.

2. Eyewitness testimony is influenced by
    A.   the fact that the details of events are often inferred rather than observed.
    B.   memory errors that increase when the races of the suspect and witness differ.
    C.   the wording of questions.
    D.   all of the above.

3. Why does the tendency to reconstruct memories present a particularly serious problem in the courtrooms?
    A.   Witnesses will lie to cover their memory errors.
    B.   Reconstructed memories are almost always wrong.
    C.   Witnesses who have reconstructed testimony will fail lie detector tests.
    D.   Witnesses sometimes can't distinguish between what they actually saw and what they have reconstructed.

4. Multiple choice is to essay as
    A.   recall is to relearning.   B.   recall is to recognition.
    C.   priming is to recall.   D.   recognition is to recall.

5. Unconsciously remembered material that continues to have an effect on actions is
    A.   semantic memory.   B.   implicit memory.
    C.   explicit memory.   D.   declarative memory.

6. Comparing the mind to a computer and speaking in terms of inputs and outputs reflects the
    A.   parallel distributed processing model of memory.
    B.   cognitive model of memory.
    C.   information-processing model of memory.
    D.   connectionist model of memory.

7. According to the "three-box" model, which is the first step in memory?
    A.   short-term memory   B.   retrieval
    C.   storage   D.   sensory memory

8. Which of the following is not a basic memory process?
    A.   encoding   B.   retrieval
    C.   storage   D.   perception

9. Which model maintains that knowledge is represented in the brain as connections among thousands of interacting processing units that are distributed in a vast network and operate in parallel?
   A. "three box" model
   B. information-processing model
   C. parallel distributed processing model
   D. all of the above

10. Why does the parallel distributed processing model reject the computer metaphor?
    A. Unlike computers, the brain does not process information sequentially.
    B. The brain is not as complex as a computer.
    C. Unlike the brain, computers process information in a parallel manner.
    D. The brain recognizes bits of information, rather than patterns all at once.

11. Which of the following describes the function of sensory memory?
    A. It holds information that has been retrieved from LTM for temporary use.
    B. It acts as a holding bin until we select items for attention.
    C. It retains information for up to 30 seconds.
    D. It aids in the retrieval of information from short-term memory.

12. By most estimates, information can be kept in STM for _____ without rehearsal.
    A. one half to two seconds
    B. up to 10 seconds
    C. up to 30 seconds
    D. up to 5 minutes

13. One way to increase the amount of information held in STM is to
    A. group information into chunks.
    B. form echoes and icons.
    C. reduce interference.
    D. use all of the above methods.

14. You call information and ask the number of your favorite restaurant. How long do you have to dial the number before you forget?
    A. 10 seconds
    B. up to 10 minutes
    C. up to 30 seconds
    D. 3 to 5 minutes

15. What could you do to extend the time that you remember this information?
    A. maintenance rehearsal
    B. deep processing
    C. elaborative rehearsal
    D. all of the above

16. Which of the following helps transfer information from short-term memory to long-term memory?
    A. deep processing
    B. chunking
    C. elaborative rehearsal
    D. all of the above

17. Information is stored by subject, category and associations in
    A. the sensory register.
    B. short-term memory.
    C. the sensory memory.
    D. long-term memory.

18. You recall from the chapter on learning that B.F. Skinner was involved in the development of operant conditioning. Your ability to remember this information demonstrates which type of memory?
    A. declarative
    B. semantic
    C. explicit
    D. all of the above

19. Learning to type, swim or drive is a function of which type of memory?
    A. semantic
    B. episodic
    C. procedural
    D. declarative

20. Semantic and episodic memories
    A. are types of declarative memories.
    B. are types of implicit memories.
    C. are examples of procedural memories.
    D. exhibit the primacy effect.

21. How does the "three-box" model account for the recency effect?
    A. Recent items are recalled because they have the best chance of getting into LTM.
    B. Short-term memory is empty when recent items are entered.
    C. At the time of recall, recent items are still in short-term memory and have not been dumped yet.
    D. all of the above.

22. A list of words has been read to you. You are retested on them one hour later and find that you recall more words at the end of the list. This demonstrates
    A. the primacy effect.
    B. a problem with the explanation provided by the "three-box" model of the recency effect.
    C. ways to extend the length of time information can remain in short-term memory.
    D. the effects of sensory memory.

23. Physiologically, short-term memory involves changes in _____, whereas long-term memory involves
    A. the neuron's ability to release neurotransmitters; permanent structural changes in the brain.
    B. permanent structural changes in the brain; changes in the neurons
    C. the hippocampus; the cortex
    D. long-term potentiation; changes in the neuron's ability to release neurotransmitters

24. Synaptic responsiveness
    A. is influenced by long-term memory.
    B. increases are known as long-term potentiation.
    C. increases during the formation of long-term memories.
    D. has all of the above characteristics.

25. Pat learned to speak Italian at home as a child. Now when she studies Spanish, she can recall only the Italian words. This is an example of

A.   retroactive interference.   B.   motivated forgetting.
C.   proactive interference.   D.   decay.

26.   Decay theory does not seem to explain forgetting in long-term memory as evidenced by the fact that
      A.   it is not uncommon to forget an event from years ago while remembering what happened yesterday.
      B.   it is not uncommon to forget an event from yesterday while remembering what happened years ago.
      C.   people who took Spanish in high school did not do well on Spanish tests 30 years later.
      D.   people generally don't remember high school algebra by the time they go to college.

27.   The idea that you will remember better if you study for a test in the same environment in which you will be tested is an example of
      A.   state-dependent memory.   B.   elaborated rehearsal.
      C.   cue-dependent memory.   D.   deja-vu.

28.   Jocelyn is convinced that she remembers an event that occurred when she was six months old. This is impossible because
      A.   parts of the brain are not well developed for some years after birth.
      B.   cognitive processes are not in place at that age.
      C.   at that age encoding is much less elaborate.
      D.   all of the above are reasons.

29.   Why is it difficult to remember events earlier than the third or fourth year of life?
      A.   The brain systems involved in memory take up to three or four years to develop.
      B.   Adults use different schema than children.
      C.   Children use different encoding methods than adults.
      D.   All of the above.

30.   Which of the following best describes the relationship between a person's "life story" and actual memories?
      A.   Both are quite accurate.   B.   Only memories are accurate.
      C.   Both involve some reconstruction.   D.   Only life stories are accurate.

PRACTICE TEST 2 - Short Answer

1.   Research in which volunteers often eliminated or changed details of a story that did not make sense to them, and then added other details to make the story coherent, demonstrates that memory is a _____ process.

2.   In reconstructing their memories, people often draw on many sources. They may incorporate information from family stories, photographs, or videos in a new integrated account. Later they may not be able to separate the original experience from what they added after the fact. This phenomenon is called _____ amnesia.

3.   False memories can be as _____ over time as true ones.

4.   Eyewitness accounts of events are heavily influenced by _____ comments made during an interrogation.

5.   Short answer questions, such as these, rely on _____ method of measuring memory; whereas multiple choice questions depend on _____.

6.   Conscious recollection of an event or an item of information is called_____ memory.

7.   Suppose you had read a list of words, some of which began with the letters "def." Later you are asked to complete word stems with the first word that comes to mind. You would be more likely to complete the word fragments with words from the list than you would be if you had not seen the list. This technique for measuring _____ memory is called _____.

8.   Models of memory that borrow heavily from the language of computer programming are referred to as _____ models.

9.   We _____ information when we convert it to a form that the brain can process and use. To use it in the future we must _____ the information and be able to recover it for use, or _____ it.

10.   _____ memory holds information for a second or two, while _____ holds information for about 30 seconds.

11.   The model of memory that says the human brain does not operate like a computer is called the _____, or connectionist, model.

12. We overcome the limits of short-term memory by grouping small bits of information into larger units, or _____.

13. One way words are organized in long-term memory is by the _____ categories to which they belong.

14. Many models of long-term memory represent its contents as a vast network of interrelated concepts and propositions. These conceptualizations of memory are called _____ models.

15. _____ memories are internal representations of the world, independent of any particular context, whereas _____ memories are internal representations of personally experienced events. Both are types of _____ memories.

16. The fact that recall is best for items at the beginning and end of a list is called the _____ effect.

17. _____ rehearsal will keep information in short-term memory, but to remember things for the long haul, it is better to use _____ rehearsal which involves associating new items of information with material that has already been stored.

18. The hormones released by the adrenal glands during stress and emotional arousal, including _____, enhance memory.

19. The _____ theory of forgetting holds that memory traces fade with time if they are not "accessed" now and then.

20. A type of interference in which new information interferes with the ability to remember old information is called _____ interference. _____ interference is when old information interferes with the ability to remember new information.

21. Often, when we need to remember, we rely on _____ cues, items of information that can help us find the specific information we're looking for. The type of memory failure that occurs when we lack these cues is called _____ forgetting.

22. If your emotional arousal is especially high at the time of an event, you may remember that event best when you are in the same emotional state. This is referred to as _____ memory.

23. Memories from before the age of two are not likely to be real memories because of childhood _____.

PRACTICE TEST 3 - Essay

1.   Identify and describe the three basic processes involved in the capacity to remember.

2.   Imagine that you watched a baseball game yesterday and presently retain many details about the game. According to the "three-box" theory, what kind of sequence have such details followed?

3.   The home team brings in a new pitcher in the fifth inning. In each situation below, suggest the type of memory most likely to be the prime determinant.

     A.   Her warm-up style indicates the fluid and coordinated movements of an experienced athlete.

     B.   After several batters are walked, she tells the umpire that the calls are no better this week than last week.

     C.   As the third batter steps up, the pitcher indicates to the umpire that improper attire is being worn.

4.   Written descriptions of a fight on a school bus have been collected from several students. Explain below how memory processes are likely to influence the various descriptions.

5.   While searching the attic, Henry discovers his senior-year diary, written over 30 years ago and not seen since.

     A.   According to decay theory, what will have been forgotten and why?

     B.   The first page contains the title "Happy Times as a Senior." He tries hard to remember but is not successful until he begins reading a description of his homeroom. This triggers a flood of memories. What variable related to forgetting best explains this experience.

     C.   Henry finds another section entitled "Worst Times as a Senior." He is sure there were very few but begins to change his mind as he reads. This time there is no flood of memories, but many descriptions of unhappy moments. Henry wonders whether he was overly imaginative or whether senior year was pretty awful. What variables that influence memory best explain this?

6.   For finals week, you had to be prepared for exams in English, math, Spanish, Italian, and history. How should the sequence of study be arranged to minimize the possibility of interference?

CHAPTER ELEVEN

Emotion

LEARNING OBJECTIVES

1. Describe the components involved in the experience of emotion.

2. Describe the role of facial expressions in emotional experience. Discuss the role of social contexts.

3. Using research evidence, discuss the involvement of the right and left prefrontal cortex, the amygdala, and the cerebral cortex in the experience and expression of emotion.

4. Identify the hormones involved in emotions and describe their effects on the body.

5. Explain why most researchers do not believe the polygraph test is a valid way to ascertain whether a person is lying.

6. Define and discuss the two-factor theory of emotion.

7. Explain through the use of examples how cognitive processes can affect emotions.

8. Distinguish between primary and secondary emotions and describe contradictory views on primary emotions.

9. Discuss how culture can influence the experience and expression of emotion.

10. Compare and contrast emotional experience and expression in men and women.

BRIEF CHAPTER SUMMARY

Chapter 11 explores the elements of emotions. Emotions have a physical component that involves facial expressions, brain activity, and hormonal activity. There seem to be some basic universal facial expressions. Specific parts of the brain are associated with aspects of emotion. The physiological component does not result directly in the experience of emotion. Events are interpreted, and our perception of events influences our emotional experience. The final element that influences our emotions and their expression is culture. Cultural rules govern how and when emotions may be expressed. Researchers have searched for primary, or universal, emotions. The search for primary emotions is controversial to those who feel that culture influences even biologically based emotions. The research on gender differences in emotions suggests that men and women experience similar emotions though they differ somewhat in their physiological responses and their perceptions and expectations about emotional experiences.

PREVIEW OUTLINE

Before you read the chapter, review the preview outline for each section of the text.   After you have read the chapter, close this book and try to <u>re-create</u> the outlines on a blank piece of paper.

I.   **ELEMENTS OF EMOTION 1: THE BODY**
   A.   **Primary emotions** are considered to be universal and biologically based, whereas secondary emotions are more culture-specific
   B.   **The face of emotion**
      1.   Darwin said facial expressions of emotion had survival function
      2.   Ekman's found seven universal facial expressions of emotion: anger, happiness, fear, surprise, disgust, sadness, and contempt
      3.   Facial feedback - facial expressions can influence feelings
      4.   Research on babies shows they use emotions to communicate
      5.   Facial expressions may have different meanings depending on the context
   C.   **The brain and emotion**
      1.   **Amygdala** - gives quick appraisal of sensory information, especially important for fear
      2.   **Cerebral cortex** - more accurate appraisal of sensory information
      3.   **Left prefrontal cortex** - associated with motivation to approach others
      4.   **Right prefrontal cortex** - associated with withdrawal from others
   D.   **Hormones and emotion** - produce the energy to respond to alarm signals
      1.   Epinephrine and norepinephrine produce state of arousal
      2.   Emotions differ from one another biochemically

E. **Detecting emotions: Does the body lie?**
    1.   The polygraph machine and lie detection - based on idea that lying associated with increased autonomic nervous system activity (increased heart rate, respiration)
    2.   Most researchers see polygraph tests as invalid because no physiological response is uniquely associated with lying.

II. ELEMENTS OF EMOTION 2: THE MIND
A. **How thoughts create emotions**
    1.   Two-factor theory of emotion - emotion depends on physiological arousal and cognitive interpretation of events
    2.   Attributions and emotion - how perceptions and explanations of events (attributions) affect emotions
        a.   Appraising events for their personal implications affects emotions
        b.   Cognitions involved range from immediate perceptions of an event to general philosophy of life

B. **Cognitions and emotional complexity** - people can learn how their thinking affects their emotions and then they can learn to change their thinking

III. ELEMENTS OF EMOTION 3: THE CULTURE
A. **Cultural and emotional variation** - are some emotions specific to culture?
    1.   Language and emotion - words for certain emotional states exist in some languages and not in others
    2.   Culture affects which emotions are defined as "primary"
    3.   Culture affects whether people think emotion comes from within or from situation

B. **The rules of emotional regulation**
    1.   Display rules - cultural rules govern how, when emotions are expressed
        a.   They are learned effortlessly
        b.   Not knowing the rules can cause misunderstandings
    2.   Body language - nonverbal signals; movement, posture, gesture, gaze
    3.   Emotion work - how, when to show an emotion we don't feel

IV. PUTTING THE ELEMENTS TOGETHER: EMOTION AND GENDER
A. **Physiology**
    1.   Men are more physiologically reactive than women, which might explain their greater discomfort with conflict in marriages
    2.   May be due to more sensitive and reactive autonomic nervous systems
    3.   Men more likely than women to rehearse negative thoughts

B. **Sensitivity to other people's emotions** - ability to "read" emotional signals depends on:
1. The sex of the sender and the receiver - better with same sex
2. How well the two people know each other - better with close others
3. How expressive the sender is - better with expressive sender
4. Who has the power - people with less power can read people with more power better
5. Stereotypes and expectations - better when emotions are what's expected

C. **Cognitions**
1. Men and women differ in perceptions and interpretations that create emotions
2. They differ in the kinds of everyday events that provoke their anger

D. **Expressiveness**
1. Women willing to and permitted to express more emotions while men expected to control them
2. Women smile more than men do and are more likely to cry
3. Men are more likely to express anger toward strangers
4. Gender differences in expressiveness are affected by gender roles, cultural norms, and the specific situation

E. **Emotion Work**
1. Women tend to try and persuade others they're happy or friendly
2. Men tend to try and persuade others they're unemotional or aggressive

PRACTICE TEST 1 - Multiple Choice

1. The elements of emotion include
    A. the face and body.   B. the mind.
    C. the culture.   D. all of the above.

2. Ekman's studies found that
    A. there are 15 universal facial expressions of emotion.
    B. there are really no universal facial expressions of emotion because of the different meaning each culture attaches to the expressions.
    C. there are seven basic facial expressions of emotion.
    D. all facial expressions are learned.

3. The reason that certain emotions are registered on the face is that facial expressions
    A. help us communicate with others.
    B. help teach young children which emotions are appropriate.
    C. can cause problems for those who do not wish their emotions to be known.
    D. are physiologically uncontrollable.

4. The ability of our forbears to tell at a glance the difference between a friendly stranger and a hostile one have survival value and serve a(n) _____ function.
    A. primary   B. evolutionary
    C. biological   D. cultural

5. Ekman's cross-cultural studies on facial expressions suggest
    A. certain facial expressions are universal in their emotional meaning.
    B. people from different cultures can recognize the emotions in pictures of people who are entirely foreign to them.
    C. that in the cultures they studied most people recognized the emotional expressions portrayed by people in other cultures.
    D. all of the above.

6. Dr. Varga is smiling. Based on the research, what can you conclude about what she feels?
    A. She definitely is feeling happy.
    B. She is experiencing a primary emotion.
    C. You cannot be sure what she is feeling since facial expressions can communicate states besides emotions.
    D. She is experiencing something positive, though you cannot be sure what.

7.   "When I clenched my jaw and knitted my brows, I suddenly felt angry." This reflects the
A.   two-factor theory.   B.   prototype theory.
C.   facial-feedback hypothesis.   D.   neuro-cultural theory.

8.   Research with infants demonstrates that facial expressions help us
A.   express internal states.
B.   communicate with others.
C.   evoke a response from others.
D.   to achieve all of the above.

9.   A limitation of the role of facial expressions in the experience of emotion includes
A.   the fact that facial expressions can have different meanings depending on the context.
B.   the fact that there is emotion without facial expression and facial expression without emotion.
C.   the fact that there is no way to "peek under the mask" of what people choose to display.
D.   all of the above.

10.   The part of the brain that is able to process immediate perceptions of danger or threat is the
A.   left cerebral hemisphere.   B.   frontal lobe.
C.   amygdala.   D.   cerebellum.

11.   With a more accurate appraisal of the situation, the _____ can override the response described in the previous question.
A.   limbic system   B.   cortex
C.   temporal lobe   D.   corpus callosum

12.   Left prefrontal cortex activation is associated with tendencies to _____, while right prefrontal cortex activation is associated with tendencies to _____ .
A.   withdraw; approach   B.   approach; withdraw
C.   withdraw; withdraw   D.   approach; approach

13.   Which of the following is one of the hormones that provides the energy of an emotion?
A.   Epinephrine   B.   Dopamine
C.   insulin   D.   Serotonin

14. One function of arousal appears to be that it
    A. prepares the body to cope with danger or threat.
    B. exhausts and calms the body.
    C. responds to all emotional states with the same pattern.
    D. makes one feel nauseated and seek protection.

15. Which is(are) involved in the physiological experience of emotion?
    A. amygdala   B. prefrontal cortex
    C. autonomic nervous system   D. all of the above

16. The longer Dr. Varga smiles, the more her mood improves. What best accounts for this?
    A. two-factor theory   B. neuro-cultural theory
    C. theory of primary emotions   D. facial-feedback hypothesis

17. You feel a tap on your shoulder outside the dorm at night. What brain structure helps you to evaluate whether this is a dangerous situation?
    A. limbic system   B. cortex
    C. amygdala   D. all of the above

18. My heart is beating, I'm hyperventilating and my pupils are dilated. Which of the following is involved in this response?
    A. epinephrine   B. adrenal glands
    C. norepinephrine   D. all of the above

19. The two-factor theory suggests that both
    A. facial features and the limbic system are necessary to experience emotion.
    B. physiological arousal and cognitive interpretation are involved in emotion.
    C. primary and secondary emotions are necessary to experience emotion.
    D. display rules and emotion work are involved in emotional experiencing.

20. According to the two-factor theory of emotion, if you are physiologically aroused and don't know why,
    A. you will not feel a need to explain the changes in your body.
    B. your interpretations of events will not produce a true emotion.
    C. you will try to label your feeling, using interpretation of events around you.
    D. you will become irritable and angry.

21. In a series of experiments, students reported occasions in which they had succeeded or failed on an exam. Researchers found that the students' emotions were most closely associated with
   A. whether they had passed or failed the exam.
   B. their explanations for their success or failure.
   C. other peoples' perceptions of their performance.
   D. past experiences with success or failure.

22. A study of Olympic athletes found that sometimes the third place winners were happier than the second place winners. Their emotional response depended on their
   A. ability to rationalize.   B. desire to win.
   C. interpretations of their award.   D. country of origin.

23. Many researchers argue against the use of polygraphs because
   A. they break often and it is not always easy to get an accurate reading.
   B. no physiological patterns of responses are specific to lying.
   C. they often let the guilty go free.
   D. of the corruption associated with their use.

24. What have studies shown about whether people can learn about the effects of their thinking on their emotions?
   A. People have shown little success at being able to change their thinking.
   B. There is little evidence that changing thinking affects emotions.
   C. People can learn how their thinking affects their emotions and change their thinking accordingly.
   D. People can learn how their thinking affects their emotions, but people's emotions are very irrational and do not respond to reason.

25. Primary emotions
   A. indicate that in all cultures certain behaviors are considered acceptable.
   B. include emotions that are morally superior.
   C. are thought to be experienced universally.
   D. incorporate all of the above.

26. Which of the following represents the position of those who disagree with the search for primary emotions?
   A. There is little agreement in what most people think of as primary.
   B. There is a cultural influence on every aspect of emotional experience.
   C. Some emotions may be "basic" in some cultures and not in others.
   D. All of the above.

27. Primary emotions are _____, whereas secondary emotions are _____.
    A. universal; culture-specific
    B. desirable; undesirable
    C. culture specific; subculture-specific
    D. agreed upon; controversial

28. Culture can affect
    A. what people feel emotional about.
    B. how particular emotions might be expressed.
    C. the meaning of expressions of emotion.
    D. all of the above.

29. Which of the following statements is true?
    A. Women feel emotions more often and more intensely than men.
    B. Men are more likely than women to reveal negative emotions, such as sadness and fear.
    C. Men and women are fairly similar in how often they experience normal, everyday emotions.
    D. Powerful people are more sensitive to subordinates' nonverbal signals than vice versa.

30. Where are gender differences in emotion found?
    A. There are some physiological difference in response to conflict.
    B. There are differences in the perceptions and expectations that generate certain emotions.
    C. There are different display rules.
    D. All of the above.

PRACTICE TEST 2 - Short Answer

1. The most obvious place to look for emotion is on the _____, where the expression of emotion can be most visible.

2. Ekman's research found seven _____ facial expressions.

3. The _____ hypothesis would predict that the longer you smiled, the happier you would begin to feel.

4. The _____, a small structure in the limbic system, appears to be responsible for evaluating sensory information and quickly determining its emotional importance. The _____ subsequently provides a more accurate appraisal of incoming information.

5. When you are in a situation requiring the body to respond, the _____ nervous system sends out two hormones, _____ and _____, that produce a state of arousal.

6. Each emotion may be associated with somewhat different _____ of autonomic activity that produces differences in the way we experience emotions.

7. Schachter and Singer's two-factor theory of emotion proposed that emotion depends on _____ arousal and the _____ interpretation of such arousal.

8. _____, or how we explain events or behavior, affect our emotional responses.

9. Cognitive _____ refer to the meanings that people attribute to events, including their thoughts, perceptions, interpretations and explanations.

10. An understanding of the reciprocal interaction between thoughts and feelings helps us to see that just as _____ affect emotions, so do _____ affect cognitions.

11. Most psychologists believe that it is possible to identify a number of _____ emotions that seem to be universal and _____ emotions that are more culture-specific.

12. Some evidence for the existence of primary emotions comes from the fact that most languages have emotion _____, or agreed upon core examples of the concept emotion.

13. Whatever the emotion, every society has _____ governing how and when emotions may be expressed.

14. Acting out an emotion we don't really feel is called emotion _____.

15. Emotions are expressed by body language, the countless _____ signals of body movement, posture, gesture, and gaze.

16. Although some basic signals of body language seem to be universal, most aspects of body language are specific to particular languages and _____.

17. If we define being "more emotional" in terms of physiological reactivity to _____, then men are more emotional than women. One possible explanation for this is that the male's autonomic nervous system is, on the average, more _____ than the female's.

18. From a cognitive standpoint, men and women often differ in their _____ of the same event.

19. Sensitivity to other people's emotional states depends on the sex of the sender and receiver, how well the two people know each other, and who has the _____.

20. The one gender difference that undoubtedly contributes most to the stereotype that women are "more emotional" than men is women's greater willingness to _____ their feelings, nonverbally and verbally.

PRACTICE TEST 3 - Essay

1. A. While enacting a role, performers sometimes report being lost in the feelings they are depicting. How might this be explained by the facial-feedback hypothesis?

   B. Successful negotiators and gamblers are often described as having poker faces. What does such a phenomenon indicate about the outward expression of emotion?

   C. Emotion work is the acting out of emotions the person does not truly feel. From the standpoint of facial expression and body language, how might this concept be defined?

   D. Body language is specific to cultures and is not good as a universal indicator of emotions. However, when facial expression is the clue, the ability to identify emotions universally rises dramatically. How might Charles Darwin explain this?

2. A. A nurse looks in on a patient shortly before surgery. The patient's heart rate and blood pressure are elevated, breathing is rapid, the pupils are dilated and the patient appears flushed. The nurse concludes that the patient is fearfully anticipating the surgery. What physiological mechanism produces the pattern observed by the nurse?

   B. The nurse tries to reassure the patient but he laughs and denies feeling nervous. In fact, the patient is not very cooperative and the nurse begins to feel irritated but continues to attempt to be comforting and pleasant. Explain the patient's and the nurse's behavior in terms of emotion work and display rules.

3. Larry, Curly and Moe all got a grade of 75 on a test, yet they each had different reactions to the grade. Larry felt disappointed and depressed. Curly felt relieved that he passed, though he didn't feel particularly happy or sad about the grade. Moe felt extremely happy. Using information about the influence of interpretations on feelings, identify expectations, surrounding events and interpretations of each student's emotional responses.

4.   Mary was given a surprise party for her 40th birthday. As each gift was being opened, Mary felt the following: shocked, then touched, by the pet caterpillar from her young daughter; delighted at the earrings from her sister; warmly amused at the cane, laxatives and contributions for a facelift that came from neighbors; insulted and angry over the "girdle for burgeoning hips" from her cousin; and irritated by the insensitivity of her husband's gift of a vacuum cleaner. Regardless of her true feelings, Mary warmly expressed gratitude and appreciation after each gift, and no one except her younger sister sensed Mary's true feelings. When the guests departed, Mary's husband began to assemble the vacuum cleaner. One look at Mary's face made it clear that she was angry. After prodding, Mary heatedly revealed that her own husband might have been more thoughtful. To her surprise, another package was produced. It contained 40 beautifully arranged exotic flowers from all over the world. Mary's husband had sent out for the flowers and arranged them himself, but confessed that he was too embarrassed to give this gift in front of the guests. Mary confessed that she really wanted to punch her cousin. The next day Mary's younger sister called and was virtually perfect in guessing Mary's true feeling about each gift.

A.   Why did Mary find it important to express gratitude for each gift?
B.   What type of performance is illustrated when Mary feigns gratitude for gifts that disturb her?
C.   Mary's husband easily sees anger on her face. Why isn't this surprising?
D.   Mary privately displays aggressive feelings toward her cousin. Her husband privately displays sensitivity and tenderness. What cultural mechanisms contribute to such behavior?
E.   What advantages does Mary's younger sister have over the other guests when reading Mary's feelings?
F.   Examine Mary's reactions to each gift and think about why she felt as she did. Which reactions tend to result from a process of interpretation that involves culturally determined meanings?

CHAPTER TWELVE

Motivation

LEARNING OBJECTIVES

1. Define motivation and distinguish between drives based on physiological needs and those that are psychological and social in nature.

2. Explain set-point theory and other genetic and environmental influences on weight.

3. List and explain three theories describing varieties or styles of love.

4. Discuss the impact of social and economic influences on gender differences in love.

5. Summarize the findings from biological research on sexual responses and behavior.

6. List and explain the cognitive, interpersonal and cultural factors that influence the sexual motives and behaviors of men and women.

7. Discuss the motivational factors involved in rape and coercive sexual behavior.

8. Describe the various explanations advanced to explain sexual orientation. Discuss the limitations of these hypotheses.

9. Explain the internal and external forces that motivate people to work and to achieve.

10. List and discuss three types of motivational conflicts.

11. Summarize Maslow's hierarchy of needs and discuss whether motives can be ranked.

BRIEF CHAPTER SUMMARY

Chapter 12 describes four categories of motives: motives to eat, motives to love, motives for sex, and motives to achieve. Biological and cultural explanations for eating are discussed. Three approaches to studying love are described: passionate versus companionate love, Sternberg's triangular theory, and attachment theory. Biological, psychological, and cultural influences on the sexual motive are discussed. Kinsey introduces the scientific study of sex, which was continued by Masters and Johnson. Coercive sex, or rape, is considered an act of dominance or aggression rather than an act motivated by sexual desire. Different theories that attempt to explain sexual orientation are reviewed. These theories lead to the conclusion that sexual orientation is a result of the interaction of biology, culture, learning, and circumstances. The motive to achieve is influenced by internal factors, such as one's expectations, values, and needs for achievement, and by external factors, such as working conditions.

PREVIEW OUTLINE

Before you read the chapter, review the preview outline for each section of the text. After you have read the chapter, close this book and try to <u>re-create</u> the outlines on a blank piece of paper.

I. THE HUNGRY ANIMAL: MOTIVES TO EAT
    A. **The genetics of weight**
        1. We no longer think that being overweight is related only to emotional problems or overeating
        2. Set-point - biological mechanism that keeps a body at a genetically influenced set point; genetically programmed basal metabolism rate interacts with fat cells and hormones to keep people at their set point
        3. Role of leptin in human obesity is complicated; often doesn't play major role in obesity
    B. **Culture, Psychology, and Weight**
        1. Obesity has increased greatly due to changes in diet and exercise
        2. Cultures' standards for ideal beauty influence eating and activity
    C. **Weight and Health: Biology versus Culture**
        1. Many women in cultures that value thinness become obsessed with weight and continual dieting; some develop eating disorders
            a. Bulimia involves binge eating and purges
            b. Anorexia nervosa involves eating hardly anything
            c. Ten times more common in women, begin in late adolescence
        2. Genes interact with cultural rules, psychological needs, and personal habits to influence weight

II. THE SOCIAL ANIMAL: MOTIVES TO LOVE

    A.   **The psychology of love**
1. Need for affiliation - motive to associate with other people
2. Basic predictors of love include proximity and similarity
3. Passionate (romantic) versus companionate (affectionate) love
4. Triangular theory of love (Sternberg) - passion, intimacy, commitment
5. Attachment theory of love (Shaver and Hazan)
   a. Adult attachment styles originate in infant-parent relationship; people develop "working models" of relationships
   b. Three styles are secure, avoidant, anxious

    B.   **Gender, culture, and love**
1. No evidence that one sex is more loving than the other
2. Men and women tend to express love differently

III. THE EROTIC ANIMAL: MOTIVES FOR SEX

    A.   **The biology of desire**
1. The hormone testosterone promotes sexual desire in both sexes, but it doesn't "cause" sexual behavior in a direct way
2. First scientific sex research by Kinsey, furthered by Masters and Johnson
3. Researchers disagree about whether men and women have different biologically-based "sex-drives"

    B.   **The psychology of desire**
1. Values, expectations, fantasies, beliefs affect sexual responsiveness
2. Motives for sex - enhancement, intimacy, coping, self-affirmation, partner approval, peer approval
3. Sexual coercion and rape - men and women have different experiences
   a. Motives for rape vary - primarily an act of aggression
   b. Characteristics of sexually aggressive males - insecurity, hostility toward women, defensiveness, preference for promiscuous, impersonal sex; convicted rapists' motives are more disturbed

    C.   **The culture of desire**
1. Sexual scripts - culture's rules for proper sexual behavior; they are based on gender roles, which result in different scripts
2. To explain origin of sexual scripts, evolutionary psychologists look to evolutionary processes, whereas cultural psychologists look to gender roles, economic, and social arrangements

    D.   **The riddle of sexual orientation**
1. Biological explanations for sexual orientation are inconclusive; psychological theories have not been supported
2. Sexual orientation research can have political goals

IV. THE COMPETENT ANIMAL: MOTIVES TO ACHIEVE

A. **The effects of motivation on work**
1. Level of learned need for achievement can be measured by using Thematic Apperception Test (TAT)
2. Goals are likely to improve performance when the goal is specific, challenging but achievable, and is defined as getting what you want (approach goals) versus avoiding what you don't want (avoidance goals)
3. Performance versus mastery goals
   a. Performance goals - want to do well, failure is discouraging
   b. Mastery (learning) goals - want to improve skills, failure not discouraging; feel greater intrinsic pleasure in the task
   c. Children praised for ability and intelligence rather than effort are more likely to develop performance goals
4. Expectations and self-efficacy - work harder if success expected; creates a self-fulfilling prophecy

B. **The effects of work on motivation**
1. Working conditions that influence work motivation and satisfaction - meaningfulness, ability to control aspects of work, varied tasks, clear and consistent rules, supportive relationships, useful feedback, opportunities for growth and development
2. Motivation is not increased by high pay but by how and when money is paid - incentive pay in particular
3. Motivation lower if lack of opportunity to advance (glass ceiling, racism)

V. MOTIVES, VALUES, AND WELL-BEING

A. **Kinds of motivational conflicts**
1. Approach-approach - equal attraction to two or more goals
2. Avoidance-avoidance - when you dislike two alternatives
3. Approach-avoidance - one activity has a positive and negative aspect

B. **Can motives be ranked?**
1. Maslow's Pyramid
   a. Survival needs at the bottom, self-actualization needs at the top; lower need must be met before higher needs can be addressed
   b. Popular theory but little empirical support
2. More recent ranking of needs based on study of American and South Korean college students; top needs were autonomy, competence, relatedness, self-esteem

PRACTICE TEST 1 - Multiple Choice

1. A process within a person or animal that causes that organism to move toward a goal or away from an unpleasant situation is called
   A. energy.
   B. incentive.
   C. motivation.
   D. the need for achievement.

2. Hunger and thirst are _____ motives, while achievement and affiliation are _____ motives.
   A. drives; needs
   B. primary; social
   C. learned; unlearned
   D. learned; primary

3. Social motives are
   A. biological.
   B. unlearned.
   C. learned.
   D. primary.

4. Set-point theory suggests that
   A. a genetically influenced weight range is maintained by a homeostatic mechanism that regulates food intake, fat reserves and metabolism.
   B. in almost all cases, being overweight is caused by overeating.
   C. obesity is an indicator of emotional disturbance.
   D. weight is not influenced by genes but by learned behaviors.

5. Set point is to _____ as thermostat is to _____.
   A. basal metabolic rate; furnace
   B. fat cells; temperature
   C. weight; furnace
   D. genes; temperature

6. The motive to be with others, make friends, cooperate, and love is the need for
   A. achievement.
   B. contact comfort.
   C. attachment.
   D. affiliation.

7. Jerry needs a lot of solitude and "space," while Harry needs friends and family around as much as possible. They differ on
   A. the need for affiliation.
   B. attachment needs.
   C. the need for contact comfort.
   D. love style.

8. Adult love styles originate in a person's first and most important "love relationship," the infant-parent attachment. Which approach to love does this describe?
   A. affiliation theory
   B. companionate theory
   C. attachment theory of love
   D. narrative theory of love

9.   Kinsey made which of the following observations about biological differences in sexual behavior between men and women?
      A.   Males and females are alike in their basic anatomy and physiology.
      B.   Males and females differ in frequency of masturbation and orgasm.
      C.   Females have a lesser "sexual capacity."
      D.   All of the above.

10.   Which of the following was a finding of Masters and Johnson?
      A.   Male and female arousal and orgasms are remarkably similar.
      B.   Orgasms are physiologically the same, regardless of the source of stimulation.
      C.   Women's capacity for sexual response infinitely surpasses that of men.
      D.   All of the above.

11.   Which of the following is true about gender differences in motives for sex?
      A.   Motives for sex are generally quite similar.
      B.   People rarely have sex when they don't want to.
      C.   Women engage in sex when they don't want to but men do not.
      D.   None of the above.

12.   Which characteristics were found more often in sexually aggressive males?
      A.   a history of violence and psychological problems
      B.   poor communication and feelings of insecurity
      C.   hostile attitudes and sexual promiscuity
      D.   a history of being abused and family problems

13.   Motivation for rape includes which of the following?
      A.   sexual outlet   B.   power and anger at women
      C.   crossed signals   D.   psychological disturbance

14.   In a large-scale sex survey, one fourth of the women said they had been forced to do something sexually that they did not want to do, but only about 3 percent of the men said that they ever had forced a woman into a sexual act. How might this be explained?
      A.   Women are in denial about their sexual behavior.
      B.   What many women experience as coercion is not seen as such by many men.
      C.   Women tend to overexaggerate these experiences.
      D.   Women say "no," but they mean "yes."

15.   Kissing, sexual arousal and orgasm are
      A.   natural behaviors.   B.   biologically based behaviors.
      C.   highly influenced by culture and learning.   D.   normal behaviors.

16. Talking about sexual responses and motivations in a college class is embarrassing for Maia, who is from Morocco. She feels she should not be listening to this kind of information, particularly in a public place with males present. This is an example of
A.   interpersonal scripts.   B.   intrapsychic scripts.
C.   cultural scripts.   D.   social scripts.

17. Two students from different parts of the world met in college in the United States. They fell in love and are beginning a sexual relationship. Because of their different cultural backgrounds, they
A.   would agree that kissing is enjoyable.
B.   would both enjoy kissing, but might disagree about whether it is appropriate.
C.   might disagree about whether kissing is erotic or deviant.
D.   would agree that they should not kiss until they have dated for a long time.

18. The fact that boys are motivated to impress other males with their sexual experiences and girls are taught not to indulge in sexual pleasure demonstrates the effects of
A.   hormones.   B.   sexual scripts.
C.   game-playing.   D.   sexual orientation.

19. Which of the following best describes current thinking about the origins of sexual orientation?
A.   Most research supports a genetic basis.
B.   Dominant mothers and absent/passive fathers contribute to male homosexuality.
C.   Brain differences between heterosexuals and homosexuals explain sexual orientation.
D.   Sexual identity and behavior involve an interaction of biology, culture, and experiences.

20. Which of the following explanations for homosexuality has been supported by research?
A.   bad mothering, absent fathering   B.   parental role models
C.   homosexuals have a mental disorder   D.   none of the above

21. Which of the following represents an argument against biological explanations of sexual orientation?
A.   The flexible sexual history of most lesbians.
B.   Most gay men and lesbians do not have a close gay relative.
C.   Studies on brain differences have not been reliable or replicated.
D.   All of the above.

22. Which of the following motivations influences peoples' work habits?
A.   their expectation and values   B.   how competent they feel
C.   the type of goals they have   D.   all of the above

23. Stacey is studying to be a master violin maker. When she makes a mistake she feels she has learned useful information about what to do next time. She knows that this process will take time and that she must be patient. She is motivated by
   A.   performance goals.   B.   learning and mastery goals.
   C.   self-efficacy.   D.   all of the above.

24. The person who is more likely to work hard is
   A.   someone who expects to succeed.   B.   someone with a high salary.
   C.   someone who has performance goals.   D.   none of the above.

25. You want to have Chinese food for dinner but you also have a craving for Italian food. This represents a(n)
   A.   approach-approach conflict.   B.   avoidance-avoidance conflict.
   C.   approach-avoidance conflict.   D.   no lose situation.

26. Going to the dentist or having one's teeth fall out is an example of a(n) _____ conflict; wanting to go out with Dan while continuing to date Stan is an example of a(n) _____ conflict; wanting to travel this summer but knowing that you would miss the summer with your friends is an example of a(n) _____ conflict.
   A.   avoidance-avoidance; approach-approach; approach-avoidance
   B.   approach-avoidance; approach-approach; avoidance-avoidance
   C.   approach-approach; avoidance-avoidance; approach-avoidance
   D.   approach-avoidance; approach-approach; approach-approach

27. Research on Maslow's hierarchy of needs
   A.   has supported the idea that motives are met in a hierarchy.
   B.   has not supported this theory.
   C.   has found that it is true that lower needs must be met first but that once these needs are met, all people do not necessarily go on to meet the higher needs.
   D.   has found that very few people go on to meet the higher needs.

PRACTICE TEST 2 - Short Answer

1. Motivation refers to any process that causes a person or animal to move _toward_ a goal or _away_ from an unpleasant situation.

2. _Maslow Pyramid of needs_ refer to states of tension resulting from the deprivation of physical needs, such as those for food and water.

3. One approach to weight holds that a biological mechanism keeps a person's body weight at a genetically influenced _set point_, which is the weight you stay at when you are not consciously trying to gain or lose.

4. Though there is considerable evidence that genes contribute to size and weight differences, it is also true that environmental influences such as _abundance_ _of food_ and _habit_ also play an important role.

5. One of the deepest and most universal of human motives is the need for _____, the need to be with others, make friends, cooperate, love.

6. Sternberg's _triangle_ theory of love is that the three ingredients of love are intimacy, _passion_, and _commitment_.

7. Companionate love is intimacy plus _____.

8. _Attachment_ theory of love says that the kind of relationships that people have as adults is strongly related to their reports of how their parents treated them.

9. Men and women do differ, on average, in how they _express_ love.

10. Gender differences in ways of expressing love and intimacy do not just pop up from nowhere; they reflect social, _biological_, and cultural forces.

11. The hormone _testosterone_ seems to promote sexual desire in both sexes, though it does not "cause" sexual behavior, or any other behavior, in a simple, direct way.

12. Kinsey was the first to introduce the idea that men and women are sexually _similar_, though he did think that women had lesser sexual capacity.

13. A study indicated that there were six factors underlying the many reasons that people give for having sex. The reasons are enhancement, intimacy, coping, self-affirmation, _partner_ _approval_ and _peer_ _approval_.

14. Men who coerce women into having sex have _____ that justify their behavior.

15. The argument that rape is primarily an act of ___power___ and aggression is supported by the widespread evidence of soldiers who rape captive women during war, and then often kill them.

16. A person following a gender role needs a _____ script that teaches men and women how to behave in sexual matters.

17. The most reasonable conclusion about sexual identity and behavior is that they involve an interaction of biology, _____, and experience.

18. Those in the field of _____ psychology study work motivation in the laboratory and in organizations, where they study the conditions that influence productivity and satisfaction.

19. The Thematic Apperception Test (TAT) is used to measure the strength of need for _____ .

20. Sometimes minority groups and women lack the _opportunities_ to achieve.

PRACTICE TEST 3 - Essay

1. Donna is a college student. Her work and her household responsibilities are completed and she finds that she has free time. She decides to do the following: call her friend, visit her boyfriend, do an extra credit assignment, and work on an extra project for her job. Describe the influence of motives on her behaviors.

2. You are at a party and there is a debate about what "causes" homosexuality. Jose says it is a choice that people freely make. Amy says that it is clearly biological. Describe the information that supports and refutes each of their positions. Also discuss the political implications of each point of view.

3. Identify the type of conflict associated with each example below.
    A. Hank promised the counselor that his third switch between chemistry and physics would be the last. He dreaded both courses but had to take one to fulfill requirements.
    B. When the networks put her favorite shows on at the same time, Lucy bought a VCR so she could watch one program and record the other for later viewing.
    C. David, an avid fisherman, just met new neighbors who made his day. The neighbors agreed to clean his fish and split the catch. David loved landing the fish but couldn't do the cleaning because it made him nauseous.

CHAPTER THIRTEEN

Theories of Personality

LEARNING OBJECTIVES

1. Define personality.

2. Describe characteristics of the16 Personality Factor (PF) and how it was developed.

3. Summarize the Big Five theory of personality, including cross-cultural research findings.

4. Discuss the issue of heritability of personality, temperament, and traits including cautionary considerations.

5. Describe the social-cognitive concept of reciprocal determinism.

6. Discuss how culture influences how we define our selves and our approach to time.

7. Explain the basic principles of Freud's psychoanalytic approach to the study of personality and list the emphases shared by modern psychodynamic theories.

8. Describe the structure of the personality, according to Freud, and defense mechanisms.

9. Describe the five psychosexual stages of personality development identified by Freud.

10. Discuss the challenges to psychoanalytic theory made by Horney, Jung, and the object-relations school.

11. Summarize the principles of humanistic psychology proposed by Maslow, Rogers, and May.

BRIEF CHAPTER SUMMARY

Chapter 13 defines personality and reviews the major theoretical approaches that have been advanced to explain its development. The biological approach focuses on the heritability of traits and the idea that there is a genetic basis for certain temperaments. The social-cognitive approach emphasizes the reciprocal interactions between specific situations and a person's cognitions and behaviors. Cognitions and behavior are also influenced by culture. The psychodynamic approach focuses on the role of unconscious processes and the development of the id, ego, and superego. Freud originally developed this approach, and then other theorists modified his work. The humanist and existential approaches reject the negative and deterministic views of the psychoanalytic and behavioral approaches. Instead, they focus on the positive aspects of humanity and the idea that humans have free will to shape their own destinies.

PREVIEW OUTLINE

Before you read the chapter, review the preview outline for each section of the text. After you have read the chapter, close this book and try to <u>re-create</u> the outlines on a blank piece of paper.

I. **MEASURING PERSONALITY**
   A. **Personality** is a distinctive pattern of behavior, thoughts, motives and emotions that characterizes an individual over time
   B. **Two kinds of personality tests**
      1. Projective tests - mainly used to diagnose disorders
      2. Objective tests or inventories - standardized questionnaires
   C. **Identifying central traits**
      1. Allport's trait theory - not all traits are equally important
         a. Central traits - characteristic ways of behaving
         b. Secondary traits - the more changeable aspects of personality
      2. Cattell - studied traits using factor analysis; found 16 factors and developed the 16 Personality Factors (PF) Questionnaire
      3. The "Big Five" traits - introversion versus extroversion, neuroticism, agreeableness, conscientiousness, openness to experience
         a. Big Five have been replicated in many countries, but there are some cultural differences
         b. Stable over a lifetime though some maturational changes exist

II. THE GENETIC CONTRIBUTION
    A.   **Heredity and temperament**
        1.   Temperaments are physiological dispositions to respond to the environment in relatively stable ways that may later form the basis of personality traits
        2.   Kagan's study on reactivity - highly reactive infants are excitable and nervous, whereas nonreactive infants lie there, don't cry, and are happy
    B.   **Heredity and traits**
        1.   Heritability estimates based on studies of adopted children and identical twins reared together and apart; for many traits, heritability is around .5
        2.   Genetic predisposition does not imply genetic inevitability

III. ENVIRONMENTAL INFLUENCES ON PERSONALITY
    A.   **The power of parents is weak**
        1.   The shared environment of the home has little influence on personality
        2.   Few parents use a consistent child-rearing style
        3.   Even with consistency, parental behavior may not influence children
        4.   Parents can modify extreme traits and things other than personality
    B.   **The power of peers**
        1.   Once children are in school, peer influence becomes stronger than parental influence
        2.   Peer acceptance is often more important than parental approval
    C.   **Situations and circumstances**
        1.   How reinforcement history and cognitions influence both responses and situations and vice versa - reciprocal determinism
        2.   Helps explains why a person may behave differently in different situations

IV. CULTURAL INFLUENCES ON PERSONALITY
    A.   **Culture** - program of shared rules that govern the behavior of people in a community or society
    B.   **Culture, values, and traits**
        1.   Individualistic vs. collectivist cultures
        2.   Monochronic (value time) vs. polychronic cultures (value relationships)
        3.   Culture of honor can increase male aggression
    C.   Difficult to describe cultural influences without stereotyping or exaggerating

V. PSYCHODYNAMIC INFLUENCES ON PERSONALITY

    A.   **Psychodynamic theories** emphasize unconscious, intrapsychic dynamics and the importance of early childhood experiences

    B.   **Freud and psychoanalysis**
1. The structure of personality - id (source of sexual energy and aggressive instinct), ego (source of reason), superego (source of conscience)
2. Defense mechanisms - reduce anxiety from conflict between id and society
3. The development of personality occurs in five psychosexual stages; if demands of a stage too great, a child may get fixated, or stuck at a stage
   a. The oral stage - babies take the world in through their mouths
   b. The anal stage - may become over controlled (anal retentive) or under controlled (anal expulsive)
   c. The Oedipal stage - desire for opposite-sex parent, then identification with the same-sex parent
   d. The latency stage - supposedly nonsexual stage
   e. The genital stage - beginning of mature adult sexuality
4. Psychologists disagree about the value of Freud's theory

    C.   **Other Psychodynamic Approaches**
1. Karen Horney - challenged the notion of penis envy and female inferiority
2. Jungian theory - biggest difference was the nature of the unconscious
   a. Collective unconscious contains the universal memory and history
   b. Concerned with archetypes - themes that appear in myths
3. The object-relations school - emphasizes need for human relationships
   a. Emphasis on children's need for mother, which in early years is only a representation of her
   b. Males and females both identify first with mother, then boys must separate which can result in more rigid boundaries with others

    D.   **Evaluating psychodynamic theories**
1. Principle of falsifiability violated - can't confirm or disprove ideas
2. Theories based on the patients' fallible memories and retrospective accounts, which creates an illusion of causality between events
3. In response to criticisms, some are using empirical methods and research

VI. THE INNER EXPERIENCE

    A.   **Humanist approaches** focus on a person's own view of the world and free will
1. Abraham Maslow - the traits of the self-actualized person are the most important - meaning, challenge, productivity
2. Carl Rogers - benefit of unconditional positive regard
3. Rollo May - free will accompanied by responsibility causes anxiety

    B.   Many assumptions cannot be tested; concepts are hard to define operationally

PRACTICE TEST 1 - Multiple Choice

1.   A distinctive and stable pattern of behavior, thoughts, motives and emotions that characterizes an individual over time is the definition of
   A.   traits.
   B.   temperament.
   C.   personality.
   D.   locus of control.

2.   Allport's trait theory suggests there are
   A.   central and secondary traits.
   B.   surface and source traits.
   C.   sixteen factors.
   D.   the "Big Five" traits.

3.   The "Big Five" refers to
   A.   the five main trait theories.
   B.   five types of traits, including cardinal, central, secondary, surface and source.
   C.   robust factors that are thought to be able to describe personality.
   D.   five stages of personality development.

4.   Woody is a complainer and a defeatist. He always sees the sour side of life. This demonstrates which of the following of the "Big Five" traits?
   A.   introversion
   B.   depressiveness
   C.   neuroticism
   D.   disagreeableness

5.   As a child, Petra was anxious and negative. She complained frequently about health problems even though she was not sick. As an adult, Petra will probably
   A.   outgrow these characteristics.
   B.   be equally likely to keep these characteristics or to change.
   C.   continue to have the same characteristics.
   D.   become even more negative and disturbed.

6.   The most controversial finding from the heritability studies on twins is the idea that
   A.   the only environmental effects on personality come from nonshared experiences.
   B.   environmental effects on personality come from only shared experiences.
   C.   most personality traits are highly heritable.
   D.   most personality traits are primarily a result of environmental influences.

7.   Studies of twins have found that heritability for most traits is around .50. This means that
   A.   if one twin has a trait, there is a 50 percent chance the other twin will have the same trait.
   B.   most people have a 50 percent chance of having a given trait.
   C.   within a group about 50 percent of the variance in a trait is attributable to genes.
   D.   the differences between two groups of people can be explained.

8. Based on studies of twins, which of the following environmental factors would be expected to have the greatest influence on the personality of two siblings?
    A. having the same parents
    B. going to the same schools
    C. having different extracurricular activities
    D. having the same religious training

9. A study of Finnish twins, ages 18 to 59, found that the heritability of extroversion decreased from the late teens to the late twenties. What does this suggest?
    A. Heritability of traits diminishes over time.
    B. The influence of the environment increases over time.
    C. For some traits, experiences at certain periods in life become more important.
    D. All of the above.

10. Which of the following suggests caution about the heritability of personality?
    A. Not all traits are equally heritable or unaffected by shared environment.
    B. Even highly heritable traits are not rigidly fixed.
    C. The relative influence of genes versus environment can change over time.
    D. All of the above.

11. The social-cognitive theory can explain how a person can be friendly at work and hostile at home. The explanation is
    A. based on whether the person has internal or external locus of control.
    B. the difference between a person's public and private personalities.
    C. that personality traits can change depending on the situation and on how people perceive and interpret those situations.
    D. an interaction of the id, ego and superego.

12. Which of the following is NOT one of the shared elements among psychodynamic theories?
    A. an emphasis on environmental influences
    B. the assumption that adult behavior is determined primarily by childhood experiences
    C. the emphasis on the unconscious mind
    D. the belief that psychological development occurs in fixed stages

13. Which part of the personality would be likely to want to go for a pizza rather than study for a test?
    A. id   B. superego
    C. ego   D. ego ideal

14. The function of defense mechanisms is
    A. to make us look good in the eyes of other people.
    B. to protect ourselves from negative environmental consequences.
    C. to protect us from the conflict and stress of reality.
    D. all of the above.

15. When the Ahern's brought home baby John, four-year-old Andy began acting like a baby himself by crawling around and wanting to drink out of a bottle. This is an example of
    A. regression.   B. identification.
    C. reaction formation.   D. projection.

16. The psychosexual stages of personality development identified by Freud are (in order)
    A. oral, anal, latency, phallic, genital.
    B. oral, phallic, anal, genital, latency.
    C. oral, anal, phallic, latency, genital.
    D. anal, phallic, genital, oral, latency.

17. According to Freud, the resolution of the _____ marks the emergence of the superego.
    A. anal stage   B. unconscious conflict
    C. Oedipus complex   D. latency stage

18. Priscilla is having relationship problems. Which of the following approaches to her difficulties represents one of the shared elements of psychodynamic theories?
    A. The problems are a result of her interpretation of what is going on.
    B. The problems are a result of her previous relationship history.
    C. The problems result from the lack of unconditional positive regard.
    D. The problems are determined by experiences in her early childhood.

19. "I don't want to study; let's go get pizza." "If you go get pizza, you'll fail the test." "You owe it to your parents to get good grades." Which parts of the personality would make each of these statements, according to Freudian theory?
    A. id; ego; superego   B. id; superego; ego
    C. ego; id; superego   D. superego; id; ego

20. Johnny was aggressive as a child. He now plays professional football. This is an example of
    A. regression.   B. sublimation.
    C. reaction formation.   D. projection.

21. Max has just had his sixth birthday. Freud would expect that
    A.   he has resolved the Oedipal complex.
    B.   his personality pattern is basically formed.
    C.   his superego has emerged.
    D.   all of the above have occurred.

22. The fact that several basic archetypes appear in virtually every society supports which Jungian idea?
    A.   penis envy   B.   the strength of the ego
    C.   psychosocial stages   D.   the collective unconscious

23. Julia disagrees with Dr. Sigmund's interpretation that she is very angry at her mother. Dr. Sigmund says that Julia's disagreement is denial and, therefore, confirms that she is angry at her mother. This is an example of which criticism of psychodynamic theories?
    A.   They draw universal principles from a few atypical patients.
    B.   They base theories of development on retrospective accounts of patients.
    C.   They violate the principle of falsifiability.
    D.   They are based on the illusion of causality.

24. Horney disagreed with Freud about
    A.   the nature of the unconscious.
    B.   the notion of the inferiority complex.
    C.   the notion that personality development continues into adult life.
    D.   penis envy and female inferiority.

25. The idea that the human psyche contains the universal memories and history of mankind was contributed by
    A.   Freud.   B.   Jung.
    C.   Erikson.   D.   Horney.

26. Which of the following is NOT one of the criticisms of psychodynamic theories?
    A.   It violates the principle of falsifiability.
    B.   It is based on retrospective memories.
    C.   It is overly comprehensive; it tries to explain too much.
    D.   It draws universal principles from studying selected patients.

27. Dr. West is studying depression. He has interviewed 50 subjects about their early lives and childhoods and he has identified common threads that fit an overall theory. This example represents which of the criticisms of psychodynamic theories?
    A.   It violates the principle of falsifiability.
    B.   It is a prospective study.
    C.   It is based on the retrospective memories of subjects.
    D.   People are seen as too malleable, like jellyfish.

28. The object-relations school predicts that adult males will have problems permitting close attachments because
    A. their identities are based on <u>not</u> being like women, so they develop more rigid ego boundaries.
    B. their superegos are too strong.
    C. they have great difficulty resolving the anal stage.
    D. all of the above.

29. Congruence and unconditional positive regard are part of
    A. Roger's theory.
    B. Maslow's theory.
    C. May's theory.
    D. existential philosophy.

30. Humanism focuses on
    A. full human potential.
    B. measurable traits.
    C. environmental influences.
    D. unconscious dynamics.

PRACTICE TEST 2 - Short Answer

1.   Personality refers to a distinctive pattern of _____, _____, motives, and emotions that characterize an individual over time.

2.   Personality tests fall into two categories. _____ tests are standardized questionnaires that require written responses, and _____ tests attempt to reveal the test-takers' unconscious conflicts and motivations.

3.   _____ has identified two types of traits; _____ traits that reflect a characteristic way of behavior and reacting, while secondary traits are more _____ aspects of personality, such as music preferences.

4.   The Big Five personality traits include introversion versus extroversion, neuroticism, _____, _____, and openness to experience.

5.   The fact that Joey was excitable, nervous, and overreacted to every little thing suggests that he falls into Kagan's category of a _____ temperamental style.

6.   In behavioral genetics, the _____ of an enormous range of personality traits is typically between .40 and .60.

7.   In numerous behavioral genetic studies, the only environmental contribution to personality differences comes from having unique experiences that are _____ with other family members.

8.   The process of _____ can account for why a person may be cheerful and friendly at work but hostile and obnoxious at home.

9.   Over time, people learn that some acts will be rewarded and others punished, and thus they develop generalized _____ about which situations and acts will be rewarding. Once acquired, these often create a _____ prophecy.

10. In _____ cultures, group harmony takes precedence over the wishes of the individual.

11. In _____ cultures, the needs of friends and family supersede appointments, and time is organized along parallel lines.

12. _____ theories, which are based on the work of Freud, emphasize the movement of psychological energy within the person, in the form of attachments, conflicts, and motivations.

13. According to Freud, the _____ contains two competing basic instincts, the ego bows to the _____ of life, whereas the _____ represents morality.

14. In psychodynamic theory, the ego has tools, called _____, that deny or distort reality and operate unconsciously. These tools protect us from conflict and the stresses of reality.

15. Johnny was always aggressive as a child. Now that he is in high school, he has become the top football player. From the psychodynamic perspective, Johnny's athletic success might be attributable to the defense mechanism of _____.

16. _____ challenged some of Freud's theories about women, suggesting that when women feel inferior to men, the explanation may be related to disadvantages that women live with and their second-class status.

17. Jung introduced the idea of the _____ unconscious, which contains _____, universal memories, symbols, and images that are the legacy of human history.

18. Object-relations theory states that a child creates a(n) _____ of the mother and this unconsciously affects personality throughout life.

19. One of the criticisms of psychodynamic theories is that they violate the principle of _____.

20. Abraham Maslow said that people who strive for a life that is meaningful, challenging, and productive are _____. Carl Rogers believed that to become a fully person you must receive _____ regard.

PRACTICE TEST 3 - Essay

1. Lynne is having aggressive fantasies about her husband. Over a long period, he has gotten drunk on a regular basis. Lynne remembers her alcoholic father, who was never there when she needed him. She also remembers her mother, who suffered silently for years. Lynne swears this will not happen to her, but she can't seem to make anything change. She is hostile toward her children and her neighbors. Her husband is always repentant the next day, but his sorrow never lasts more than a week. Yet, Lynne doesn't take the final step of leaving.

    Identify which approach to personality each of the following set of comments represents:

    A. The perseverance of Lynne's mother is the significant determinant in this case. Her mother's behavior taught Lynne that marriage was for better or for worse, but also that silence produces suffering. Lynne's pattern was acquired from an important role model.
    B. Aggressiveness is Lynne's outstanding characteristic and it dominates her actions and relationships with most people.
    C. Lynne's marriage to and anger with an alcoholic suggests many unresolved feelings toward her father. Her marriage to an alcoholic demonstrates her ongoing attachment to her father and the effort to resolve her issues with him. Her anger most likely is unresolved anger at her father. Her reluctance to leave reflects her desire to stay united with her father.
    D. Lynne is struggling with her choices. While marriage is important to her, she realizes that her husband's alcoholism is a source of despair. She is struggling with her values, principles, desires for growth and fulfillment, and how they should influence her choices.

2. Bernard had studied for his psychology test, but before he was finished studying, he agreed to go partying with his friends and stayed out late. The test was very difficult and he found he did not know many of the answers. The class was crowded and a good student was sitting very close to him. It would have been very easy to look over at her paper. He was worried because this test grade would make a big difference on his final grade. He struggled with whether or not he should cheat. He decided not to cheat because he felt that he would have let his parents down if he did. Instead, he decided that this grade really didn't matter so much. He felt guilty about not having studied enough and about having considered cheating.

    Indicate whether the id, ego, or superego is involved in each of the following examples and explain the basis for your answer:

    A. Bernard's studying for his test
    B. Going out partying with his friends rather than studying
    C. Wanting a good grade under any circumstance

D. Evaluating whether or not to cheat
E. Deciding not to cheat
F. Deciding that the grade did not matter so much
G. Feeling guilty about his behavior

3. Identify which defense mechanism each example represents:

A. A mother shows exaggerated concern and love for her children, even though she unconsciously feels trapped and frustrated by motherhood.

B. Bob often feels that other people don't like him and are talking behind his back.

C. Jack is unconsciously attracted to his sister-in-law and, though he seems to have no awareness of it, his sister-in-law senses these feelings.

D. Even after finding his lighter in the jacket worn the other day, Tony swears he never misplaces anything and someone must be playing a trick on him.

E. Whenever he is frustrated, Jack has a tantrum and destroys anything he can get his hands on.

F. The football coach loves to insult John and make him angry. Whenever he does this, the opposing team really suffers because then John begins to hit extra hard.

4. Identify the most likely stage of fixation demonstrated in the following descriptions:

A. A husband has had long-term marital problems due to a continuing lack of interest in sex.

B. A chain smoker begins to eat whenever he becomes the least bit upset.

C. A man is attracted to much older women because of their protective, caring ways.

D. A woman has all her CDs, tapes, and the food in her cabinets organized alphabetically, and the clothes in her closets are organized by color. The pencils on her desk all must be sharpened and her desk cleared off before she can work.

5. Below are criticisms of Freudian psychoanalysis. Identify which theorist would have been most likely to make each comment.

A. Freud saw the importance of the individual's past but failed to see the contribution of humanity's past. People have universal memories owing to the ancestry they share.

B. Freud misunderstood women. He believed they were motivated by envy for men when the true determining forces were social injustice and second-class treatment.

C. Freud emphasized a child's fear of the powerful father, but ignored the child's need for a powerful mother, especially during the baby's early years. He emphasized the dynamics of inner drives and impulses, but paid little attention to the child's relationship with others.

6. Based on the three humanistic theorists, indicate how each thinker might account for a person's failure to reach his or her full potential.

7. Using the "Big Five" trait approach, indicate which set of traits would be most useful for describing each of the individuals described below.

   A.   Bob is stable, happy to meet people and well-liked. He has many friends and few worries.

   B.   Mary is neat, timely, and dependable. She has relatively few interests or hobbies, but she is a good listener and is liked by her co-workers.

   C.   John complains constantly and worries about his health and his life in general. He reads a lot and loves going to movies and to museums, but he always goes alone.

CHAPTER FOURTEEN

Development Over the Life Span

LEARNING OBJECTIVES

1. List and summarize the stages of prenatal development and describe some possible harmful influences.

2. Describe the importance of contact comfort in early life and the research findings about attachment.

3. Describe the stages of language development.

4. Describe and evaluate Piaget's theory of cognitive development.

5. Describe and evaluate Kohlberg's theory of moral development.

6. Distinguish between gender typing and gender identity and describe the explanations that have been given for gender development. Explain how gender typing changes over the lifespan.

7. Describe the events that signal the onset of puberty in males and females and the relationship between age of onset of puberty and later adjustment.

8. Summarize the evidence on the relationship between adolescence and emotional turmoil.

9. Describe the four approaches to balancing ethnic identity and acculturation.

10. List and discuss the stages of Erikson's theory of psychosocial development.

11. Summarize the biological and emotional changes associated with midlife.

12. Discuss the effects of aging on intelligence and memory.

13. Discuss the impact of childhood experience on adulthood.

BRIEF CHAPTER SUMMARY

Chapter 14 describes the stages of prenatal development, which include the germinal stage, the embryonic stage, and the fetal stage. The newborn is capable of processing information, though there are many limitations to the newborn's abilities. According to Piaget's theory of cognitive development, thinking develops in four stages: the sensorimotor stage, the preoperational stage, the concrete operations stage, and the formal operations stage. While parts of Piaget's theory have been refuted, other parts of it have been confirmed. Language, another aspect of cognitive development, is an evolutionary adaptation of the human species. Children are responsive to aspects of language in the first months of life, and by about two years of age, they are using two to three word combinations. Moral reasoning is another aspect of cognitive development. Kohlberg's theory of moral reasoning is described. Development of gender identity is discussed. Language, thinking, gender identity, and moral reasoning are all areas of development that influence one another. Myths and realities of adolescent development are discussed. The physiology of puberty is described, along with the psychological issues of this period of development. Aspects of adulthood are examined, including mid-life and aging. Erickson's theory identifies eight stages of psychological development that occur across the lifespan.

PREVIEW OUTLINE

Before you read the chapter, review the preview outline for each section of the text. After you have read the chapter, close this book and try to <u>re-create</u> the outlines on a blank piece of paper.

I. **FROM CONCEPTION THROUGH THE FIRST YEAR**
   A. **Developmental psychologists** study universal aspects of life-span development as well as cultural and individual variations; many study socialization
   B. **Prenatal development** - maturation is the sequential unfolding of genetically influenced behavior and physical characteristics
      1. Three stages - germinal stage (fertilized egg divides and attaches to the uterine wall); embryonic stage (embryo develops); fetal stage (organs and systems develop)
      2. Harmful influences, like German measles, x-rays, sexually transmitted diseases, cigarette smoking, alcohol, drugs can cross the placental barrier
   C. **The infant's world**
      1. Physical abilities - newborns have a series of reflexes, perceptual abilities, sensations that are not fully developed, social interest, and synchrony
      2. Culture and maturation - infants all go through the same maturational sequence, but many aspects of development depend on culture

II. ATTACHMENT
A. **Contact comfort** - Harlow studies show need for being touched and held
B. **Separation and security -** separation anxiety develops between six and eight months and lasts until middle of second year; experienced by all children
  1. Ainsworth - studied attachment using the "strange situation" method
     a. secure - cry when mom leaves, happy upon return
     b. avoidant - don't care what mom does
     c. anxious/ambivilant - cry when mom leaves, resists upon return
  2. Factors that may cause insecure attachment include the mother's style, the child's genetic disposition, and stressful family circumstances
C. **How critical are the early years?** There are critical periods for perceptual development; unclear whether critical period for intellectual development

III. COGNITIVE DEVELOPMENT
A. **Language** - an evolutionary adaptation of the human species
  1. In first months, responsive to pitch, intensity and sound of language
  2. By 4 to 6 months, learn many basic sounds of own language
  3. Between 6 months to one year, become more familiar with own language
  4. At 11 months, babies develop symbolic gestures
  5. Between 18 months and 2 years, use telegraphic communication
B. **Thinking**
  1. Piaget's theory - children make two mental adaptations to new experiences
     a. Assimilation - fitting new information into existing schemas
     b. Accommodation - changing schemas because of new information
  2. Piaget proposed children go through four stages of cognitive development
     a. Sensory-motor stage - birth to 2 years old, object permanence
     b. Preoperational stage - ages 2 to 7, able to pretend
     c. Concrete operations stage - ages 7 to 12, conservation, math
     d. Formal operations stage - ages 12 to adulthood, abstract reasoning
  3. Piaget underestimated children's abilities, overestimated adults' abilities
  4. Vygotsky's theory - development depends on social/cultural context
C. **Moral reasoning**
  1. Kohlberg developed a theory with three levels of moral development
     a. Preconventional morality - fear punishment
     b. Conventional morality, ages 10 or 11 - conformity, law and order
     c. Postconventional - universal human rights
  2. Gilligan - men base moral reasoning on justice, women base moral reasoning on compassion; little research support
D. **Moral behavior**
  1. Power assertion - parent uses punishment to correct child's misbehavior
  2. Induction - parent appeals to child's sense of responsibility

IV. GENDER DEVELOPMENT

  A. **Terms**
  1. Gender identity - sense of being male or female independent of behavior
  2. Gender typing - process of learning what culture considers "appropriate"
  B. **Influences on gender development**
  1. Biological influences - toy and play preferences may be inborn
  2. Cognitive influences - children, especially boys, develop gender schemas
  3. Learning influences - gender socialization, adults' treatment of children
  C. **Gender over the life span** - gender differences are greatest in childhood

V. ADOLESCENCE

  A. **Adolescence** - period of development between puberty, the age at which a person becomes capable of sexual reproduction, and adulthood
  B. **The physiology of adolescence** - puberty and the onset of reproductive capacity
  1. Become capable of reproduction, emergence of secondary sex characteristics (e.g., deepened voice for boys)
  2. Timing of puberty depends on genes and environment; is occurring earlier
  3. Different adjustment issues related to early and late maturers
  4. Brain development – changes in prefrontal cortex and limbic system
  C. **The psychology of adolescence**
  1. Teenagers have greater conflict with parents, mood swings, risky behavior
  2. Conflict with parents can reflect teens' desire for more autonomy
  D. Adolescents try to balance ethnic identity with acculturation

VI. ADULTHOOD

  A. **Stages and ages** - Erikson identifies eight stages that can occur out of order
  1. Trust versus mistrust - first year
  2. Autonomy versus shame and doubt - toddler
  3. Initiative versus guilt - preschooler
  4. Competence versus inferiority - school-age
  5. Identity versus role confusion - adolescence
  6. Intimacy versus isolation - young adulthood
  7. Generativity versus stagnation - middle years
  8. Ego integrity versus despair - old age
  B. **The transitions of life** – the social clock tells us the "right" time for transitions
  1. Emerging adulthood - stage of life before career, marriage
  2. The middle years - for most people, the prime of life
  C. **Old age** - gerontologists have challenged stereotypes
  1. Crystallized intelligence (knowledge and skills built over a lifetime) remains stable over the life span, but fluid intelligence (independent of education and experience) declines
  2. Aging associated with improved well-being and increased happiness

VII. ARE ADULTS PRISONERS OF CHILDHOOD?

- A. Events of childhood do not necessarily have permanent effects
- B. Evidence comes from studies of children who recovered from wars, from abusive or alcoholic parents, and sexual abuse
- C. Resilience affected by personality, attention from others, positive experiences

STAGES OF COGNITIVE DEVELOPMENT ACCORDING TO PIAGET

Complete the following chart by describing the characteristics, limitations, and achievements of each stage of Piaget's theory of cognitive development.

STAGE OF DEVELOPMENT	CHARACTERISTICS	LIMITATIONS	ACHIEVEMENTS
SENSORY-MOTOR STAGE			
PREOPERATIONAL STAGE			
CONCRETE OPERATIONS STAGE			
FORMAL OPERATIONS STAGE			

PRACTICE TEST 1 - Multiple Choice

1. The order of the three stages of prenatal development is
    A. embryonic, germinal, fetal.   B. germinal, fetal, embryonic.
    C. germinal, embryonic, fetal.   D. fetal, germinal, embryonic.

2. Which of the following could be a problem during pregnancy?
    A. coffee   B. alcohol
    C. cigarettes   D. all of the above

3. Embryos that are genetically male will begin to secrete _____ during the
    _____ stage of prenatal development.
    A. adrenalin; embryonic   B. testosterone; embryonic
    C. hormones; fetal   D. estrogen; germinal

4. Jane has smoked heavily during her pregnancy. What are the risks?
    A. increased chance of miscarriage   B. premature birth
    C. her child may be hyperactive   D. all of the above

5. An infant touched on the cheek or corner of the mouth will turn in the direction from
    which he or she was touched and search for something to suck on. This is called the
    A. sucking reflex.   B. rooting reflex.
    C. sneeze reflex.   D. grasping reflex.

6. Which of the following statements is true?
    A. Synchrony refers to the coordination of one person's behavior to another's.
    B. Newborns synchronize their behavior to adult speech, street noise, and tapping.
    C. Synchrony occurs in four stages.
    D. Synchrony is critical during the first year of life but unimportant later on.

7. The deep emotional tie that babies and children develop for their primary caregivers, and
    their distress at being separated from them, is called
    A. attachment.   B. affiliation.
    C. contact comfort.   D. security.

8. Harry and Margaret Harlow's studies, in which infant rhesus monkeys ran to soft, terry
    cloth "mothers" when they were frightened or startled, demonstrated the need for
    A. affiliation.   B. food.
    C. contact comfort.   D. love.

9. Lucia's mom is not very comfortable with physical affection. Although she loves Lucia and takes good care of her, she does not hold or cuddle her. In contrast, her dad likes to hug and cuddle. Based on Harlow's experiments, to which parent would Lucia be most likely to go to when she is upset?
    A. her mom
    B. her dad
    C. either
    D. impossible to say

10. Baby Huey cries for his mother to pick him up, yet when she does, he wants to be put back down. According to Ainsworth's studies, Huey exhibits a(n)
    A. avoidant attachment style.
    B. ambivalent attachment style.
    C. secure attachment style
    D. psychological problem.

11. Ainsworth identified mother's treatment of their babies as the primary determinant of attachment styles. What are other influences on attachment?
    A. Infant temperament.
    B. Stressful events.
    C. Family circumstances.
    D. All of the above.

12. The order of Piaget's stages of cognitive development is
    A. preoperational, sensory-motor, concrete operations, formal operations.
    B. concrete operations, preoperational, sensory-motor, formal operations.
    C. sensory-motor, preoperational, formal operations, concrete operations.
    D. sensory-motor, preoperational, concrete operations, formal operations.

13. Fitting new information into your present system of knowledge and beliefs is called
    A. assimilation.
    B. organization.
    C. accommodation.
    D. sensory-motor development.

14. According to Piaget, during the concrete operations stage the child
    A. thinks egocentrically.
    B. develops object permanence.
    C. grasps conservation.
    D. can reason abstractly.

15. While on a walk with his father, Butch points to a cardinal and his father says, "Birdie." A little bit later, Butch sees a blue jay and says, "Birdie." This is an example of
    A. assimilation.
    B. conservation.
    C. accommodation.
    D. an operation.

16. During the first months, babies are highly responsive to
    A. normal adult talk.
    B. the basic sounds of their native language.
    C. the pitch, intensity and sound of language.
    D. all of the above.

17. Based on the stages of language development, which of the following would a four- to six-month-old baby be able to do?
    A. have a repertoire of symbolic gestures
    B. use telegraphic speech
    C. recognize "mommy" and "daddy"
    D. all of the above

18. In the first months of life, a baby is most likely to respond to
    A. his or her name.
    B. the words "mommy" and "daddy."
    C. the basic sounds of his or her native language.
    D. speech in which the pitch is higher and more varied and spoken with exaggerated intonation.

19. "Mama here," "go 'way bug," and "my toy" are examples of
    A. baby talk.
    B. telegraphic speech.
    C. babbling.
    D. parentese.

20. A child's fundamental sense of maleness or femaleness that exists regardless of what one wears or does is called
    A. gender schema.
    B. gender socialization.
    C. gender identity.
    D. sex-typing.

21. According to gender schema theory
    A. gender-typed behavior increases once a gender schema is developed.
    B. gender schemas do not develop until a child is about four years old.
    C. gender schemas are formed early and basically do not change throughout life.
    D. gender schemas disappear during adolescence.

22. Both Fran and Dan know that girls play with dolls and become nurses and boys play with trucks and become doctors. This demonstrates
    A. gender socialization.
    B. fixations in the oral stage.
    C. gender identity.
    D. all of the above.

23. The belief by children that bears, fire, anger, dogs, and the color black are "masculine" and butterflies, hearts, the color pink, and flowers are feminine indicates that
    A. children have accurate gender identity.
    B. children have been reinforced for these types of distinctions.
    C. children are learning gender schemas.
    D. there is a biological basis for these distinctions.

24. Kohlberg's theory describes
    A. moral emotions.
    B. moral behavior.
    C. moral reasoning.
    D. moral actions.

25. Which of the following reflects the influence of culture on children?
    A. the choice of behaviors that are valued in public figures
    B. that children are oriented to their peers
    C. a child's temperament
    D. all of the above

26. Early-maturing boys
    A. generally have a negative body image compared to late-developing boys.
    B. are more likely to smoke, drink, use drugs and break the law than later-maturing boys.
    C. feel worse about themselves than do late-developing boys at first, but they end up the healthiest group.
    D. have more self-control and emotional stability than late-developing boys.

27. Noriko is going through menopause. If she is like most women, she will
    A. experience depression and other emotional reactions.
    B. will not experience unusually severe symptoms.
    C. will regret reaching menopause.
    D. will experience severe physical discomfort.

28. The findings of gerontologists have changed our understanding of old age by
    A. reevaluating when "old age" begins.
    B. separating aging from illness.
    C. recognizing some of the benefits of aging.
    D. doing all of the above.

29. Fluid intelligence
    A. tends to remain stable or even improve over the life span.
    B. is influenced by an inherited predisposition, and it parallels other biological capacities in its growth and, in later years, decline.
    C. is the knowledge and skills that are built up over a lifetime.
    D. gives us the ability to solve math problems, define words, or summarize a president's policy.

30. According to Erikson, Heather, who is 16 years old, will
    A. experience an identity crisis.
    B. fight against stagnation.
    C. learn to share herself with another person and make a commitment.
    D. deal with her feelings of competence versus inferiority.

PRACTICE TEST 2 - Short Answer

1. The psychological and social processes by which children learn the rules and behavior expected of them by their society is called _____.

2. Prenatal development is divided into three stages: the _____ begins at conception, the _____ begins once the implantation of the _____ into the wall of the uterus is completed.

3. The _____, connected to the embryo by the umbilical cord, serves to screen out some, but not all, harmful substances. Some harmful influences, such as _____ and _____ can cross the barrier.

4. Babies have rudimentary "conversations" with those who tend them. The rhythmic dialogue is called _____.

5. In the Harlow experiments, the baby monkeys ran to the _____ "mother" when they were frightened or startled. This reaction demonstrated the need for _____.

6. A mother brings her baby into an unfamiliar room containing lots of toys. After a while a stranger comes in and attempts to play with the child. The mother leaves the baby with the stranger. She returns, plays with the child, and then the stranger leaves. Finally, the mother leaves the baby alone for three minutes and returns. This describes the research method used by _____ and it is called the _____.

7. In the research situation described in question 5, babies who did not care if their mothers left the room and made little effort to seek contact with the mothers when they returned demonstrated one of the insecure types of attachment, called _____ attachment style.

8. Ainsworth believed that attachment styles were based on the way _____ treated their babies in the first year. Subsequent research has found that other factors contribute to insecure attachment. These other factors include family circumstances, later stressful events in childhood and the child's _____.

9. Jennifer is about _____ months old, and she has started to smack her lips when she is hungry, to blow on something to show that it is hot, and to shrug her shoulders to indicate that she doesn't know an answer to a question. Jennifer is demonstrating her developing repertoire of _____ gestures.

10. The Swiss psychologist, _____, proposed a theory of cognitive development.

11. When Leah learns a _____ for birdies, she is able to identify robins, cardinals, and pet parakeets, as birdies. This demonstrates Piaget's concept of _____, or fitting new information into existing categories.

12. Jean-Paul is 12 months old. When his mother puts his favorite toy out-of-sight at meal time, he still cries for it. Jean-Paul has developed _____.

13. Hillary's dad asks her advice about a birthday present for her mom. Five-year-old Hillary suggests that they buy mom one of Hillary's favorite toys. Piaget's theory proposes that Hillary is demonstrating _____. Hillary is in Piaget's _____ stage of cognitive development.

14. Jack understands the principles of conservation and cause and effect, yet he cannot think in abstractions or use logical deductions. He is in the _____ stage of cognitive development.

15. Bill will not jay walk even when he is on a small road and there is no traffic in sight. He says "It is the law, and it is important that we obey the laws we have chosen because society is based on them." Based on this reasoning, Bill would be in the _____ stage of Kohlberg's theory of moral development.

16. Learning theorists point to the role of _____, or the reinforcers and societal messages children get about what "girls" and "boys" do.

17. The onset of menstruation is called _____. The cessation of menstruation is called _____.

18. When teenagers have conflicts with their parents over autonomy, they are usually trying to _____, to develop their own opinions, values, and style of dress and look.

19. Ethnic _____ have a strong sense of ethnic identity but weak feelings of _____.

20. Erik Erikson wrote that all individuals go through _____ stages in their lives, resolving an inevitable _____ at each one.

21. _____ intelligence is relatively independent of education and experience and in later years it _____. _____ intelligence depends heavily on culture, education, and experience, and it tends to remain _____ over the life span.

PRACTICE TEST 3 - Essay

1. Prenatal development is associated with several dangers. Identify the dangers associated with
    A. x-rays   B. cigarettes
    C. alcohol   D. drugs

2. A. You are part of a pediatric medical team and you are conducting an evaluation of a newborn infant. Discuss all the behaviors and sensory abilities that a normal newborn should have.
    B. Many people think newborn attachment is instinctive. Discuss behaviors that contribute to attachment between the newborn and the caregiver.

3. A. A four-year-old girl insists small people must live in the TV because they are right there behind the glass. Identify her stage of cognitive development and the phenomenon being displayed by this child.
    B. A child adept at roller skating goes ice skating for the first time. She keeps trying to stand and move just as she would on roller skates but she falls again and again. According to Piaget, what is necessary for mastery of this new skill?
    C. A child threatened to tell his parents when his older brother gave him only one of the three candy bars they were supposed to share. The older child then broke his brother's bar in half and gave him two pieces. This satisfied both children because they each had two pieces. Identify the cognitive stages of these children and the disadvantage that allows the younger child to be cheated.
    D. Previously, whenever Johnny banged with a spoon, his mother would put it in a drawer and Johnny would quickly move on to something else. Now that he's eight months old, this isn't working. The child continues to demand the spoon even though he can't see it. Identify the cognitive stage of this child and the change that has taken place.

4. Harold has been babysitting for Jennie since she was an infant. She is now 23 months old. Harold has always tried to get Jennie to speak. He is now trying to get her to say, "The apple is on the table." Describe what Jennie's response might have been at 4 months old, 10 months old, 14 months old, and 23 months old.

5. Five people have been asked to explain why stealing is wrong. From the explanations provided, identify the most likely level of moral reasoning.
    A. Jim believes stealing is wrong because it hurts the feelings of others.
    B. Joshua believes stealing is wrong because it violates the principle that everyone should work hard to acquire his or her own things.
    C. Jennifer believes most stealing is wrong, but in some cases, like saving someone's life, it can be justified.
    D. Joe believes stealing is wrong because you could be caught and punished.

CHAPTER
FIFTEEN

Health, Stress, and Coping

LEARNING OBJECTIVES

1. Describe Selye's stages of stress response and compare his theory to current theories.

2. Describe the functioning of the immune system.

3. Summarize the aims of psychoneuroimmunology and health psychology.

4. Discuss the relationship between emotions and illness.

5. Compare optimistic and pessimistic explanatory styles and describe their relationship to illness and coping with stress.

6. Define locus of control and explain its relationship with health and well-being.

7. Distinguish between primary and secondary control and explain how culture influences their use.

8. List and explain the major methods of coping with stress.

9. Discuss the relationship between social networks and health and well-being.

10. Discuss to what degree we have control over our health.

BRIEF CHAPTER SUMMARY

Chapter 15 examines the effects of stress on our lives. Hans Selye began the modern era of stress research and identified a stress response cycle. This cycle includes an alarm phase, a resistance phase, and an exhaustion phase. Health psychologists study the relationship between psychological factors and health. Stress is no longer considered a purely biological condition that leads directly to illness, but rather an interaction between aspects of the individual and aspects of the environment. The area of psychoneuroimmunology examines the relationship among psychological processes, the nervous and endocrine systems, and the immune system. The current view of the relationship between stress and illness considers aspects of the external stressor, characteristics of the individual, emotional style of the individual, and perceived coping abilities. Several coping methods are reviewed, including reducing bodily arousal, solving the problem, thinking about the problem differently, and drawing on social support. Finally, the chapter examines the extent to which we can control our health.

PREVIEW OUTLINE

Before you read the chapter, review the preview outline for each section of the text. After you have read the chapter, close this book and try to <u>re-create</u> the outlines on a blank piece of paper.

I. **THE NATURE OF STRESS**
    A.   **Definitions**
        1.   Stress - refers to recurring conflicts, traumatic experience, continuing pressures that seem uncontrollable, and small irritations
        2.   Stressors - environmental factors that throw the body out of balance
        3.   Health psychology studies the sources of wellness and illness to learn why some people succumb to stress and disease and others do not
    B.   **The stress-illness mystery -** The following may threaten health:
        1.   Noise
        2.   Bereavement and loss (e.g., through divorce or death)
        3.   Work-related problems
        4.   Poverty and powerlessness - related to health care, diet, continuous environmental stressors (crime, discrimination, housing)
    C.   **The physiology of stress**
        1.   Hans Selye's General Adaptation Syndrome
            a.   Alarm phase - the body mobilizes to meet threat
            b.   Resistance phase - resists or copes with a stressor which makes the body more susceptible to *other* stressors
            c.   Exhaustion phase - occurs if the stressor persists; body's resources are depleted and vulnerability to illness increases

2.   Some stress is positive; but it is important to minimize its negative effects

3.   Current approaches - "fight or flight" response initiates activity along the HPA axis for increased energy; long-term activation can be harmful

D.   The mind-body link

1.   Researchers study mechanisms that link mind and body; interdisciplinary specialty is called psychoneuroimmunology (PNI)

2.   PNI researchers study psychological factors that influence the immune system (e.g., feeling crowded) as well as the white blood cells of the immune system (which recognize foreign substances and destroy or deactivate them)

II. THE PSYCHOLOGY OF STRESS

A.   Emotions and illness

1.   Evidence that negative emotions affect the course of illness once a person has a medical condition; less clear whether negative emotions <u>cause</u> illness

2.   Hostility and heart disease

    a.   Early research on the Type A pattern as risk factor for heart disease

    b.   Cynical or antagonistic hostility found to be related to heart disease

3.   Depression may be a risk factor for heart disease and other diseases, but the evidence is somewhat contradictory

4.   Emotional inhibition

    a.   Trying to avoid bothersome thoughts has the opposite effect

    b.   Suppressors (those who deny feelings of anxiety, anger, or fear) have the trait of emotional inhibition and are at greater risk of becoming ill than those who acknowledge their fears

B.   Letting grievances go

1.   "Confessing" worries and fears can reduce chance of illness if it produces insight and understanding

2.   Feeling positive emotions is associated with longevity

C.   Explanatory styles (optimism, pessimism, or defensive pessimism)

1.   Pessimistic style associated lower achievement, illness, slower recovery from trauma, self-destructive behavior

2.   Optimistic style associated with "positive illusions" (not denial), active problem solving, persistence, better health habits

D.   The sense of control

1.   Locus of control - your expectation of whether you can control the things that happen to you

    a.   Internal locus of control - those who believe they are responsible for what happens to them

    b.   External locus of control - those who believe they are victims of circumstances

2.　　The benefits of control
　　　a.　　Difficult events more tolerable if more predictable or controllable
　　　b.　　Feeling in control reduces chronic pain, improves adjustment to surgery and illness, speeds up recovery from diseases
3.　　The limits of control
　　　a.　　Trying to control the uncontrollable or blaming control are problems
　　　b.　　Ideas about control are influenced by culture: primary control (modify situation) vs. secondary control (modify desires)
　　　c.　　Goal is to avoid guilt and self-blame while retaining self-efficacy

III. COPING WITH STRESS
A.　**Coping** - what people do to control, tolerate, or reduce the effects of stressors
B.　**Cooling off** - techniques that reduce bodily arousal have a variety of benefits, such as relaxation, massage and "contact comfort," and exercise
C.　**Solving the problem**
　　1.　Emotion-focused coping - giving in to emotions right after tragedy
　　2.　Problem-focused coping - learning information about how to cope
D.　**Rethinking the problem**
　　1.　Reappraising the situation - thinking about a problem differently which changes a person's emotional response
　　2.　Learning from experience - finding benefit from a bad experience
　　3.　Making social comparisons - comparing self to others less fortunate
　　4.　Cultivating a sense of humor - can help with sense of control
E.　**Drawing on social support**
　　1.　Studies show positive effects of friends on health and longevity
　　2.　Friends can be source of stress when there is arguing and hostility
F.　**Healing through helping** - there are benefits associated with giving support

IV. HOW MUCH CONTROL DO WE HAVE OVER OUR HEALTH?
A.　**Relationship between stress and illness** – is not direct
　　1.　Many factors influence outcome, such as personality traits, biological vulnerabilities, emotional inhibition, explanatory styles, coping strategies
　　2.　Behavior (smoking, diet, exercise) has a strong influence on health
B.　**Avoid oversimplification or emotional reasoning about health**

PRACTICE TEST 1 - Multiple Choice

1. According to Selye, the body mobilizes to meet a threat during which stage?
    A. alarm
    B. resistance
    C. activation
    D. exhaustion

2. Ellen is in finals week and she has been getting by on very little sleep. She is managing to prepare for her tests, but she is more irritable than usual and feels like she might be getting the flu. This would be compatible with the _____ of Selye's model.
    A. alarm stage
    B. exhaustion stage
    C. resistance stage
    D. activation stage

3. You have the flu. The _____ are designed to recognize this foreign substance and _____ it.
    A. white blood cells; destroy
    B. brain chemicals; transform
    C. antigens; heal
    D. red blood cells; stimulate

4. White blood cells of the immune system are designed to recognize
    A. foreign substances.
    B. flu viruses and bacteria.
    C. antigens.
    D. all of the above.

5. Jerry has been under stress for a long period of time. He is lonely at college, he is under pressure to do well, and he is in the middle of finals. Which of the following is true?
    A. He is at higher risk for getting sick.
    B. Persistent stress depletes the body of energy.
    C. How he responds will depend on his coping skills.
    D. All of the above are true.

6. Dr. Weller is conducting research on the health behaviors of people who become ill and those who do not. What field of study does this represent?
    A. health psychology
    B. psychoneuroimmunology
    C. psychosomatic medicine
    D. any of the above

7. Hank is stuck in a traffic jam and he is already late for his important appointment. This type of stressor
    A. does not pose much threat to health.
    B. increases the risk of illness.
    C. is related to heart disease.
    D. decreases the risk of illness.

8. Crowding is most stressful
    A. in a small room.
    B. on a hot day.
    C. in a crowd of strangers.
    D. when you feel crowded.

9.	Which of the following would most stress researchers believe to be the most serious threat to health?
	A.	being chronically unemployed
	B.	crowding
	C.	traffic jams
	D.	the demands of a deadline

10.	Scientists interested in exploring the links between psychological processes and the immune system created an interdisciplinary field called
	A.	health psychology.
	B.	psychosomatic medicine.
	C.	psychoneuroimmunology.
	D.	behavioral medicine.

11.	Negative emotions
	A.	are influential in affecting the course of the illness, once a person is already ill.
	B.	are influential in causing an illness.
	C.	have an impact on a person's psychological, not physical, well being.
	D.	are directly related to heart disease and cancer.

12.	The stressfulness of noise depends on _____.
	A.	whether the noise is your choice of noise.
	B.	whether it is unpleasant.
	C.	the type of noise it is.
	D.	how loud it is.

13.	The part of the Type A personality pattern that seems to be hazardous to health is
	A.	a fast work pace.
	B.	intensity.
	C.	an achievement orientation.
	D.	hostility.

14.	Who among the following men has a higher risk for coronary heart disease?
	A.	John is intense, ambitious, hard-driving and successful.
	B.	Ron is complaining and irritable.
	C.	Don is aggressive, confrontational, rude, cynical and uncooperative.
	D.	Lon is easy-going and calm.

15.	Which of the following is NOT one of the hypothesized relationships between emotion and illness?
	A.	Emotions may contribute to illness, but illness also influences emotions.
	B.	Specific emotions are known to cause certain diseases.
	C.	Researchers disagree about the strength of the link between emotion and illness.
	D.	The mind and body interact.

16.	A person _____ is at greater risk of becoming ill.
	A.	who expresses his or her emotions
	B.	with a problem-focused coping style
	C.	who is emotionally inhibited
	D.	who has an optimistic explanatory style

17. Optimists
    A. are the best judges of reality.
    B. have positive illusions.
    C. deny that problems exist.
    D. don't take care of themselves.

18. Which of the following is likely to have been said by someone with a pessimistic explanatory style?
    A. "This problem is all my fault and it's going to ruin my life."
    B. "I couldn't do anything about this."
    C. "I have had terrible luck today."
    D. "Everything will be fine."

19. "To lose is to win" and "The true tolerance is to tolerate the intolerable" are statements that reflect
    A. primary control.
    B. secondary control.
    C. locus of control.
    D. external locus of control.

20. Scheduled exams should be less stressful than pop quizzes because
    A. students can vent their emotions.
    B. students are more optimistic.
    C. students have more control.
    D. students can get more rest.

21. Compared to Western cultures, Eastern cultures, such as Japan's, emphasize
    A. primary control.
    B. internal control.
    C. secondary control.
    D. external control.

22. Which of the following demonstrates a problem that can result from the belief that an event is controllable?
    A. People could be unrealistically confident and try to control the uncontrollable.
    B. People could blame themselves for a problem they could not control.
    C. For some people, the realities of their lives are less controllable than for others.
    D. All of the above.

23. Identifying a problem and learning as much as possible about it is part of
    A. emotion-focused coping.
    B. rethinking the problem.
    C. problem-focused coping.
    D. cooling off.

24. _____ tends to increase self-efficacy, reduce anger, anxiety, and psychological stress.
    A. problem-focused coping.
    B. avoidance.
    C. external locus of control.
    D. looking outward.

25. When is it best to use emotion-focused coping and when should one use problem-focused coping?
   A. Problem-focused coping should be used at all times; it is never desirable to use emotion-focused coping.
   B. Emotion-focused coping is useful following a trauma but a shift should be made to problem-focused coping.
   C. Emotion-focused coping is called for when stressors are continuous or can be prepared for; problem-focused coping should be used when the stressor is sudden.
   D. Emotion-focused coping should be used by people with Type A personalities, and problem-focused coping is appropriate for those with emotional inhibition.

26. Amanda has experienced high levels of stress lately. She is coping by meditating regularly and exercising daily. Which category of coping techniques is she using?
   A. solving the problem
   B. reappraising of the problem
   C. reducing bodily arousal
   D. making social comparisons

27. The positive effects of social supports may be a result of
   A. providing attachment.
   B. improved immune function.
   C. help evaluating problems.
   D. all of the above.

28. Social support
   A. helps heart rate return to normal more quickly after a stressful episode.
   B. can extend the survival time of people with serious illnesses, in some cases.
   C. can contribute to longer life.
   D. all of the above.

29. Social support can actually be harmful if
   A. the two parties frequently argue.
   B. friends resist positive changes.
   C. friends try to stem grief prematurely.
   D. all of the above conditions exist.

30. Anne has quit drinking. Her friend, Carl, continually asks her to join their group for drinks after work. This is an example of
   A. a situation in which a friend might contribute to stress.
   B. a way that friends can help reduce the effects of stress.
   C. an example of healing through helping.
   D. external locus of control.

31. Which of the following is a psychological factor that is thought to be important to good health?
   A. social support
   B. ability to relax
   C. feelings of control
   D. all of the above

PRACTICE TEST 2 - Short Answer

1. _____ psychology is concerned with the psychological factors that influence how people stay healthy, why they become ill, and how they respond when they do get ill.

2. _____ introduced the modern era of stress research. He concluded that "stress" consists of a series of physiological reactions that occur in three phases: the _____ phase, the _____ phase, and the _____ phase.

3. Divorced and _____ people are more vulnerable to illness, perhaps because they feel unhappy, don't sleep or eat well, and they consume more drugs and cigarettes.

4. People who live in poverty or have little power in their lives have _____ health and _____ mortality rates for almost every disease and medical condition than do those at the higher end of the socioeconomic scale.

5. When an _____ invades the body, the _____ system deploys white blood cells that produce chemicals that go to the brain.

6. The interdisciplinary specialty that investigates the exact mechanisms that link mind and body, and studies how stress causes problems is called _____.

7. Negative emotions, like loneliness and worry, can suppress the _____ system.

8. The factor that can be dangerous for health in the behavior of some Type A personalities is _____.

9. People who tend to deny feelings of anxiety, anger, or fear and pretend that everything is fine exhibit a personality trait called _____.

10. People with an _____ explanatory style tend to live longer and may engage in unrealistic, but healthy, positive _____.

11. People can tolerate all kinds of stressors if they feel able to _____ them. For example, the crowd you choose to join for a football game is not as stressful as being trapped in a crowd on a busy street.

12. If you do not like a situation, you are supposed to change it or fight it. This represents _____ control, whereas if you try to accommodate to reality by changing your own desires, you are demonstrating _____ control.

13. All the things people do to control, tolerate, or reduce the effects of life's stressors is called _____.

14. _____ coping in which a person focuses on the anger, anxiety, or grief the problem has caused is normal after a tragedy or trauma. However, over time _____ coping strategies are associated with better adjustment.

15. _____ the situation can help a person to think about the problem differently.

16. In a difficult situation, successful copers often _____ themselves to others who are less fortunate.

17. Friends and social supports can both _____ and _____ stress.

18. Debate continues to rage over the extent to which _____ factors are involved in the onset or course of some illnesses.

19. Health professionals worry about the _____ industry that oversimplifies findings from health research.

20. It is important to avoid _____ thinking when a person is deciding about treatments for health problems.

21. Many diseases, such as tuberculosis and ulcers, were once thought to be caused exclusively by _____ factors, until the _____ that actually do cause them were identified.

PRACTICE TEST 3 - Essay

1.   Indicate which member of each pair is likely to experience greater stress. Explain why.

    A.   Air traffic controllers versus fishermen
    B.   Type A personalities versus Type B personalities
    C.   Subjects with an external locus of control versus subjects with an internal locus of control
    D.   Subjects with a large social network versus single subjects
    E.   Subjects with an optimistic versus pessimistic explanatory style

2.   Apply Hans Selye's phases of stress response to people being held hostage. Describe what they would experience in the alarm, resistance, and exhaustion phases.

3.   Over a period of years, David has been under treatment for a variety of disorders, including depression and ulcers. Visits to the doctor and prescriptions have been fairly regular because symptoms recur or new ones break out whenever medication is stopped. The doctor is now beginning to suggest that the origin of the problems must be related to stress or his depression.

    A.   How could stress make recurring symptoms possible?
    B.   What are some possible relationships that might exist between David's depression and his illnesses?
    C.   What must David examine about himself and his life?

4.   Assume that a group of hostages has been held by terrorists for several years. For each description, indicate whether stress has been reduced through attempts to solve, reappraise or live with the problem, and identify the specific coping strategy being used.

    A.   Margaret has decided her captors have no bad intentions and are just trying to make an important philosophical point.
    B.   Frank believes escape would be difficult but not impossible. He keeps formulating escape plans and explaining them to others.
    C.   Joe believes this disaster has a bright side. Had another terrorist group taken them, there might have been torture as well as captivity.
    D.   Like Frank, Tony believes escape is possible, but only if the terrorists unexpectedly slip-up. His goal is to remain as calm as possible and look for an opportunity. He refuses to waste energy and lose hope by developing or considering unrealistic escape plans.
    E.   Joan believes the group will remain in captivity virtually forever. Her goal is to eat as regularly as possible and combat inactivity through exercise.

CHAPTER
SIXTEEN

Psychological Disorders

LEARNING OBJECTIVES

1. Describe three perspectives on mental disorders and distinguish mental disorder from abnormal behavior and from the legal definition of insanity.

2. Describe the five axes of the Diagnostic and Statistical Manual of Mental Disorders (DSM) on which clinicians can evaluate a person.

3. Summarize the positions supporting and criticizing the DSM.

4. List and describe the principle characteristics of the anxiety disorders.

5. Distinguish between major depression and bipolar disorder.

6. Explain the various theories that attempt to account for depression.

7. List the general features of personality disorders and three specific personality disorders.

8. Describe the features of antisocial personality disorder and theories explaining the causes.

9. List and discuss the characteristics of dissociative identity disorder.

10. Describe the current controversy about the validity and nature of dissociative identity disorder (multiple personality disorder).

11. List the signs of substance abuse.

12. Distinguish between the biological and the learning models of addiction.

13. List the components that interact to influence addiction and abuse.

14. Describe the symptoms of schizophrenia.

15. Discuss the four areas that researchers are investigating to understand schizophrenia.

BRIEF CHAPTER SUMMARY

Chapter 16 defines mental disorders and distinguishes abnormal behavior from mental disorders. The issues and difficulties involved in developing a reliable and valid diagnostic system are also discussed. The *Diagnostic and Statistical Manual of Mental Disorders* (DSM), which is the manual that contains descriptions of all diagnostic categories of mental disorders, is reviewed. Some of the problems with this diagnostic system are described. Six general categories of disorders are reviewed. They consist of anxiety disorders (e.g., PTSD, phobias), mood disorders (e.g., depression, bipolar disorder), personality disorders (e.g., narcissistic personality disorder, antisocial personality disorder), addictions, dissociative disorders (e.g., amnesia, dissociative identity disorder), and schizophrenia. The text describes symptoms, predisposing factors and theories of causation for specific mental disorders under each broad disorder category.

PREVIEW OUTLINE

Before you read the chapter, review the preview outline for each section of the text. After you have read the chapter, close this book and try to <u>re-create</u> the outlines on a blank piece of paper.

I. **DILEMMAS OF DIAGNOSIS**
    A. **Defining mental disorders** - abnormal behavior is not the same as mental disorder
        1. Legal definition - awareness of the consequences of one's actions
        2. Violation of cultural standards - depends on the culture and time
        3. Maladaptive or harmful behavior
        4. Emotional distress
    B. **Text's definition** - any behavior or emotional state that causes an individual great or worry; is self-defeating or self-destructive; or is maladaptive and disrupts the person's relationships or the larger community
    C. **Diagnosis: art or science?**
        1. *The Diagnostic and Statistical Manual of Mental Disorders* (DSM) - standard reference used to diagnose disorders; primary aim is descriptive
            a. Lists symptoms and associated information for each disorder
            b. Classifies each disorder according to five axes or dimensions:
                (1) Primary clinical problem
                (2) Ingrained aspects of the individual's personality
                (3) Medical conditions relevant to the disorder
                (4) Social and environmental problems
                (5) Global assessment of the patient's overall functioning

2. Problems with the DSM - danger of overdiagnosis, power of diagnostic labels, confusion of serious mental disorders with normal problems, the illusion of objectivity – beliefs about what is "normal" can change

3. Benefits of the DSM - new studies are improving empirical support for its categories, improves accuracy of diagnosis, biases in certain diagnosis can be corrected with awareness and better research

D. **Dilemmas of measurement**

1. Projective tests are used to infer a person's motives and conflicts based on interpretation of ambiguous stimuli (e.g., Rorschach Inkblot Test)

2. Objective tests - standardized questionnaires requiring written responses (e.g., MMPI-2)

II. ANXIETY DISORDERS

A. **Anxiety and panic**

1. Generalized anxiety disorder

   a. Characteristics - continuous and uncontrollable anxiety, feelings of dread, restlessness, difficulty concentrating, sleep disturbance

   b. May occur without specific anxiety-producing event, but may be related to physiological tendency to experience anxiety

2. Posttraumatic stress disorder (PTSD) - anxiety results from uncontrollable and unpredictable danger such as rape, war, torture, or natural disasters

   a. Symptoms include reliving the trauma, "psychic numbing," increased arousal, inability to feel happy, detachment from others

   b. Associated with damage to hippocampus

3. Panic disorder - recurring attacks of intense fear or panic

   a. Symptoms include trembling, dizziness, heart palpitations, feelings of unreality, fear of dying, going crazy, or losing control

   b. Difference between those who develop panic disorder and those who don't is how they interpret bodily reactions

B. **Fears and phobias - exaggerated fear of a specific situation, activity, etc.**

1. Some may have evolutionary basis

2. Social phobia - fear of being observed by others

3. Agoraphobia - fear of being alone in a public place from which escape might be difficult or help unavailable

C. **Obsessions and compulsions**

1. Obsessions - recurrent, persistent, unwished-for thoughts that are frightening or repugnant

2. Compulsions - repetitive, ritualized behaviors over which people feel a lack of control (e.g., hand washing, counting, checking)

3. Most sufferers know the behavior is senseless and don't enjoy it

4. PET scans find parts of the brain are hyperactive in people with OCD

III. MOOD DISORDERS

A. **Depression** - emotional, behavioral, cognitive, physical changes; more common in women than men

B. **Bipolar disorder - depression alternates with mania, an abnormally high state of exhilaration, where person is full of energy, ambition, self-esteem**

C. **Theories of depression**

1. Biological explanations emphasize genetics, brain chemistry (deficiencies in serotonin and norepinephrine) and shrinkage of some brain structures

2. Life experiences explanations emphasize stressful circumstances of people's lives; may explain gender differences in depression rates

3. Problems with close relationships (e.g., separations and losses)

4. Cognitive explanations emphasize habits of thinking and interpreting events - depressed people have a pessimistic explanatory style

5. "Vulnerability-stress" explanations draw on all four previous explanations as an interaction between individual vulnerability and environmental stress

IV. PERSONALITY DISORDERS

A. **Definition** - rigid, maladaptive traits that cause great distress or inability to get along with others

B. **Problem personalities**

1. Narcissistic personality disorder - exaggerated sense of self-importance

2. Borderline personality disorder - intense but unstable relationships, fear of abandonment, unrealistic self-image, emotional volatility

C. **Antisocial personality disorder**

1. Individuals who lack a connection to anyone so they can cheat, con, and kill without any problem; used to be called psychopaths or sociopaths

2. Symptoms include - repeated law-breaking, deception, acting impulsively, fighting, disregarding safety, lacking remorse

3. Often begin with problem behaviors in childhood; more common in males

4. Causes of APD

    a. CNS abnormalities - inability to feel emotional arousal

    b. Genetically influenced problems with impulse control

    c. Brain damage from physical abuse or neglect

V. DRUG ABUSE AND ADDICTION

A. **DSM definition of substance abuse** - maladaptive pattern of substance use leading to clinically significant impairment or distress

B. **Biology and addiction** - addiction is a biochemical process influenced by genes

1. Biological model - addiction due to biochemistry, metabolism and genetics

2. Genetic factors may cause high levels of dopamine production

3. Causal relationship also works the other way: heavy drinking reduces endorphins, shrinks cortex, damages liver

C. **Learning, culture, and addiction** - challenges the biological model
    1. Addiction patterns vary with cultural practices and social environment
    2. Policies of total abstinence tend to increase rates of addiction
    3. Not all addicts go through withdrawal symptoms when they stop the drug
    4. Addiction depends on the drug AND the reason the person is taking it

D. **Debating the causes of addiction**
    1. Biological and learning models contribute to our understanding
    2. Theoretical differences have treatment implications
    3. Most heated disagreement is about controlled drinking; research finds that many people can switch to moderate drinking under certain conditions

VI. DISSOCIATIVE DISORDERS

A. **Definition** - disorders in which consciousness, behavior and identity are split off

B. **Psychogenic amnesia** - inability to remember important personal information, usually of a traumatic nature, that cannot be explained by ordinary forgetfulness

C. **Dissociative identity disorder ("multiple personality")**
    1. The appearance of two or more distinct identities within one person
    2. The MPD controversy - two views among mental health professionals
        a. A real disorder, common but often under-diagnosed; usually develops in childhood as a response to repeated trauma
        b. A creation of mental health clinicians who believe in it - pressure and suggestion by clinicians elicit additional personalities
    3. The sociocognitive explanation - an extreme form of a normal ability to present different aspects of our personalities to others

VII. SCHIZOPHRENIA

A. **Schizophrenia** - a psychosis or condition involving distorted perceptions of reality and an inability to function in most aspects of life

B. **Symptoms of schizophrenia**
    1. Active or positive symptoms - distortions of normal thinking and behavior
        a. Bizarre delusions - false beliefs
        b. Hallucinations - usually auditory - seem intensely real
        c. Disorganized, incoherent speech - illogical jumble of ideas
        d. Grossly disorganized and inappropriate behavior
    2. Negative symptoms - loss of former abilities
        a. Loss of motivation - inability to pursue goals
        b. Poverty of speech - empty replies reflecting diminished thought
        c. Emotional flatness - general unresponsiveness

C. **Theories of schizophrenia** - many variations and symptoms
    1. Genetic predispositions exist though no specific genes identified
    2. Structural brain abnormalities (enlarged ventricles, smaller hippocampus)
    3. Neurotransmitter abnormalities (e.g., high activity in dopamine areas)
    4. Prenatal problems possibly related to malnutrition or a virus

PSYCHOLOGICAL DISORDERS

Complete the following chart indicating the major symptoms, predisposing factors and explanatory theories for each of the disorders described in the left-hand column.

TYPE OF DISORDER	MAJOR SYMPTOMS	PREDISPOSING FACTORS	EXPLANATORY THEORIES
ANXIETY DISORDERS **Generalized Anxiety Disorder**			
Social Phobia			
Agoraphobia			
Panic Attack			
Obsessive-Compulsive Disorder			
MOOD DISORDERS **Major Depression**			
Bipolar Disorder			
PERSONALITY DISORDERS **Borderline**			
Narcissistic			
Antisocial			
DISSOCIATIVE DISORDERS **Dissociative Identity Disorder**			
Amnesia			
SUBSTANCE ABUSE			
SCHIZOPHRENIA			

PRACTICE TEST 1 - Multiple Choice

1. According to the _____ definition of mental disorder, a person who shows a total lack of sexual interest exhibits abnormal behavior.
    A. maladaptive behavior
    B. violation of cultural standards
    C. emotional distress
    D. impaired judgment

2. Which of the following is <u>NOT</u> one of the definitions of mental disorder?
    A. statistical deviation
    B. lack of self-control
    C. violation of cultural standards
    D. emotional distress

3. Whether a person is aware of the consequences of his or her actions and can control his or her behavior is at the heart of the legal term,
    A. mental disorder.
    B. insanity.
    C. neurotic.
    D. psychotic.

4. The primary aim of the *Diagnostic and Statistical Manual of Mental Disorders* (DSM) is
    A. to provide clear criteria of diagnostic categories.
    B. to describe the causes of particular disorders.
    C. to describe the best course of treatment for a particular disorder.
    D. all of the above.

5. Clinicians are encouraged to evaluate each client according to five axes, or dimensions, in the DSM. The third dimension is
    A. the primary clinical problem.
    B. ingrained aspects of the client's personality.
    C. medical conditions that are relevant to the disorder.
    D. social and environmental problems that can make the disorder worse.

6. Which of the following is <u>NOT</u> one of the criticisms of the DSM?
    A. It confounds serious "mental disorders" with normal problems in living.
    B. Its heavy emphasis on theory may alienate clinicians from different perspectives.
    C. It gives the illusion of objectivity.
    D. It may foster overdiagnosis and self-fulfilling prophecies.

7. The diagnoses of Disorder of Written Expression and Caffeine-Induced Sleep Disorder represent which criticism of the DSM?
    A. the idea that diagnosis can be made objectively scientific
    B. misusing diagnoses for social and political purposes
    C. confounding serious "mental disorders" with normal problems in living
    D. the fostering of overdiagnosis and self-fulfilling prophecies

8.   Generalized anxiety disorder is marked by
       A.   unrealistic fears of specific things or situations.
       B.   continuous, uncontrollable anxiety or worry.
       C.   the sudden onset of intense fear or terror.
       D.   unwished-for thoughts and repetitive behaviors.

9.   The most disabling fear disorder that accounts for more than half of the phobia cases for
       which people seek treatment is called
       A.   panic disorder.   B.   social phobia.
       C.   claustrophobia.   D.   agoraphobia.

10.   Checking the furnace repeatedly before one can sleep and washing one's hands many
       times in one hour are examples of
       A.   obsessions.   B.   phobias.
       C.   compulsions.   D.   superstitions.

11.   Unlike normal sadness or grief, major depression involves
       A.   panic attacks.   B.   low self-esteem.
       C.   a lack of interest in outside activities.   D.   a negative mood.

12.   Recently John has been overeating, having difficulty sleeping through the night,
       experiencing a lack of energy and interest and having trouble concentrating. These
       physical changes can be signs of
       A.   a phobia.   B.   mania.
       C.   depression.   D.   panic disorder.

13.   Mania is an abnormally
       A.   chronic state of depression.   B.   apathetic state.
       C.   intense feeling of despair.   D.   high state of exhilaration.

14.   Most manic episodes alternate with
       A.   episodes of depression.   B.   panic attacks.
       C.   obsessive-compulsive episodes.   D.   periods of elation.

15.   More women receive a diagnosis of depression than men. Which of the following is a
       possible explanation for this gender difference in depression?
       A.   Women are more likely to have a history of sexual abuse.
       B.   Women are more likely to lack fulfilling jobs.
       C.   Mothers are vulnerable to depression.
       D.   All of the above.

16. Social theories of depression suggest that women are more likely to be depressed than men because they are more likely to lack
    A. endorphins and key neurotransmitters.
    B. positive self-images.
    C. fulfilling work and family relations.
    D. a stable network of friends.

17. Duane is taking antidepressants. How do they alleviate symptoms of depression?
    A. They decrease levels of dopamine.
    B. They increase levels of serotonin and norepinephrine.
    C. They decrease levels of serotonin and norepinephrine.
    D. They increase levels of dopamine.

18. Individuals suffering from antisocial personality disorder are often charming and can be highly successful
    A. psychotherapists.
    B. con men.
    C. actors.
    D. business executives.

19. Hypothesized causes of antisocial personality disorder include
    A. problems in behavioral inhibition.
    B. neurological impairments.
    C. social deprivation.
    D. all of the above.

20. Having a genetic disposition toward impulsivity, addiction, hyperactivity; being neglected or rejected by parents; having a history of physical abuse or birth complications are all
    A. contributors to mood disorders.
    B. risk factors for antisocial personality disorder.
    C. foundations for any mental disorder.
    D. paths to dissociative disorders.

21. According to the DSM-IV, the key feature of substance abuse is
    A. the length of time a person has been using the drug.
    B. the inability to stop using the drug or to cut down on use.
    C. a maladaptive pattern of use leading to significant impairment or distress.
    D. all of the above.

22. The disease model of addiction
    A. requires abstinence.
    B. maintains that people have an inherited predisposition for alcoholism.
    C. holds that addiction is related to biochemistry, metabolism, and genetics.
    D. incorporates all of the above.

23. At the heart of the debate between the disease and learning models of addiction is the question of whether
   A. moderate drinking is possible for former alcoholics.
   B. alcoholics should be blamed for their alcoholism.
   C. there is an alcoholic personality.
   D. alcoholics are "bad" or "sick."

24. A sudden inability to remember certain important personal information describes
   A. psychogenic amnesia.   B. obsessive-compulsive disorder.
   C. dissociative identity disorder.   D. post-traumatic stress disorder.

25. The controversy among mental health professionals about dissociative identity disorder has to do with
   A. whether it is a common and underdiagnosed disorder or whether it is concocted by mental health professionals and suggestible patients.
   B. whether it should be treated with traditional techniques or whether special treatments should be utilized.
   C. whether it is a biologically-based disorder or whether it results from psychosocial factors.
   D. whether the alternate personalities should be "seen" in treatment or whether they should be ignored by the therapist.

26. Elizabeth thinks she is Madonna. When she speaks she often does not make any sense at all and at times she appears to be talking to herself. She is experiencing
   A. positive symptoms of schizophrenia.
   B. negative symptoms of schizophrenia.
   C. catatonic symptoms of schizophrenia.
   D. emotional flatness.

27. Bizarre delusions, hallucinations, incoherent speech, disorganized and inappropriate behavior are _____ symptoms of schizophrenia.
   A. positive or active   B. negative
   C. catatonic   D. maladaptive

28. Negative symptoms of schizophrenia
   A. may begin before and continue after positive symptoms.
   B. include loss of motivation.
   C. include diminished thought and emotional flatness.
   D. include all of the above.

29. Support for the idea of an infectious virus during prenatal development as a cause of schizophrenia comes from the fact that
   A. there is a significant association between a mother's exposure to a virus during prenatal development.
   B. most schizophrenics have very low immune functioning.
   C. most schizophrenics show abnormalities on chromosome 5.
   D. most schizophrenics have extra dopamine receptors.

30. Which of the following has been advanced as one of the biological explanations of schizophrenia?
   A. brain abnormalities
   B. extra dopamine receptors
   C. genes
   D. all of the above

31. The idea that genetic or brain abnormalities combine with family or other pressures to trigger schizophrenia reflects the
   A. interactionist model
   B. learning theory model
   C. vulnerability-stress model
   D. biology-pressure model

32. Brain abnormalities that have been found to be associated with schizophrenia include
   A. decreased brain weight.
   B. reduced numbers of neurons in specific layers of the prefrontal cortex.
   C. enlarged ventricles.
   D. all of the above.

PRACTICE TEST 2 - Short Answer

1.   One perspective defines mental disorders as a violation of _____ standards.

2.   The official manual describing the major categories of mental disorder is the
        _____.

3.   The fact that Attention Deficit/Hyperactivity Disorder is the fastest-growing disorder in
        America (where it is diagnosed at least ten times as often as it is in Europe) supports the
        criticism of the DSM that it fosters _____.

4.   _____ anxiety disorder is continuous, uncontrollable anxiety or worry.

5.   Typical anxiety symptoms of _____ include reliving the trauma in recurrent,
        intrusive thoughts or dreams.

6.   The essential difference between people who develop panic disorder and those who do
        not lies in how they _____ their bodily reactions.

7.   John will not take a class if a class presentation is one of the requirements. He is terrified
        of speaking in class because he worries that he will do or say something humiliating or
        embarrassing. The most likely diagnosis for John is _____.

8.   The most disabling fear disorder which accounts for more than half of the phobia cases
        for which people seek treatment is _____.

9.   _____ are recurrent, persistent, unwished-for thoughts or images, whereas
        _____ are repetitive, ritualized, stereotyped behaviors that the person feels must be
        carried out to avoid disaster. If the person does not carry out the behaviors, he or she will
        experience high levels of _____.

10.   People who suffer from major depression experience emotional, _____, and
        _____ changes severe enough to disrupt their ordinary functioning.

11.   _____ occurs two or three times as often among women as among men, all over the
        world.

12.   _____ explanations of depression emphasize problems with close relationships.

13.   The DSM-IV describes _____ disorders as "an enduring pattern of inner experience and behavior that deviates markedly from the expectations of the individual's culture [and] is pervasive and inflexible."

14.   People with antisocial personality disorder may have problems in behavioral _____, the ability to control responses to frustration and provocation.

15.   The _____ model of APD says that disorder is more likely to develop when biological predispositions are combined with physical abuse, parental neglect, lack of love, or other environmental _____.

16.   In psychogenic _____, a person is unable to remember important personal information, usually of a traumatic nature. In a related disorder called dissociative _____, a person forgets his or her identity entirely and wanders far from home.

17.   On one side of the MPD controversy, there are those who think MPD is _____, but often misdiagnosed. On the other side are those who believe that most cases of MPD are generated by _____, either knowingly or unknowingly.

18.   The _____ explanation of MPD holds that it is simply an extreme form of the ability we all have to present different aspects of our personalities to others.

19.   The biological model holds that addiction, whether to alcohol or any other drug, is due primarily to a person's _____, metabolism, and genetic predisposition.

20.   The fact that within a particular country, addiction rates can rise or fall rapidly in response to cultural changes supports the _____ model of addiction.

21.   Schizophrenia is an example of a _____, a mental condition that involves distorted perceptions of reality and an inability to function in most aspects of life.

22.   Two active or positive symptoms of schizophrenia include bizarre _____ or false beliefs, and _____.

23.   There is good evidence for the existence of a _____ contribution to schizophrenia. In addition, _____ abnormalities are associated with schizophrenia.

24.   An infectious _____ during prenatal development may affect the likelihood of schizophrenia developing.

PRACTICE TEST 3 - Essay

1. Jason spends all day at the shopping mall. Every day he stops people who look in his direction and literally begs for their forgiveness. Jason's boldly colored sweatshirts make Jason quite noticeable. These are worn every day, over his coat when it's cold, and each one has exactly the same inscription: "Jason is not a thief." Discuss the aspect of Jason's behavior that conforms to each of the following definitions of mental disorder.

   A. Violation of cultural standards
   B. Maladaptive behavior
   C. Emotional distress
   D. Impaired judgment and self-control

2. In the formulation of Jason's diagnosis according to the DSM-IV, indicate whether the types of information identified below would be included. Explain your answers.

   A. A diagnostic label for Jason's condition
   B. The suspected cause(s) for Jason's symptoms
   C. An estimate of potential treatment effects
   D. How well Jason is functioning
   E. Any medical condition that Jason might have

3. For each description below, indicate whether the anxiety that is present is normal or abnormal. When it is abnormal, suggest the most likely diagnostic category.

   A. Carl loves the racetrack but he will not go there again. The last time he was there he suddenly felt his heart racing, he was gasping for breath, his hands began to tremble and he broke out into a cold sweat.
   B. Sandy is very clean! She feels contaminated unless she bathes and changes her clothes at least four times a day, and she is meticulous about the house as well. Every room is scrubbed at least twice a week and the bathroom is cleaned daily.
   C. A college student becomes anxious whenever assigned a project that requires speaking in front of class. The anxiety motivates meticulous preparation and the student rehearses material again and again.
   D. Marsha was stranded in a building for over two hours. The stairway was blocked by men moving large cartons, and the only way down was the elevators. Elevators cause Marsha to sweat, tremble and suffer from images of being crushed. She decided to wait rather than take the elevator.
   E. Harry has had problems since returning from Vietnam. He is listless and quarrelsome, and has fitful sleeps, reliving his past in nightmarish dreams.

4. Decide whether each of the statements below is correct or incorrect. When it is incorrect, rewrite it in a more factual form.

   A. Mood disorders consist primarily of emotional symptoms and have little impact on behavioral, cognitive or physical functioning.
   B. In bipolar disorder, periods of sluggishness alternate with active attempts to commit suicide.
   C. Antidepressant drugs work by altering the activity level of the limbic system.
   D. Lack of fulfilling work and family relationships are a good predictor of depression.
   E. Negatively distorted thinking is the result, not the cause, of depression.
   F. Repeated failure is an unlikely source of major depressive episodes.

5. Josephine is highly mistrustful of airline personnel. She believes that airplanes dirty the streets and sidewalks by dripping oil and that pilots have a power called "telectic penetration." On hearing a plane, Josephine becomes introspective and claims she is being used as radar. She feels the pilots are tuning in to her latitude and longitude and asking her questions about her location. She is unable to speak until they are through.

   A. Does Josephine have delusions? If so, what?
   B. Is Josephine hallucinating? If so, describe her hallucinations.
   C. Is Josephine having any disorganized or incoherent speech? If so, describe.
   D. Is Josephine demonstrating any disorganized or inappropriate behavior? If so, what?
   E. Is Josephine demonstrating emotional flatness? If so, describe.

CHAPTER
SEVENTEEN

Approaches to Treatment and Therapy

LEARNING OBJECTIVES

1. Discuss the uses of antipsychotic drugs, antidepressants, tranquilizers and lithium in treating emotional disorders.

2. Summarize the problems inherent in treating psychological disorders with drugs.

3. Describe the procedures used in attempts to alter brain function directly.

4. List and explain the goals and principles of the four major schools of psychotherapy.

5. Explain the scientist-practitioner gap and why it has developed.

6. Describe the results of efforts to evaluate the effectiveness of psychotherapy.

7. Discuss the factors most likely to lead to successful therapy and discuss the role of the therapeutic alliance.

8. Discuss which therapies work best for specific problems.

9. Discuss the circumstances under which therapy can be harmful.

10. Explain the limitations of psychotherapy.

BRIEF CHAPTER SUMMARY

Chapter 17 describes various approaches to the treatment of mental disorders. Three general types of approaches are reviewed. Medical approaches include drug treatments, psychosurgery, and electroconvulsive therapy. Drug treatments include medications that treat psychoses (antipsychotic medications like Haldol and Clozaril), depression (antidepressants like MAOIs and Prozac), anxiety (tranquilizers like Valium and Xanax), and bipolar disorder (lithium carbonate). Although drugs have contributed to significant advances in the treatment of mental disorders, they require great caution in their use. Psychosurgery, which was used more commonly in the 1950s, is rarely used any longer because of its serious and irreversible side effects. Electroconvulsive therapy is still used for serious cases of depression that do not respond to other treatments. Types of psychotherapy exist based on each of the major perspectives (e.g., psychodynamic, humanistic). The general principles and techniques of each of these approaches are reviewed along with research on their effectiveness. Although there are certain commonalities among all the different types of psychotherapy, research indicates that some approaches are more effective for particular problems.

PREVIEW OUTLINE

Before you read the chapter, review the preview outline for each section of the text. After you have read the chapter, close this book and try to re-create the outlines on a blank piece of paper.

I. BIOLOGICAL TREATMENTS
   A. **The question of drugs**
   1. Biological treatments are enjoying a resurgence because of evidence that some disorders have a biological component
   2. Drugs commonly prescribed for mental disorders
       a. Antipsychotic drugs (neuroleptics) for schizophrenia and other psychoses; more effective on positive than negative symptoms
       b. Antidepressant drugs - include (MAO) inhibitors, tricyclics, and SSRIs - nonaddictive, but can have unpleasant side effects
       c. Tranquilizers - increase activity of GABA
       d. Lithium carbonate - prescribed for bipolar disorder; must be administered in the correct dose or can be dangerous
   3. Cautions about drugs include overprescription, relapse and drop-out rates, dosage problems, and placebo effect (to what extent is the effectiveness of a drug due simply to belief in the drug's effectiveness?)

B. **Surgery and electroshock**

    1.   Psychosurgery - surgery to destroy selected areas of the brain (e.g., prefrontal lobotomy, transcranial magnetic stimulation)

    2.   Electroconvulsive therapy (ECT) - works for severely depressed people, though it is unclear why it works

II. KINDS OF PSYCHOTHERAPY

A. **Commonalities among psychotherapies** - help clients think about their lives in new ways and find solutions to their problems

B. **Psychodynamic therapy**

    1.   Probes the past and the unconscious with techniques such as free association and transference

    2.   Traditional psychoanalysis evolved into psychodynamic therapies

    3.   They do not aim to solve an individual's immediate problem - symptoms are seen as the tip of the iceberg

C. **Behavioral and cognitive therapy** - focus is behavior change not insight

    1.   Behavioral techniques - derived from classical and operant conditioning

        a.   Systematic desensitization - step by step process of "desensitizing" a client to a feared object or experience; uses counterconditioning

        b.   Exposure treatment (or flooding) - therapist accompanies client into the feared situation

        c.   Behavioral records and contracts

        d.   Skills training - practice in behaviors necessary for achieving goals

    2.   Cognitive techniques

        a.   Aim is to identify thoughts, beliefs and expectations that might be prolonging a person's problems

        b.   Albert Ellis and rational emotive behavior therapy - therapist challenges unrealistic beliefs directly with rational arguments

        c.   Beck's approach uses other, less direct, techniques

D. **Humanistic and existential therapy**

    1.   Humanistic therapies - assume that people seek self-actualization

    2.   Do not delve into the past; help people to feel better about themselves

    3.   Client-centered or nondirective therapy by Carl Rogers - unconditional positive regard and empathy by therapist

    4.   Existential therapy - helps client explore meaning of existence, choose a destiny and accept self-responsibility

E. **Therapy in social context**

    1.   Family therapy - believes that the problem developed and is maintained in the social context, and that is where change must occur

    2.   The family as a changing pattern in which all parts affect each other and efforts to treat a single member are doomed to fail; observing the family together reveals family tensions and imbalances

F. **Psychotherapy in practice** - integrative approach

III. EVALUATING PSYCHOTHERAPY

A. **The scientist-practitioner gap**
   1. Conflict between scientists and practitioners about the relevance of research findings to clinical practice
   2. Breach between scientists and therapists has widened, partly due to professional schools that are unconnected to academic departments

B. **The therapeutic alliance**
   1. Some participants will do better than others in therapy (e.g., those motivated to improve or who have family support)
   2. Understanding role of the client's culture is also important

C. **When therapy helps**
   1. Randomized controlled trials reveal empirically validated treatments
   2. Which therapy for which problem?
      a. Behavior and cognitive therapies are the method of choice for depression, anxiety disorders, anger and impulsive violence, health problems, sleeps disorders, and childhood behavior problems
      b. Family intervention therapies help schizophrenics by teaching their families skills for dealing with the schizophrenic children

D. **When therapy harms**
   1. Sexual intimacies or other unethical behavior
   2. Prejudice or cultural ignorance on the part of a therapist
   3. Inappropriate or coercive influence
   4. Use of empirically unsupported, potentially dangerous techniques

IV. THE VALUE AND VALUES OF PSYCHOTHERAPY

A. **Does psychotherapy promise too much or foster a preoccupation with the self?**

B. **Make wise decisions when choosing a therapist, choosing a therapy, and deciding when to leave**

APPROACHES TO PSYCHOTHERAPY

Complete the following chart by listing specific techniques and general goals of therapy for each of the approaches in the left-hand column.

THERAPY APPROACH	SPECIFIC TECHNIQUES	GENERAL GOALS OF THERAPY
PSYCHODYNAMIC APPROACHES		
BEHAVIORAL APPROACH		
COGNITIVE APPROACHES		
HUMANISTIC APPROACHES		
FAMILY THERAPY		

PRACTICE TEST 1 - Multiple Choice

1.   The most widespread biological treatment is
        A.   medication.   B.   psychosurgery.
        C.   ECT.   D.   psychotherapy.

2.   Antipsychotic drugs do <u>NOT</u>
        A.   restore normal thought patterns.   B.   lessen hallucinations.
        C.   reduce dramatic symptoms.   D.   have side effects.

3.   Randolf is taking antipsychotic medication. Which of the following should concern him?
        A.   the possibility of tardive dyskinesia
        B.   the fact that while the more dramatic symptoms may be helped, normal thinking
                may not
        C.   though he may be well enough to be released from a hospital, he may not be able
                to care for himself
        D.   All of the above are concerns.

4.   Lithium carbonate is often effective in treating people who
        A.   have schizophrenia.   B.   have tardive dyskinesia.
        C.   complain of unhappiness or anxiety.   D.   have bipolar disorder.

5.   Jay is taking a medication that elevates the levels of norepinephrine and serotonin in his
        brain. What is his most probable diagnosis?
        A.   depression   B.   an anxiety disorder
        C.   bipolar disorder   D.   a psychosis

6.   Felicia has been prescribed an antidepressant. Based on the cautions about drug
        treatment, Felicia should probably have concerns about
        A.   whether the drug is more effective than a placebo.
        B.   whether the drug has been tested for long-term use.
        C.   whether the right dosage has been identified.
        D.   all of the above.

7.   A problem with using drugs in treating psychological disorders is that
        A.   there are high drop-out rates.
        B.   tests of drug effects in long-term usage are often missing.
        C.   there is a strong placebo effect in evaluating their effectiveness.
        D.   all of the above are potential problems.

8. The original intention of prefrontal lobotomy was to
   A. reduce the patient's emotional discomfort without impairing intellectual capacity.
   B. "ventilate" evil impulses or mental pressures.
   C. remove an abnormal organic condition, such as a tumor.
   D. replace drugs and electroconvulsive therapy, which were considered dangerous.

9. Among the following patients, who would be a likely candidate for electroconvulsive therapy (ECT)?
   A. Fran is suicidally depressed.
   B. Dan is anxious.
   C. Stan is moderately depressed.
   D. ECT should not be used on any of them, since it is outdated and barbaric.

10. Critics of ECT say that it
   A. only helps people with minor psychological problems.
   B. is too often used improperly, and it can damage the brain.
   C. requires high voltages that could be fatal.
   D. causes epileptic seizures.

11. In psychodynamic therapies, the patient's displacement of emotional elements in his or her inner life onto the therapist is called
   A. free association.   B. transference.
   C. insight.   D. dynamic focus.

12. A type of therapy that takes the individual right into the most feared situation is called
   A. systematic desensitization.   B. aversive conditioning.
   C. flooding or exposure treatment. D. brief psychodynamic therapy.

13. Systematic desensitization, aversive conditioning, flooding and skills training are all
   A. techniques used in cognitive therapies. B. psychodynamic techniques.
   C. methods employed by humanists.   D. behavioral techniques.

14. To help Bob with his fear of flying, Dr. Rose teaches Bob to relax while they proceed through a series of steps that go from reading a story about an airplane, to visiting an airport, to boarding a plane, to taking a short flight. This _____ technique is called

   _____.
   A. cognitive; rational emotive therapy   B. humanistic; flooding
   C. behavioral; systematic desensitization D. behavioral; flooding

15. Cognitive therapies focus on changing _____, whereas humanistic therapies focus on

   _____.
   A. beliefs; self-acceptance   B. behaviors; changing families
   C. behaviors; insight into the past D. thoughts; skills

16. Which two therapies often borrow each other's methods, so that a combination of the two is more common than either method alone?
   A. psychoanalysis; behavior therapy
   B. family therapy; group therapy
   C. cognitive therapy; behavior therapy
   D. support groups; group therapy

17. In which approach does the therapist challenge the client's illogical beliefs?
   A. cognitive therapy
   B. humanistic therapy
   C. psychodynamic therapy
   D. existential therapy

18. What type of therapist would try to provide unconditional positive regard?
   A. cognitive
   B. humanistic
   C. psychodynamic
   D. existential

19. Which type of therapist might make use of insight, transference, and free association?
   A. a humanistic therapist
   B. a behaviorist therapist
   C. a psychodynamic therapist
   D. a cognitive therapist

20. Professionals who help those who are physically disabled to work and live independently are called
   A. behavioral psychologists.
   B. family therapists.
   C. rehabilitation psychologists.
   D. group therapists.

21. Based on controlled clinical trials, which of the following is true about the effectiveness of therapy?
   A. Psychotherapy is better than doing nothing at all.
   B. People who do best in psychotherapy are those who have less serious problems and are motivated to improve.
   C. For the common emotional problems of life, short-term treatment is usually sufficient.
   D. All of the above

22. Good therapeutic candidates are those who
   A. are introspective and want to talk about their childhoods.
   B. want a chance to talk about their feelings without any limits.
   C. recognize the expertise of the therapist.
   D. are unhappy and motivated enough to want to work on their problems.

23. A therapeutic alliance is
   A. an organization of therapists who advocate for the benefits of therapy.
   B. a group of consumers who were harmed because of a therapist's incompetence or unethical methods.
   C. a bond between the client and therapist that depends on their ability to understand each other.
   D. a support group in which people share common problems.

24. Depth therapies work best for
    A. anxiety disorders.
    B. people who are introspective and want to explore their pasts and examine their current lives.
    C. people with sex problems.
    D. people who are drug abusers.

25. Research suggests that cognitive and behavioral approaches are very successful with many types of problems, however, they are NOT thought to work well for
    A. personality disorders and psychoses.
    B. phobias and panic disorder.
    C. moderate depression.
    D. agoraphobia and anxiety disorders.

26. In which of the following cases is Melina most likely to find the therapeutic experience harmful?
    A. Her therapist firmly believes that Melina was sexually abused in childhood, though she has no memories of this and does not believe it is so.
    B. Her therapist disagrees with her about several issues.
    C. Her therapist does not always give her an immediate appointment when she calls.
    D. All of the above may be harmful.

27. Which factors can cause psychotherapy to be harmful?
    A. coercion   B. bias
    C. therapist-induced disorders   D. all of the above

28. A realistic expectation for the outcome of psychotherapy is
    A. to learn that any change is possible.
    B. to help make decisions and clarify values and goals.
    C. to be happy all, or almost all, of the time.
    D. to help eliminate the problems from one's life.

PRACTICE TEST 2 - Short Answer

1. Neuroleptics, or antipsychotic drugs, are used in the treatment of _____ and other _____.

2. One of the side effects of the antipsychotic drugs is a neurological disorder called _____, which is characterized by hand tremors and other involuntary muscle movements.

3. Monoamine oxidase inhibitors, tricyclics, and selective serotonin reuptake inhibitors are all examples of _____ drugs.

4. _____ is a special category of drug which often helps people who suffer from bipolar disorder.

5. People who take antidepressant drugs without also learning how to cope with their problems are more likely to _____ in the future.

6. A form of psychosurgery that was supposed to reduce the patient's emotional symptoms without impairing intellectual ability, called a _____, left many patients apathetic, withdrawn, and unable to care for themselves.

7. _____ is used as a treatment for severe depression, for patients who are at risk of committing suicide who cannot wait for antidepressants or psychotherapy to take effect.

8. To bring unconscious conflicts to awareness, _____ therapists often ask the client to say whatever comes to mind. This technique is called _____.

9. Bob has been seeing Dr. Sigmund. Bob has always felt that his mother rejected him and now he finds that he is furious at Dr. Sigmund for planning a vacation. This element of psychodynamic therapy is called _____.

10. _____ is one of the _____ techniques that involves a step-by-step process of desensitizing a client to a feared object or experience.

11. The technique of _____ involves having clients who are suffering from specific anxieties confront the feared situation or memory directly.

12. Cognitive therapists require clients to examine the _____ for their beliefs and to consider other _____ of events that might result in less disturbing emotions.

13. One of the best known schools of cognitive therapy was developed by Albert Ellis and is now called rational _____ behavior therapy.

14. _____ therapy, developed by Carl Rogers, the therapist listens to the client in an accepting, nonjudgmental way and offers _____ positive regard.

15. _____ therapists maintain that problems develop in a social context, and that any changes a person makes in therapy will affect that context.

16. The scientist-practitioner gap refers to the breach between scientists and therapists about the importance of _____ methods and findings on the practice of psychotherapy.

17. In some cases, psychotherapy has been found to be harmful because the therapist may be _____, inducing the client to produce the symptoms the therapist is looking for.

18. The personality of the therapist is also critical to the success of any therapy, particularly the qualities that Carl Rogers praised: _____, expressiveness, warmth, and _____.

19. A task force from the American Psychological Association found that _____treatment is particularly effective for depression and _____ disorders.

20. The APA task force also found that young adults with schizophrenia are greatly helped by family therapies that teach parents _____ skills in dealing with their troubled children.

21. _____ to accept the therapist's advice, sexual intimacies, or other unethical behavior can result in harm to the client.

22. Therapist influence is a likely reason for the growing number of people diagnosed with _____ disorder in the 1980s and 1990s.

23. _____ psychologists set up programs to help people who are mentally ill in their own communities rather than in hospitals. _____ psychologists are concerned with the assessment and treatment of people who ar physically disabled.

PRACTICE TEST 3 - Essay

1. Identify the three major categories of approaches to psychological problems and briefly describe the help they offer. Indicate under what circumstances each would be desirable.

2. Identify the drugs typically prescribed for each of the disorders listed below and then briefly explain why drugs alone may not be sufficient treatment.

    A. Anxiety disorders
    B. Mood disorders
    C. Psychotic disorders

3. Summarize the major features of each of the five major approaches to psychotherapy. Specify the goals and common techniques of each.

4. Identify the features of the client, the therapist, and their relationship that are associated with therapeutic success.

5. Identify and briefly describe the factors that contribute to therapeutic harm.

APPENDIX A

Statistical Methods

LEARNING OBJECTIVES

1. Describe a frequency distribution and explain how one is constructed.

2. Describe the different types of graphs and explain how graphs can mask or exaggerate differences.

3. Describe the three measures of central tendency and how each is calculated.

4. Define standard deviation and describe how it is calculated.

5. Compare and contrast percentile scores and z-scores.

6. Describe a normal distribution and the two types of skewed distributions.

7. Describe the characteristics of a normal curve.

8. Distinguish between the null and the alternative hypothesis.

9. Explain what is meant by statistical significance, and discuss the relationship between statistical significance and psychological importance.

10. Define sampling distribution.

PREVIEW OUTLINE

Before you read the appendix, review the preview outline for each section. After you have read the appendix, close this book and try to <u>re-create</u> the outlines on a blank piece of paper.

I. ORGANIZING DATA

    A.   **Constructing a frequency distribution** - often the first step in organizing data
          1.   Shows how often each possible score actually occurred
          2.   Grouped frequency distributions (groups adjacent scores into equal-sized classes or intervals) are sometimes used with many possible scores

    B.   **Graphing the data**
          1.   A graph is a picture that depicts numerical relationships
          2.   Types of graphs
                a.   Histogram or bar graph - draw rectangles or bars above each score indicating the number of times it occurred from the bar's height
                b.   Frequency polygon, or line graph - each score is indicated by a dot placed directly over the score on the horizontal axis
          3.   Caution about graphs - they can mask or exaggerate differences

II. DESCRIBING DATA

    A.   **Measuring central tendency** - single representative number for a set of data
          1.   The mean or "average"
                a.   Add up a set of scores and divide by the total number of scores
                b.   Means can be misleading because very high or very low scores can dramatically raise or lower the mean
          2.   The median
                a.   The median is the midpoint in a set of scores ordered
                b.   A more representative measure when extreme scores occur
          3.   The mode
                a.   The score that occurs most often
                b.   Used less often than other measures of central tendency

    B.   **Measuring variability** - tells whether the scores are clustered closely around the mean or widely scattered
          1.   The mode - simplest measure of variability - found by subtracting the lowest score from the highest one
          2.   The standard deviation - tells how much, on the average, scores in a distribution differ from the mean
                a.   To compute the standard deviation - Subtract the mean from each score yielding deviation scores, square deviation scores, average the squared deviation scores, then take the square root of the result
                b.   Large standard deviations signify that scores are widely scattered and the mean is probably not very representative

C. **Transforming scores** - used when researchers don't want to work directly with raw scores

    1.   Percentile scores - percentage of people scoring at or below a given raw score

    2.   Z-scores or standard scores

        a.   Tell how far a given raw score is above or below the mean, using the standard deviation as the unit of measurement

        b.   They preserve the relative spacing of the original raw scores

        c.   Z-scores comparisons must be done with caution

D. **Curves** - or the pattern of the distribution

    1.   A normal distribution has a symmetrical, bell-shaped form when plotted in a frequency polygon - called a normal curve

    2.   Characteristics of a normal curve - symmetrical, all measures of central tendency (mean, median, mode) have the same value

    3.   Not all types of observations are distributed normally; some are lopsided or skewed

        a.   When the tail goes to the left, it is a negative skew

        b.   When the tail goes to the right, it is a positive skew

III. DRAWING INFERENCES with inferential statistics

A. **The null versus the alternative hypothesis**

    1.   The null hypothesis states the possibility that the experimental manipulations will have no effect on the subjects' behavior

    2.   The alternative hypothesis states that the average experimental group score will differ from the average control group score

    3.   The goal is to reject the null hypothesis

B. **Testing hypotheses**

    1.   Goal - to be reasonably certain the difference did not occur by chance

    2.   Sampling distribution is used - the theoretical distribution of differences between means

    3.   When the null hypothesis is true, there is no difference between groups

    4.   If there is a difference, how likely is it to occur by chance?

    5.   If it is highly improbable that a result occurs by chance, it is said to be statistically significant

    6.   Characteristics of statistical significance

        a.   Finding accepted as statistically significant if the likelihood of its occurring by chance is five percent or less ($p < .05$)

        b.   Statistically significant results are not always psychologically interesting or important

        c.   Statistical significance is related to sample size - results from a large sample are likely to be found statistically significant

PRACTICE TEST 1 - Multiple Choice

1. The first step in organizing raw data is to
   A. get a measure of the central tendency.
   B. establish the range.
   C. construct a frequency distribution.
   D. identify standard deviation.

2. Dr. Starr gives 10-question quizzes in her psychology class. When she returns quizzes, she puts on the board how many people scored a 10, 9, 8, 7, 6, 5, 4, 3, 2 and 1. This is called a
   A. normal curve.
   B. frequency distribution.
   C. frequency polygon.
   D. histogram.

3. A "histogram" is the technical term that describes a
   A. bar graph.
   B. polygon.
   C. mean.
   D. line graph.

4. A histogram is to a polygon as
   A. a line is to a bar.
   B. null is to alternative.
   C. a bar is to a line.
   D. normal is to skewed.

5. The most frequently occurring score in a distribution is called the
   A. mean.
   B. median.
   C. standard deviation.
   D. mode.

6. The mean, median and mode are
   A. measures of central tendency.
   B. measures of variability.
   C. characteristics of a normal distribution, but not a skewed distribution.
   D. characteristics of a skewed distribution, but not a normal distribution.

7. A measure of variability that indicates the average difference between scores in a distribution and their mean is called the
   A. range.
   B. standard deviation.
   C. mode.
   D. z-score.

8. A score that indicates how far a given score is from the mean is called a
   A. range.
   B. mode.
   C. standard deviation.
   D. z-score.

9. Students in Dr. Friedlander's class got the following scores on their first test: 75, 77, 87, 63, 93, 77, 72, 80, 57, 68, 76. What is the mode?
   A. 77
   B. 75
   C. 36
   D. 76

10. What is the median in the distribution of scores in question 9?
    A. 77   B. 75
    C. 36   D. 76

11. What is the range in the distribution of scores in question 9?
    A. 77   B. 36
    C. 30   D. 76

12. If the mean is 10, and the standard deviation is 2, a person with a raw score of 8 has a z-score of
    A. 8.   B. -1.
    C. 1.   D. 2.

13. A lopsided distribution in which scores cluster at the high or low end of the distribution is referred to as
    A. normal.   B. bimodal.
    C. skewed.   D. standard.

14. What asserts that experimental manipulations have no effect?
    A. null hypothesis   B. sampling distribution
    C. alternative hypothesis   D. statistical significance

15. If the null hypothesis is true, differences between experimental and control groups are due to
    A. standard deviations.   B. skew.
    C. chance fluctuations.   D. true differences.

16. Results that are not attributable to chance are referred to as
    A. non-chance fluctuations.   B. skewed.
    C. statistically significant.   D. all of the above.

17. The theoretical distribution of the results of the entire population is called the
    A. null hypothesis.   B. sampling distribution.
    C. statistical significance.   D. random error.

18. Statistical significance
    A. suggests that a result would be highly improbable by chance alone.
    B. does not necessarily have anything to do with psychological importance.
    C. is a likely outcome with a large sample.
    D. incorporates all of the above.

PRACTICE TEST 2 - Short Answer

1.   A _____ distribution shows how often each possible score occurs.

2.   In a frequency _____, each score is indicated by a dot placed on a horizontal axis at the appropriate height on the vertical axis.

3.   The _____ is calculated by adding up a set of scores and dividing by the number of scores in the set. The _____ is the score that occurs most often.

4.   The above terms are ways of characterizing an entire set of data in terms of a representative number. They are measures of _____ tendency.

5.   The _____ is the simplest measure of variability, whereas the standard _____ tells how much, on average, scores in a distribution differ from the _____.

6.   When researchers don't want to work directly with raw scores, they can convert the scores to either _____ or to _____.

7.   A _____ distribution has a symmetrical, bell-shaped form when plotted on a frequency polygon.

8.   When a distribution of scores is lopsided and the longer tail goes to the left, it is characterized as _____ skewed.

9.   The _____ hypothesis states the possibility that the experimental manipulations will have no effect on the behavior of the participants.

10.   If it is highly improbable that a result occurs by chance, it is said to be _____ significant.

PRACTICE TEST 3 - Essay

1. Researchers organize and describe data in a variety of ways. Below, different statistical devices have been grouped together. Examine each grouping and describe the common purpose of the statistics within each.

    A.   Mean, median, mode
    B.   Range and standard deviation
    C.   Frequency distributions, bar graphs (histograms) and line graphs (frequency polygons)
    D.   Percentile scores and z-scores

2. Assume that the height of the male population is normally distributed with a mean of 70 inches and a standard deviation of 3 inches. Given such information, examine each of the statements below and decide whether it is justified or unjustified. Explain the basis for your answer.

    A.   The most frequently occurring male height is 70 inches.
    B.   The percentage of men above 70 inches is much higher than the percentage below this height.
    C.   If the height requirement for entering the police academy were set at 73 inches, less than half the male population would qualify.
    D.   A curve depicting the height of players in professional basketball would also be normally distributed.

3. Below are two inaccurate statements about hypothesis testing and statistical significance. Revise each statement so that it is accurate.

    A.   The null hypothesis is accepted whenever results are statistically significant.
    B.   Statistical significance is a measure of the relative strengths of experimental and control treatments.

A N S W E R   K E Y

ANSWER KEYS FOR CHAPTER ONE

ANSWER KEY - PRACTICE TEST 1 - MULTIPLE CHOICE

1.	B	2.	B	3.	B	4.	A
5.	D	6.	D	7.	A	8.	C
9.	D	10.	D	11.	A	12.	A
13.	C	14.	A	15.	D	16.	A
17.	B	18.	B	19.	D	20.	D
21.	B	22.	A	23.	A	24.	C
25.	C	26.	D	27.	A	28.	B
29.	C	30.	D				

ANSWER KEY - PRACTICE TEST 2 - SHORT ANSWER

1.   behavior and mental processes
2.   empirical
3.   critical thinking
4.   any two of the following: ask questions, define your terms, examine the evidence, analyze assumptions and biases, avoid emotional reasoning, don't oversimplify, consider other interpretations, tolerate uncertainty
5.   predict, modify
6.   trained introspection
7.   structuralism
8.   conflicts and traumas from early childhood
9.   psychodynamic
10.   biological, learning, cognitive, sociocultural, psychodynamic
11.   learning
12.   free will
13.   cognitive
14.   social and cultural forces
15.   social rules and roles, groups, authority and how we are affected by other people; cultural
16.   feminist
17.   basic; applied
18.   industrial/occupational; educational
19.   nonclinical
20.   clinical psychology, counseling psychology, school psychology
21.   developmental
22.   license; doctorate
23.   psychotherapist, psychoanalyst, psychiatrist
24.   psychiatrists; psychotherapists
25.   social workers, school counselors, marriage, family and child counselors

ANSWER KEY - PRACTICE TEST 3 - ESSAY

1 A. This activity is an area of basic psychology because this research is not applying the measurement of intelligence for a particular use. This falls in the area of psychometrics, which is a nonclinical specialty.

  B. The study of vision falls in the area of basic research, since the findings are not concerned with the practical uses of its findings. This research is conducted by experimental psychologists because they conduct laboratory studies of sensation as well as other areas. Experimental psychology is a nonclinical specialty.

  C. Piaget's work is an example of basic psychology because the theory does not address practical uses of the knowledge. This activity falls in the area of developmental psychology because Piaget studied how people change and grow over time. It is a nonclinical area.

  D. Studying work motivations falls in the basic psychology area because this project does not involve direct use or application of the findings. This type of research falls into the specialty area of industrial or organizational psychology, which studies behavior in the workplace. It is a nonclinical specialty.

  E. Milgram's study represents basic psychology because there is no direct application of the findings. It falls under the nonclinical specialty area, social psychology. The study examines how the social context influences individuals.

  F. Strupp's study is basic research because direct application for these findings is not part of the purpose of the study. It falls under the specialty of clinical psychology, which is interested in treating mental or emotional problems and is a clinical specialty area.

  G. The study of children's self-esteem is applied research, since it was used to make changes in the school systems. This type of research falls under the specialty area of developmental psychology, since it deals with how people change and grow over time. Developmental psychology is a nonclinical specialty.

  H. Using findings from career development research to assist students is an example of applied psychology. This activity falls into the specialty of counseling psychology, a clinical area, because it is dealing with problems of everyday life rather than with mental disorders.

2. Learning theory or behaviorism would explore how Harold learned his behavior and how his environmental conditions encouraged his drug abuse. Specifically, behaviorists would be interested in the payoffs or rewards that result from the drug use. Social learning theorists might wonder if Harold had learned this behavior from observing or imitating others, such as peers or parents.

Psychologists from a psychodynamic perspective would understand Harold's drug abuse as a result of unconscious conflicts that remain unresolved from his early childhood. Harold is unaware of his true motivations because they are unconscious.

The biological perspective understands Harold's drug abuse as a direct result of addictive processes by which the body comes to crave and depend on drugs. If Harold were to attempt to discontinue his drug use, he would experience unpleasant bodily sensations related to withdrawal. Therefore, to avoid bodily withdrawal symptoms, his drug use is continued. Biological predispositions may be operating that may have made Harold more sensitive to drug exposure.

Cognitive psychologists would be interested in Harold's perception and reasoning about drug use. Are his ideas about drugs irrational or unreasonable? What does he tell himself about drug use or nonuse? For example, does he believe that he must use drugs to be accepted by his peers? Cognitive psychologists would be interested in whether Harold believes he has control of himself or whether he sees his drug use as a problem. Sociocultural psychologists would look to the attitude in the culture toward alcohol use. They would understand the role alcohol plays for people and how it is expected to be used. For example, attitudes and expectations for alcohol use are different in other countries where alcohol is used as a beverage at meals and is consumed at meal times by adolescents and sometimes children.

According to humanists, Harold's drug abuse represents a choice. He is freely choosing to use drugs and is equally free to choose not to do so. Humanists may inquire whether he believes it assists him in dealing with questions about reaching his full potential.

Feminist psychologists would be interested in gender differences in drug abuse. They would see Harold's drug use as a way of dealing with emotions that are compatible with the male gender role in this society. Since the expression of certain emotions is not considered masculine, they might speculate that drug use would be a way of dealing with "unmasculine" emotions.

3.   A psychologist would use psychotherapy based on psychological theories to treat Juanita's depression. The psychologist would have formal training and would hold either a Ph.D., an Ed.D., or a Psy.D. A psychiatrist would be likely to prescribe medication for Juanita's depression. A psychiatrist is a medical doctor (M.D.) with a residency in psychiatry. A psychoanalyst would use psychoanalysis, which is a type of psychotherapy based on the work of Sigmund Freud. To practice psychoanalysis, specialized training at a recognized psychoanalytic institute is required. A psychotherapist would use psychotherapy. A psychotherapist may or may not have formal education in psychology or a related field.

ANSWER KEYS FOR CHAPTER TWO

ANSWER KEY - PRACTICE TEST 1 - MULTIPLE CHOICE

1.	B	2.	A	3.	C	4.	D
5.	A	6.	C	7.	A	8.	B
9.	D	10.	D	11.	C	12.	A
13.	B	14.	B	15.	C	16.	D
17.	C	18.	B	19.	B	20.	C
21.	C	22.	B	23.	A	24.	D
25.	B	26.	C	27.	D	28.	A
29.	D	30.	A	31.	A	32.	B
33.	D	34.	A	35.	D		

ANSWER KEY - PRACTICE TEST 2 - SHORT ANSWER

1. unfounded belief
2. hypothesis
3. operational
4. principle of falsifiability
5. replicated
6. descriptive
7. case study
8. naturalistic observational studies
9. objective; projective
10. norms
11. reliability
12. validity
13. criterion validity
14. representative
15. volunteer
16. correlation; variables
17. positively; a causal relationship
18. experimental method
19. independent; dependent
20. experimental; control
21. placebo; expectations
22. single
23. descriptive
24. significant
25. cross-sectional; longitudinal

ANSWER KEY - PRACTICE TEST 3 - ESSAY

1.   A.   Survey. Adolescents constitute a large population and the information sought should be accessible through questionnaires or interviews. Care is needed to construct a sample that is representative of the population under consideration.

        B.   Psychological tests. The goal is to measure psychological qualities within an individual. Other methods (e.g., case history, naturalistic observation) might be employed, but they are more time-consuming and do not offer the degree of standardization, reliability and validity found in a well-constructed test.

        C.   Experiment. Cause-and-effect information is being sought. In science this information is obtained through experiments in which the proposed causal variable is manipulated under controlled conditions.

        D.   Correlation. This technique is used to determine if and how strongly two variables are related. Establishing that a correlation exists, however, does not address the problem of why two things are related.

        E.   Naturalistic observation. A description of behavior as it occurs in a real-life situation is being sought. Making the observations without arousing suspicion in subjects could be problematic.

        F.   Case study. Making this determination requires in-depth information about the way a variety of psychological factors - expectation, values, motives, past experiences, and so forth - blend together within the person. This kind of information is unique to the person under consideration and could not be assessed through standardized tests.

        G.   Laboratory observation. The goal is to identify what the parents are doing that may be contributing to the child's problems and help them to parent differently. To ascertain what is currently going on in the family, observing them interact in the laboratory would be the best way to actually see what is occurring. Information could be collected with an interview or questionnaire, but parents may not be aware of what they are doing.

2.   A.   Hypothesis: Caffeine improves studying
              Independent variable and its operational definition: caffeine; ounces
              Dependent variable and its operational definition: studying; test score
              Experimental condition: group receiving caffeine
              Control group: group receiving decaffeinated beverage

B. Hypothesis: Heavy metal music increases aggression
Independent variable and its operational definition: music; jazz, classical, heavy metal
Dependent variable and its operational definition: aggression; amount of time spent punching bag
Experimental condition: groups exposed to jazz, classical and heavy metal music
Control group: group exposed to white noise machine

C. Hypothesis: Exercise increases relaxation
Independent variable and its operational definition: exercise; aerobics, number of sit-ups and push-ups
Dependent variable and its operational definition: relaxation; heart rate, muscle tension, respiration, blood pressure
Experimental condition: groups engaging in aerobics, sit-ups and push-ups
Control group: group having supervised study session

3. A. Positive   B. Negative
    C. Negative   D. Positive
    E. Zero   F. Negative
    G. Negative   H. Positive
    I. Negative   J. Zero

4. A. Unethical. Requiring research participation for a course, without providing an alternate way of satisfying the course requirement, violates the principle of voluntary consent.
    B. Unethical. Not only should subjects be free to withdraw at any time, but they should also be informed of this right before they begin to participate.
    C. Ethical. Although it is controversial, outright deception has not been ruled out by the American Psychological Association's guidelines.
    D. Ethical. Under the American Psychological Association's guidelines, the use of animals is acceptable in research that reduces human suffering and promotes human welfare.
    E. Ethical. The investigator is obligated to protect subjects from physical and mental discomfort by using both voluntary and informed consent.

ANSWER KEYS FOR CHAPTER THREE

ANSWER KEY - PRACTICE TEST 1 - MULTIPLE CHOICE

1. C	2. B	3. C	4. D
5. A	6. C	7. C	8. A
9. A	10. B	11. B	12. D
13. B	14. A	15. B	16. C
17. D	18. C	19. D	20. D
21. B	22. C	23. D	24. A
25. B	26. A	27. B	28. C
29. D	30. B	31. B	32. D

ANSWER KEY - PRACTICE TEST 2 - SHORT ANSWER

1. Genes; chromosomes
2. genome
3. linkage
4. evolutionary
5. evolution
6. mutate
7. natural selection
8. modules
9. language; mating
10. rules; elements
11. surface; deep
12. Chomsky; acquisition
13. similar stages
14. critical period
15. sociobiologists
16. analogy; commonalities
17. stereotypes
18. heritability
19. individuals
20. identical (monozygotic); fraternal (dizygotic)
21. .50; .60 -.80
22. group
23. prenatal care; malnutrition or exposure to toxins or large family size or stressful family circumstances

ANSWER KEY - PRACTICE TEST 3 - ESSAY

1. A. The basic elements of DNA within the genes influence protein synthesis in the body by specifying the sequence of amino acids, which are the building blocks of the proteins. The sequence of amino acids are affected by the arrangement of the basic elements, which comprises a chemical code. Proteins then go on to affect virtually all structural and biochemical characteristics of the organism. Genes for alcoholism might influence the basic elements of DNA or their arrangement, which then go on to influence the amino acids, the proteins and the structures or biochemistry of the body.

   B. This statement misinterprets heritability estimates. Heritability estimates do <u>NOT</u> apply to individuals, only to variations within a group. No one can determine the impact of heredity on any particular individual's trait. For one person, genes may make a tremendous difference; for another, the environment may be more important. This statement ignores the fact that even highly heritable traits can be modified by the environment. This statement ignores environmental influences.

   C. One might use a linkage study, which would examine large families in which alcoholism is common.

2. A. The feeling of disgust may have been useful in warding off contamination from disease and contagion.
   B. Intuition may have allowed people to anticipate others' behaviors based on their beliefs and desires and thereby prepare for problems.
   C. Self-concept may have been useful in knowing one's value to others.
   D. Feelings of kinship may have promoted protection and help to one's kin, thereby insuring their survival.
   E. Male promiscuity has the effect of increasing the offspring of any individual male, thereby continuing his genes.
   F. Female selectivity increases the chances of conceiving with the best genes.

3. Until the middle of this century, views about language acquisition suggested that language is learned (not inborn) bit by bit and that children learn to speak by imitating adults and paying attention when adults correct their mistakes. Chomsky stated that language was too complex to learn in this way. He said that children learn not only which sounds form words, but can apply the rules of syntax and discern underlying meaning. He said that the capacity for language is inborn and that the brain has a language acquisition device, or a "mental module" that allows children to develop language if they are exposed to an adequate sampling of speech. According to Chomsky, human beings are designed to use language. The following support his position:
   1. Children everywhere seem to go through similar stages of linguistic development.
   2. Children combine words in ways that adults never would, and so could not simply be imitating.
   3. Adults do not consistently correct their children's syntax.
   4. Even children who are profoundly retarded acquire language.

4.   A.   The study would use pairs of identical twins reared apart. IQ tests would be given to both members of the pairs and the following comparisons would be made:

1. Scores of both members of the pairs of identical twins
2. Scores of identical twins reared together
3. Scores of siblings reared apart
4. Scores of siblings reared together
5. Scores of unrelated people

The conclusions would depend on the results of these comparisons. Similarity of IQ scores based on genetic similarity, regardless of shared environment, would be supportive evidence for heritability estimates. Cautionary statements would include:

1. Heritable does not mean the same thing as genetic.
2. Heritability applies only to a particular group living in a particular environment, and estimates may differ for different groups.
3. Heritability estimates do not apply to individuals, only to variations within a group.
4. Even highly heritable traits can be modified by the environment.

    B.   The following recommendations would be made:

1. Develop a prenatal care program for mothers-to-be that involves education about drug use, nutrition, health, environmental pollutants
2. Nutrition program for young children
3. Assistance related to exposure to toxins
4. Information on the importance of mental stimulation
5. Family therapy and support to reduce stressful family circumstances
6. Training in parent-child interactions

ANSWER KEYS FOR CHAPTER FOUR

ANSWER KEY - PRACTICE TEST 1 - MULTIPLE CHOICE

1. D	2. B	3. A	4. D
5. A	6. C	7. C	8. D
9. A	10. B	11. A	12. A
13. B	14. C	15. B	16. D
17. B	18. B	19. C	20. A
21. B	22. D	23. D	24. B
25. A	26. A	27. B	28. C
29. D	30. B		

ANSWER KEY - PRACTICE TEST 2 - SHORT ANSWER

1. central; peripheral
2. somatic; autonomic
3. sympathetic; parasympathetic
4. cell body
5. dendrites; axon
6. myelin sheath
7. synapse
8. axon terminal; neurotransmitters
9. all or none
10. Endorphins; neurotransmitters
11. endocrine
12. norepinephrine and serotonin; acetylcholine
13. androgens; estrogen; progesterone
14. electroencephalogram
15. magnetic resonance imaging
16. reticular activating
17. pons; medulla; cerebellum
18. thalamus
19. hypothalamus
20. limbic
21. hippocampus
22. occipital; parietal; temporal; frontal
23. corpus callosum
24. Wernicke's; temporal; Broca's; frontal
25. behavior

ANSWER KEY - PRACTICE TEST 3 - ESSAY

1.   A.   The dendrites of neurons in the ear are stimulated and the message is sent to the cell body, which causes an inflow of sodium ions and an outflow of potassium ions that result in a wave of electrical voltage travelling down the axon. At the end of the axon, synaptic vesicles held in the synaptic end bulb release neurotransmitters, which cross the synaptic cleft and lock into receptor sites on the next neuron.

        B.   The sound causes neurons in the ear to fire, via sensory neurons to the thalamus, which directs the message to the auditory cortex in the temporal lobes, to the prefrontal lobes to figure out what to do and make a plan, to the motor cortex in the frontal lobe, out of the brain via motor neurons to the skeletal muscles to get up and move.

        C.   Information from the ears goes to the brain via the somatic nervous system of the peripheral nervous system. Once at the thalamus, it is in the central nervous system. As information exits the brain from the motor cortex, the somatic nervous system gets involved again as messages go to the muscles that allow you to cross the room. Your feeling nervous involves the autonomic nervous system, which carries messages from the central nervous system about your preparedness for the test to the glands and organs.

2.   A.   Hypothalamus
        B.   Thalamus
        C.   Prefrontal lobe
        D.   Broca's area
        E.   Hippocampus
        F.   Cerebellum

3.   It is difficult to say exactly, but the cerebrum, which is responsible for higher functioning, has been damaged. Parts of the brain stem, specifically the medulla, which is responsible for heart rate and respiration, are still in tact, but because Helen is not conscious, it is possible that the pons, which is responsible for sleeping and waking, may be damaged.

4.   A.   Frontal lobes; personality, planning, initiative
        B.   Parietal lobes; body senses and location
        C.   Occipital lobes; vision

5.   A.   Right
        B.   Left
        C.   Right
        D.   Left
        E.   There are problems with functions controlled by the left hemisphere, but not with the right hemisphere.

ANSWER KEYS FOR CHAPTER FIVE

ANSWER KEY - PRACTICE TEST 1 - MULTIPLE CHOICE

1. B	2. C	3. B	4. B
5. D	6. C	7. B	8. D
9. D	10. D	11. A	12. C
13. B	14. C	15. B	16. C
17. B	18. C	19. C	20. D
21. D	22. B	23. C	24. D
25. C	26. D	27. A	28. C
29. C			

ANSWER KEY - PRACTICE TEST 2 - SHORT ANSWER

1. consciousness
2. circadian
3. suprachiasmatic nucleus
4. hormone levels; the menstrual cycle (among others)
5. desynchronization
6. hormones
7. REM sleep
8. spindles
9. inactive; active
10. lucid
11. manifest; latent
12. mental housekeeping
13. interpreted brain activity
14. Psychoactive
15. central nervous system
16. stimulants
17. tolerance
18. neurotransmitter
19. physical factors, experience with the drug, environmental setting, or mental set
20. "think-drink" effect
21. hidden observer
22. pseudomemories
23. dissociation
24. medical and psychological
25. sociocognitive

ANSWER KEY - PRACTICE TEST 3 - ESSAY

1. A.   Ultradian, because the cycle repeats several times a day
    B.   Infradian, because the cycle repeats less than once a day
    C.   Ultradian, because the cycle repeats several times a day
    D.   Could be circadian if cycle repeats daily; could be ultradian if cycle repeats more than once a day; could be infradian if cycle repeats less than once a day
    E.   Ultradian, because the cycle repeats several times a day
    F.   Infradian, because the cycle repeats less than once a day

2. A.   The definition of PMS is important because physical and emotional symptoms often appear on the same questionnaire.   Because many women may experience physical symptoms, they are likely to have a higher score than if these two categories of symptoms were presented separately.
    B.   Negative moods are likely to be attributed to PMS when they occur just prior to the onset of menstruation, whereas negative moods that occur at different stages of the menstrual cycle are likely to be attributed to other factors.   Another problem related to the self-reporting of PMS symptoms is the tendency to notice negative moods that occur before menstruation, and to ignore the absence of negative moods before menstruation.
    C.   Expectations can influence perceptions.   The very title of a widely used questionnaire, the Menstrual Distress Questionnaire, can bias responders to look for and find certain symptoms, while ignoring other, more positive, symptoms.
    D.   Research findings include
         1.   Women and men do not differ in the emotional symptoms or number of mood swings they experience over the course of a month.
         2.   For most women, the relationship between cycle stage and symptoms is weak or nonexistent.
         3.   There is no reliable relationship between cycle stage and behaviors that matter in real life.
         4.   Women do not consistently report negative psychological changes from one cycle to the next.

3. A.   Sleep consists of REM and four distinct non-REM periods.
    B.   The extra alertness results from the fact that the body is synchronized to wake itself up as the morning approaches. Loss of sleep is not invigorating.
    C.   Although theorists do not agree on the exact functions of sleep, rest is one of its presumed functions. We can "catch up" on several nights of sleep deprivation in just one night.
    D.   Though people can function pretty well after losing a single night's sleep, mental flexibility, originality and other aspects of creative thinking may suffer.
    E.   We display four to five REM periods each night, and laboratory research indicates that we dream every night.

4.   A.   Activation-synthesis theory or dreams as interpreted brain activity
       B.   Dreams as information processing
       C.   Dreams as unconscious wishes or psychoanalytic theory
       D.   Dreams as problem-solving

5.   A1.   Depressant
       A2.   Disinhibition, anxiety reduction, slower reaction times, memory loss, poor coordination
       A3.   Death, psychosis, organic damage, blackouts

       B1.   Depressant
       B2.   Sedation, anxiety and guilt reduction, release of tension
       B3.   Tolerance and addiction, sensory and motor impairment, coma, death

       C1.   Opiate
       C2.   Pain reduction, euphoria
       C3.   Addiction, convulsions, nausea, death

       D1.   Stimulant
       D2.   Elevated metabolism and mood, increased wakefulness
       D3.   Nervousness, delusions, psychosis, death

       E1.   Stimulant
       E2.   Appetite suppression, excitability, euphoria
       E3.   Sleeplessness, sweating, paranoia, depression

       F1.   Psychedelic
       F2.   Hallucinations and visions, feelings of insight, exhilaration
       F3.   Psychosis, panic, paranoia

       G1.   Classification unclear, some say mild psychedelic
       G2.   Relaxation, increased appetite, culturally determined effects
       G3.   Controversial abusive effects

ANSWER KEY - PRACTICE TEST 1 - MULTIPLE CHOICE

1.	C	2.	C	3.	A	4.	C
5.	B	6.	A	7.	A	8.	C
9.	D	10.	A	11.	B	12.	A
13.	B	14.	C	15.	D	16.	D
17.	C	18.	B	19.	D	20.	D
21.	A	22.	B	23.	C	24.	A
25.	B	26.	A	27.	B	28.	C
29.	C	30.	A	31.	B	32.	D

ANSWER KEY - PRACTICE TEST 2 - SHORT ANSWER.

1. Perception
2. anatomical; functional
3. psychophysics
4. absolute
5. just noticeable difference (j.n.d.)
6. sensory; decision
7. adaptation
8. brightness
9. retina
10. rods; cones
11. Feature-detector
12. ground
13. closure
14. constancies
15. off
16. basilar membrane; cochlea
17. intensity or amplitude
18. salty, sour, bitter, and sweet; umami
19. culture
20. touch (or pressure), warmth, cold, pain
21. gate-control
22. kinesthesis; equilibrium
23. visual cliff
24. emotions, expectations
25. Extrasensory perception

ANSWER KEY - PRACTICE TEST 3 - ESSAY

1.   A.   When a person compares two stimuli (the scarf and the car), the size of the change necessary to produce a just noticeable difference is a constant proportion of the original stimulus. In this case, $2.00 is a much larger proportion of $10 than it is of $10,000. Therefore, $2.00 on the price of a car would not produce a just noticeable difference. Two dollars represents 1/5 of the price of the scarf. One-fifth of the price of the car would be $2,000 and would produce a j.n.d.

       B.   Signal detection theory indicates that active decision-making is involved in determining an absolute threshold. The fatigue, as well as attention, of subjects may be interfering with decision making.

       C.   A reduction in sensitivity results from unchanging, repetitious stimulation or sensory adaptation. John may be having trouble feeling the glasses on his head because they have been there for a long time.

       D.   When people find themselves in a state of sensory overload, they often cope by blocking out unimportant sights and sounds and focusing only on those they find useful. Unimportant sounds are not fully processed by the brain. This capacity for selective attention protects us from being overwhelmed by all the sensory signals impinging on our receptors.

2.   Light, the stimulus for vision, travels in the form of waves. Waves have certain physical properties: length, which corresponds to hue or color; amplitude, which corresponds to brightness; and complexity, which corresponds to saturation or colorfulness. The light enters the cornea and is bent by the lens to focus. The amount of light that enters the eye is controlled by muscles in the iris, which surrounds the pupil. The pupil widens or dilates to influence the amount of light let in. The light goes to the retina located in the back of the eye. The retina contains rods and cones, which are the visual receptors. The cones are responsible for color vision; the rods for black-and-white vision and seeing things in dim light. The fovea, where vision is sharpest, is in the center of the retina and contains only cones. Rods and cones are connected to bipolar neurons that communicate with ganglion cells. The axons of the ganglion cells converge to form the optic nerve, which carries information out through the back of the eye and on to the brain.

3.   A.   Three colors will be needed - blue, red and green - corresponding to three types of cones. Combining such colors produces the human color spectrum.

       B.   Four colors will be needed - blue, yellow, red and green. They must be paired in a way that allows them to function as opposites.

4.   A.   Loudness is increasing as indicated by changes in the amplitude of the waves.

       B.   Pitch changes are related to changes in wave frequency.

       C.   The quality of sound, called timbre, is being altered by mixing various waves.

5.   A.   Proximity is the tendency to perceive objects that are close together as a group.
      B.   Closure is the tendency to fill in gaps to perceive complete forms.
      C.   Similarity is the tendency to see things that are alike as belonging together.
      D.   Continuity is the tendency for lines and patterns to be perceived as continuous.

6.   A.   Your expectation could influence your interpretation of what you saw and what happened.
      B.   Your belief about your neighbor's character could influence your perception that he was sneaking around.
      C.   Your emotions could influence your perception that someone was at the door.

ANSWER KEYS FOR CHAPTER SEVEN

ANSWER KEY - PRACTICE TEST 1 - MULTIPLE CHOICE

1. C	2. B	3. A	4. D
5. A	6. C	7. A	8. A
9. B	10. C	11. D	12. B
13. C	14. D	15. B	16. C
17. A	18. C	19. A	20. B
21. C	22. A	23. C	24. A
25. B	26. C	27. C	28. C
29. C	30. A	31. A	32. B
33. B			

ANSWER KEY - PRACTICE TEST 2 - SHORT ANSWER

1. learning
2. conditioned stimulus
3. extinction
4. higher-order
5. generalization
6. discrimination
7. predicts
8. counterconditioning
9. operant; consequences
10. reinforcement
11. reflexive; complex
12. primary; secondary
13. positive; negative
14. negative; punishment
15. reduces; increases
16. intermittent (or partial)
17. fixed-ratio
18. fixed-interval
19. shaping
20. extinction; reinforcement
21. extrinsic; intrinsic
22. biological
23. latent
24. observational
25. social-cognitive

ANSWER KEY - PRACTICE TEST 3 - ESSAY

1. A. CS = first and middle name; US = father's anger; UR = anxiety; CR = anxiety
    B. CS = closet and leash; US = walk; UR = excitement; CR = excitement
    C. CS = perfume; US = true love; UR = happy; CR = happy
    D. CS = Park Place and Main Street; US = accident; UR = fear; CR = anxiety

2. A. Dogs are often disciplined by being swatted (US) with rolled-up newspapers (CS). Fear is a natural response (UR) to being hit and a learned response to such objects (CR). Furthermore, stimulus generalization is demonstrated in that the dog gives the CR to other types of rolled-up papers.
    B. When attacked (US) by a Doberman (CS) in the past, Joan experienced fear (US). Since that time, she has been nervous about all Dobermans (stimulus generalization), though not around other dogs (stimulus discrimination). Her reduction of fear toward Dobermans represents extinction.
    C. The sudden noise of screeching tires (CS) often causes people to tense up and flinch (CR). The lack of response during a car race is stimulus discrimination.
    D. Getting sick (UR) from spoiled chicken (US) caused Bill to experience stimulus generalization to turkey (CS), which is similar to the chicken on which he originally became ill, and to experience a CR to the turkey.

3. A. The tendency to buckle-up is strengthened through negative reinforcement (the desire to eliminate the sound of the buzzer).
    B. Punishment is weakening the tendency to smoke around the roommate. This becomes more complicated because of the addictive process, which negatively reinforces smoking by removing uncomfortable withdrawal symptoms.
    C. Reinforcement is strengthening Warren's dishwashing behavior.
    D. Punishment is weakening Fred's tendency to go down the most difficult slopes.

4. A. Sara is on a partial reinforcement schedule. While this may be enough to maintain a behavior once it is well established, when a response is weak it should be reinforced each time it occurs (continuous reinforcement).
    B. By picking him up sometimes in response to his cries, Ari's parents have put him on a partial reinforcement schedule, which causes behaviors to be very persistent and difficult to extinguish. To change this pattern, they must consistently respond by not picking him up when he cries and eventually the behavior will extinguish. It will take longer to do so now that he is on this intermittent schedule.
    C. It appears that all the things the teacher is trying to use as punishment are reinforcing Sue's behavior. They all involve extra attention, so by finding a consequence that is unpleasant and does not involve attention, this behavior might be decreased by using punishment. She might also try teaching her and then reinforcing her for other types of attention.

5.   The initial punishment occurs long after the marks are made and therefore may not be associated with the behavior that is being punished. The parent is also scolding the child when he or she is feeling angry and therefore he or she may be harsher than usual. The child may also be aroused because of the punishment. Ideally, the behavior should be directed to an appropriate medium, such as paper or coloring books, and then that behavior should be reinforced.

6.   A.   Variable-interval
      B.   Fixed-ratio
      C.   Fixed-interval
      D.   Fixed-ratio

7.   Similarities
      1.   Agree about the importance of laws of operant and classical conditioning
      2.   Recognize the importance of reinforcers and the environment

      Differences
      1.   In addition to behaviors, study attitudes, beliefs, and expectations
      2.   Emphasize interaction between individuals and their environment

ANSWER KEYS FOR CHAPTER EIGHT

ANSWER KEY - PRACTICE TEST 1 - MULTIPLE CHOICE

1. A	2. B	3. B	4. B
5. B	6. D	7. D	8. A
9. A	10. D	11. C	12. B
13. A	14. C	15. D	16. B
17. A	18. C	19. C	20. D
21. D	22. A	23. C	24. C
25. A	26. D	27. D	28. C
29. A	30. D	31. B	32. A

ANSWER KEY - PRACTICE TEST 2 - SHORT ANSWER

1. Roles
2. two-thirds
3. roles
4. manners; entrapment
5. cognition
6. situational
7. dispositional; situational; fundamental
8. self-serving bias
9. just-world hypothesis
10. attitude
11. validity
12. coercive
13. obedience; conformity
14. groupthink
15. diffusion of responsibility
16. uninteresting
17. Deindividuation
18. Altrusim
19. social
20. ethnocentrism
21. stereotype; prejudice
22. emphasize; underestimate
23. distrust
24. social

ANSWER KEY - PRACTICE TEST 3 - ESSAY

1. The prison study   The students were either playing the roles of prison guards or prisoners. These roles were governed by norms of how prisoners and guards should behave. The students knew the roles and the norms that governed them and played the parts.

   The obedience study   The roles of the research subject and authority figure were known to the study participants, who then played the role of subject. Knowing the norms for both sets of roles made it difficult for subjects to violate their roles and defy the authority figure.

2.
   A.   Dispositional attribution
   B.   Just-world hypothesis
   C.   Situational attribution - self-serving bias
   D.   Situational attribution

3. You might want to use some techniques of friendly persuasion. You could use the validity effect by repeating that you have worked very hard in this class. Repeatedly referring to your effort may make it seem more believable to the faculty member. You also might want to make a reference to a class you have taken by a well-respected colleague in which you did very well. This is attempting to influence your teacher's attitude by using the respected colleague's opinion. Finally you might try to link your message with a good feeling by telling your professor how much you enjoyed the class.

4. To reduce social loafing, Dr. Wong should make sure each student is responsible for a different part of the project that is essential to the whole project. She might make part of the grade an individual grade and part of the grade a group grade. To reduce groupthink, she might want to make grades dependent on the presentation of multiple points of view and different positions and approaches. She will want to structure the project so that success depends on the cooperation and interdependence of all students. Finally, to promote altruism and independent action, she might want students to volunteer at a homeless shelter to get to know some homeless people personally.

5.
   A.   Underestimating differences within other groups
   B.   Accentuating differences between groups
   C.   Producing selective perceptions
   D.   Illusory correlations

6. Factors that contribute to the persistence of prejudice include
   1. Socialization - children learn prejudices from their parents.
   2. Social benefits - prejudices bring support from others who share them and the threat of losing support when one abandons the prejudice.
   3. Economic benefits and justification of discrimination - when economic or social times are difficult, prejudice increases.

Reducing prejudice: efforts that have not been particularly successful include - the contact hypothesis, efforts aimed at individuals, such as education, and the legal approach.

A program to reduce prejudice must include - multiple efforts, the cooperation of both sides, equal status and economic standing of both sides, comprehensive support from authorities and the opportunity to work and socialize together, formally and informally.

ANSWER KEYS FOR CHAPTER NINE

ANSWER KEY - PRACTICE TEST 1 - MULTIPLE CHOICE

1. C	2. A	3. C	4. C
5. D	6. C	7. A	8. D
9. A	10. D	11. B	12. B
13. C	14. B	15. B	16. B
17. A	18. B	19. C	20. C
21. C	22. B	23. D	24. C
25. D	26. B	27. C	

ANSWER KEY - PRACTICE TEST 2 - SHORT ANSWER

1. mental
2. concept
3. basic
4. proposition; cognitive schema
5. subconscious
6. nonconscious
7. must; is probably
8. formal; algorithm
9. dialectical reasoning
10. reflective
11. quasi-reflective
12. mental sets
13. availability heuristic
14. dissonance
15. achievement; aptitude
16. psychometric approach; cognitive approach
17. biased; culture
18. general; multiple
19. triarchic; contextual
20. componential, experiential, contextual
21. motivation; cultural attitudes
22. lower
23. displacement; productivity
24. anthropomorphism

ANSWER KEY - PRACTICE TEST 3 - ESSAY

1. A. Coat   B. Horse
    C. Dog   D. Uncle

2. A. The ship's position must be deduced. The position of the North Star and the formula are two premises that, once known, will allow the conclusion to be determined with certainty.
    B. Scientists of all types rely on inductive reasoning. Enough cases must be collected before a conclusion can be drawn.
    C. The overall process is dialectical reasoning, which is likely to incorporate inductive and deductive reasoning. It will be necessary to assess potential outcomes, risks, losses and appropriate considerations.
    D. Again, the overall process is dialectical reasoning, which will probably incorporate inductive and deductive reasoning.

3. A. Availability heuristic   B. Cognitive dissonance
    C. Confirmation bias

4. A. Componential intelligence   B. Contextual intelligence
    C. Experiential intelligence

5. A. Evidence supporting cognitive abilities in nonhumans
    1. Evidence on herons, sea otters and assassin bugs related to their food gathering habits reflects behaviors that appear intelligent.
    2. Some chimpanzees use objects as rudimentary tools, and there is evidence for some summing abilities and the use of numerals to label quantities.
    3. Some primates demonstrate the ability to use some aspects of language like - learning signs from sign language, understanding words and some sentences, using signs to converse with each other, ability to manipulate keyboard symbols to request food without formal training, use of some simple grammatical rules.
    4. Other evidence exists from dolphins and parrots.

    B. Evidence against cognitive abilities in nonhumans
    1. The meaning of these abilities is questioned; human meaning may be attributed to these actions.
    2. Early studies were overinterpreted and biased.
    3. It's unclear whether the use of signs and symbols were strung together without any particular order or syntax.
    4. While an animal may be "conscious," in the sense of being aware of its environment, it does not know that it knows and is unable to think about its own thoughts in the way that human beings do.

ANSWER KEYS FOR CHAPTER TEN

ANSWER KEY - PRACTICE TEST 1 - MULTIPLE CHOICE

1.	A	2.	D	3.	D	4.	D
5.	B	6.	C	7.	D	8.	D
9.	C	10.	A	11.	B	12.	C
13.	A	14.	C	15.	D	16.	D
17.	D	18.	A	19.	C	20.	A
21.	C	22.	B	23.	A	24.	D
25.	A	26.	B	27.	C	28.	D
29.	D	30.	C				

ANSWER KEY - PRACTICE TEST 2 - SHORT ANSWER

1. reconstructive
2. source
3. stable
4. suggestive
5. recall; recognition
6. explicit
7. implicit; priming
8. information processing
9. encode; store; retrieve
10. sensory; short-term
11. parallel distributed processing
12. chunks
13. semantic
14. network
15. semantic; episodic; declarative
16. serial position
17. maintenance; elaborative
18. epinephrine
19. decay
20. retroactive; proactive
21. retrieval; cue-dependent
22. state-dependent
23. amnesia

ANSWER KEY - PRACTICE TEST 3 - ESSAY

1. To be remembered, material first must be encoded into the form in which it is to be retained. Storage takes place in various areas of the brain, which appears to correspond to structural changes in the brain. Retrieval is the process by which stored material is located for current use.

2. Information entering through the senses is briefly held in sensory memory, where preliminary sorting and encoding take place. It is then transferred to short-term storage, where it is rehearsed. Finally, as a result of deep processing or elaborative rehearsal, it is forwarded to long-term storage, where it is indexed and organized to become part of the network of more permanent material.

3. A.   Procedural memory
    B.   Episodic memory
    C.   Semantic memory

4. Memory processes are subject to distortion in recall. Selection pressures bias information within sensory memory. Short-term memory simplifies, condenses and even adds meaning as information is being processed. In long-term storage, information is organized and indexed within the pre-existing framework, allowing memories to become intermixed. As information is retrieved, distortion can result from interferences and reasoning involved in reconstructing the event.

5. A.   According to decay theory, virtually all the details should be forgotten because of the long time interval involved. The only memories remaining should be those used from time to time as the person grew older.
    B.   The absence of retrieval cues is often a source of forgetting. The example suggests that the mental image created by the description of the homeroom was a cue that released a set of associated memories.
    C.   Some emotionally unpleasant situations may be forgotten more rapidly and may be harder to recall than other situations. For the sake of emotional comfort, Henry may be motivated to forget situations associated with personal distress.

6. Interference arises as memory incorporates similar material in succession. Assuming there is greatest similarity between Italian and Spanish, these should be kept as separate as possible, as well as overlearned and frequently reviewed. Breaks would also help as you go from one topic of study to another. A sequence like Italian, math, English, history and Spanish would be better than Spanish, Italian, English, math and history.

ANSWER KEYS FOR CHAPTER ELEVEN

ANSWER KEY - PRACTICE TEST 1 - MULTIPLE CHOICE

1. D	2. C	3. A	4. B
5. D	6. C	7. C	8. B
9. D	10. C	11. B	12. B
13. A	14. A	15. D	16. D
17. B	18. D	19. B	20. C
21. B	22. C	23. B	24. C
25. C	26. D	27. A	28. D
29. C	30. D		

ANSWER KEY - PRACTICE TEST 2 - SHORT ANSWER

1.   face
2.   basic
3.   facial feedback
4.   amygdala; cerebral cortex
5.   sympathetic (or autonomic); epinephrine, norepinephrine
6.   patterns
7.   physiological; cognitive
8.   attributions
9.   appraisals
10. cognitions; emotions
11. primary; secondary
12. prototypes
13. display rules
14. work
15. nonverbal
16. cultures
17. provocation; sensitive
18. perceptions
19. power
20. express

ANSWER KEY - PRACTICE TEST 3 - ESSAY

1. A.   The facial-feedback hypothesis assumes that emotion and facial expression are intimately interconnected. Distinct facial expressions not only identify emotions but contribute to them as well. By posing the face, performers may actually engender emotions in themselves.

    B.   They indicate that outward expressions can be masked or even faked. More importantly, they indicate that learning is important in the expression of emotion.

    C.   Emotion work might be defined as the ability to intentionally alter facial expression and body language to simulate a chosen emotion.

    D.   For Darwin, facial expression was biologically wired because of its adaptive communication value. Because the face rather than the body is the focal point of social interaction, body expressions need not be similarly wired.

2. A.   An increase in epinephrine and norepinephrine is brought about by the adrenal glands and under the control of the autonomic nervous system. Involvement of the amygdala, limbic system and cortex contribute to this arousal response.

    B.   The patient is functioning according to the display rules for men, which dictate that men should not feel fear or anxiety. The nurse is doing the emotion work associated with the role of a nurse. Nurses are supposed to be comforting and pleasant to patients.

3. These results are consistent with the idea that it is our interpretation of events that is instrumental in the experiencing of emotion rather than the event. The students' reactions are based on their explanations and interpretations of why they got those grades. Larry studied hard and expected a better grade. His depressive reaction may have to do with the fact that since he studied and did not do better, he may see himself as stupid, which is an internal and stable interpretation. Curly studied a little bit for the test so he felt relieved that he got a C. The grade has no bearing on his view of himself. He did not expect to fail, but did not really expect a better grade. Moe did not study at all so he interpreted the grade as very lucky. The grade did not influence his view of himself, but rather he interpreted it as due to external luck.

4. A.   Display rules govern the recipients of gifts.
    B.   Emotion work involves acting out emotions not truly felt.
    C.   The facial expression of anger is universally recognizable. Moreover, the husband's familiarity with Mary should make any idiosyncratic expressive features easily identifiable.
    D.   The emotion work is implied by gender roles.
    E.   She has a combination of lower status, high familiarity, sexual similarity, and gender.
    F.   All of the reactions do.

ANSWER KEYS FOR CHAPTER TWELVE

ANSWER KEY - PRACTICE TEST 1 - MULTIPLE CHOICE

1. C	2. B	3. C	4. A
5. A	6. D	7. A	8. C
9. D	10. D	11. A	12. C
13. B	14. B	15. C	16. C
17. C	18. B	19. D	20. D
21. D	22. D	23. B	24. A
25. A	26. A	27. B	

ANSWER KEY - PRACTICE TEST 2 - SHORT ANSWER

1. toward; away
2. drives
3. set point
4. diet; exercise
5. affiliation
6. triangle; passion; commitment
7. commitment
8. Attachment
9. express
10. economic
11. testosterone
12. similar
13. partner approval; peer approval
14. misperceptions
15. dominance
16. sexual
17. cultural norms
18. industrial/organizational
19. achievement
20. opportunity

ANSWER KEY - PRACTICE TEST 3 - ESSAY

1. We cannot be certain what motivates any given behavior. Each behavior described may be activated by a variety of different motives. Below are some possible explanations.
    a. Calling her friend shows need for affiliation.
    b. Visiting her boyfriend demonstrates the motivation for love.
    c. Doing extra credit assignments and an extra work project could reflect need for achievement, performance goals or learning goals.

2. <u>Information that supports homosexuality as a choice and refutes the biological argument</u>
    a. The fluidity of women's experiences
    b. There are flaws in the biological evidence
        *Methodological problems in the findings on brain differences
        *The majority of homosexuals do not have a close gay relative
    c. Psychological theories have not been well-supported

    <u>Information that supports the biological information and refutes the choice position</u>
    a. Research findings that women with a history of prenatal exposure to estrogen are more likely to become bisexual or lesbian
    b. Research findings on differences in brain structures of homosexual and heterosexual men
    c. Studies that show a moderate heritability

    <u>Political implications include</u> If homosexuality is biological, then it is a fact of nature and not a choice, and therefore, people should not be prejudiced. Those who are prejudiced against homosexuals suggest that the biological evidence says that it is a "defect" and should be eradicated or "cured." Those who say it is a choice, say it can be "unchosen."

3. A. Avoidance-avoidance conflict
    B. Approach-approach conflict
    C. Approach-avoidance conflict

ANSWER KEYS FOR CHAPTER THIRTEEN

ANSWER KEY - PRACTICE TEST 1 - MULTIPLE CHOICE

1. C	2. A	3. C	4. C
5. C	6. A	7. C	8. C
9. D	10. D	11. C	12. A
13. A	14. C	15. A	16. C
17. C	18. D	19. A	20. B
21. D	22. D	23. C	24. D
25. B	26. C	27. C	28. A
29. A	30. A		

ANSWER KEY - PRACTICE TEST 2 - SHORT ANSWER

1. behavior; thoughts
2. objective; projective
3. Allport; central; secondary
4. agreeableness; conscientiousness
5. reactive
6. heritability
7. nonshared
8. reciprocal determinism
9. expectations; self-fulfilling
10. collectivist
11. polychronic
12. Psychodynamic
13. id; realities; superego
14. defense mechanisms
15. sublimation
16. Horney
17. collective; archetypes
18. representation
19. falsifiability
20. self-actualized; functioning; unconditional positive

ANSWER KEY - PRACTICE TEST 3 - ESSAY

1. A. Cognitive social learning approach
    B. Trait approach
    C. Psychodynamic approach
    D. Humanistic approach

2.   A.   According to the reality principle, the ego would seek to prepare for the test.

        B.   The id seeks pleasure and immediate gratification, according to the pleasure principle.

        C.   The id seeks pleasure and is not concerned with the consequences of reality.

        D.   The ego is appraising reality.

        E.   The internalized parental values of the superego are discouraging him from cheating.

        F.   The ego is defending against threats from the superego.

        G.   Violations of the superego produce guilt.

3.   A.   Reaction formation   D.   Denial

        B.   Projection   E.   Regression

        C.   Repression   F.   Displacement

4.   A.   Phallic stage   C.   Phallic stage

        B.   Oral stage   D.   Anal stage

5.   A.   Adler

        B.   Jung

        C.   Horney

        D.   Object-relations school

6.   Abraham Maslow

Self-actualization was a basic need for Maslow. However, its achievement depended on gratifying even more fundamental needs, such as physiological drives and social needs.

Rollo May

May believes that alienation, loneliness and helplessness are basic components of human existence. The person strives to overcome these through effective choices.

Carl Rogers

According to Rogers, self-actualization and full functioning are related to the presence of unconditional positive regard. However, most children and adults live in situations in which they receive conditional positive regard.

7.   A.   Low levels of neuroticism, high levels of extroversion and agreeableness

        B.   High levels of conscientiousness, and probably agreeableness, and a low level of openness to experience

        C.   High levels of neuroticism and openness to experience, but a low level of extroversion

ANSWER KEYS FOR CHAPTER FOURTEEN

ANSWER KEY - PRACTICE TEST 1 - MULTIPLE CHOICE

1.	A	2.	D	3.	B	4.	D
5.	B	6.	A	7.	A	8.	C
9.	B	10.	B	11.	D	12.	D
13.	A	14.	C	15.	A	16.	D
17.	D	18.	C	19.	B	20.	C
21.	B	22.	C	23.	C	24.	C
25.	D	26.	B	27.	B	28.	D
29.	D	30.	A				

ANSWER KEY - PRACTICE TEST 2 - SHORT ANSWER

1. socialization
2. germinal; embryonic
3. placenta; x-rays; drugs
4. synchrony
5. terry cloth; contact comfort
6. Ainsworth; strange situation
7. avoidant
8. mothers; temperament
9. eleven; symbolic
10. Piaget
11. schema; assimilation
12. object permanence
13. egocentrism; preoperational
14. concrete operations
15. conventional
16. socialization
17. menarche; menopause
18. individuate
19. separatists; acculturation
20. eight; crisis
21. Fluid; declines; Crystallized; stable

ANSWER KEY - PRACTICE TEST 3 - ESSAY

1.   A.   Fetal abnormalities and deformities
      B.   There is an increased likelihood of miscarriage, premature birth, abnormal fetal heartbeat and underweight babies; after the child's birth, there are increased rates of sickness and Sudden Infant Death Syndrome; in later childhood, hyperactivity and difficulties in school.
      C.   Fetal alcohol syndrome
      D.   Effects vary with specific drugs; extreme caution must be exercised, even with prescribed and over-the-counter drugs.

2.   A.   Newborns should have the following reflexes: rooting, sucking, swallowing, Moro, Babinski, grasp, stepping. They should follow a moving light with their eyes and turn toward a familiar sound. They should be able to distinguish contrasts, shadows and edges, and be able to discriminate their primary caregiver.
      B.   Newborns are sociable from birth and show a preference for the human face. They can distinguish their primary caregiver by smell, sight or sound almost immediately. They establish synchrony with the primary caregiver very early.

3.   A.   The child is in the preoperational stage and is demonstrating egocentric thinking.
      B.   The child is incorrectly trying to use assimilation; she should use accommodation.
      C.   The younger child is in the preoperational stage and lacks the ability to conserve; the older child is in the concrete operations stage.
      D.   Johnny is in the sensory-motor stage and has developed object permanence.

4.   At 4 months old - Jennie would cry and coo and respond to high-pitched and more varied verbalizations in which the intonation is exaggerated. She can recognize her own name.
At 10 months old - she would be increasingly familiar with the sound structure of her native language. She might be making babbling sounds such as "ba-ba" or "goo-goo".
At 14 months old - she could begin using gestures.
At 23 months old - she would use telegraphic speech because she is not yet able to use article and auxiliary words. She would probably say, "Apple table."

5.   A.   Conventional morality
      B.   Postconventional morality
      C.   Postconventional morality
      D.   Preconventional morality

ANSWER KEYS FOR CHAPTER FIFTEEN

ANSWER KEY - PRACTICE TEST 1 - MULTIPLE CHOICE

1. A	2. C	3. A	4. D
5. D	6. D	7. A	8. D
9. A	10. D	11. A	12. A
13. D	14. C	15. B	16. C
17. B	18. A	19. B	20. C
21. C	22. D	23. C	24. A
25. B	26. C	27. D	28. D
29. D	30. A	31. D	

ANSWER KEY - PRACTICE TEST 2 - SHORT ANSWER

1. Health
2. Selye; alarm; resistance; exhaustion
3. widowed
4. worse; higher
5. antigen; immune
6. psychoneuroimmunology
7. immune
8. hostility
9. emotional inhibition
10. optimistic; illusions
11. control
12. primary; secondary
13. coping
14. Emotion-focused; problem-focused
15. Reappraising
16. compare
17. reduce; cause
18. psychological
19. "pop-health"
20. either-or
21. emotional; bacteria

ANSWER KEY - PRACTICE TEST 3 - ESSAY

1.   A.   Air traffic controllers are likely to face a higher degree of daily irritation and uncontrollable events than fishermen.

           B.   Type A people, particularly if they have antagonistic hostility and experience greater stress.

           C.   Those with an external locus of control are less likely to feel that they can predict and control their environments, and prediction and control reduce stress.

           D.   Generally, those with social networks experience buffers to stress.

           E.   Pessimistic explanatory styles result in the perception that the stressor is unchangeable, therefore these people will feel less control over the stress.

2.   A.   The alarm phase will be the most prominent as the person is being captured. Bodily resources will be mobilized as the person attempts to fight or flee.

           B.   Resistance will coincide with early captivity. Its duration is related to the victim's capacity to manage potentially overwhelming events. Signs of arousal will be prominent and bodily preparedness is the rule. Biologically, use of energy resources will be above normal. Psychologically, the victim is actively fighting the situation.

           C.   The timing of exhaustion depends on individual characteristics, such as coping styles. Biologically, it is signaled by bodily fatigue and susceptibility to illness. Psychologically, the person shows signs of giving up and wearing down.

3.   A.   Prolonged stress is capable of suppressing the disease and infection fighting cells of the immune system. As this happens, bodily defenses are impaired and susceptibility to symptoms increases.

           B.   Though the evidence is mixed, it is possible that the depression is contributing to his illness by affecting the immune system. It is also possible, however, that his continuous illness is contributing to the depression. It may be that poor health habits are causing both or that an entirely different thing is causing both. Finally, the depression and the illnesses could be mutually influencing each other.

           C.   David must examine his personality for antagonistic hostility; his personal style of evaluating and managing changes, daily hassles, and problems; the quality and quantity of his social relationships and interest; and everyday habits relating to rest exercise, and diet.

4.   A.   Margaret is rethinking the problem and using some denial.

           B.   The situation is being directly attacked with a problem-focused strategy.

           C.   Frank is reappraising the problem using social comparisons.

           D.   Tony is using an emotion-focused strategy.

           E.   Joan is trying to live with the problem.

ANSWER KEYS FOR CHAPTER SIXTEEN

ANSWER KEY - PRACTICE TEST 1 - MULTIPLE CHOICE

1. B	2. A	3. B	4. A
5. C	6. B	7. C	8. B
9. D	10. C	11. B	12. C
13. D	14. A	15. D	16. C
17. B	18. B	19. D	20. B
21. C	22. D	23. A	24. A
25. A	26. A	27. A	28. D
29. A	30. D	31. C	32. D

ANSWER KEY - PRACTICE TEST 2 - SHORT ANSWER

1.   cultural
2.   Diagnostic and Statistical Manual of Mental Disorders (DSM-IV)
3.   overdiagnosis
4.   Generalized
5.   post-traumatic stress disorder
6.   interpret
7.   social phobia
8.   agoraphobia
9.   Obsessions; compulsions; anxiety
10. behavioral, cognitive
11. Depression
12. attachment
13. personality
14. inhibition
15. vulnerability-stress; stresses
16. amnesia; fugue
17. common; clinicians
18. sociocognitive
19. biochemistry
20. learning
21. psychosis
22. delusions; hallucinations
23. genetic; prenatal
24. virus

ANSWER KEY - PRACTICE TEST 3 - ESSAY

1.   A.   This definition considers the violation of norms and standards to be abnormal. Jason violates norms governing social interaction, appearance and good taste.

        B.   Maladaptive behavior is behavior that results in disharmony and distress. Jason is behaving disruptively toward others.

        C.   This definition relies on signs of distress. Jason is apparently seeking forgiveness based on some internal experience of guilt or distress.

        D.   Jason does not seem to be able to distinguish between acceptable and unacceptable behavior, or, if he makes this distinction, he is unable to control himself.

2.   A.   Included

        B.   Excluded

        C.   Excluded

        D.   Included

        E.   Included

Explanation - The DSM-IV classifies disorders on five axes: primary diagnosis, ingrained aspects of personality, relevant medical conditions, current stressors and overall level of functioning. The included items reflect those axes and the others do not.

3.   A.   Abnormal: panic attack

        B.   Abnormal: obsessive-compulsive disorder

        C.   Normal

        D.   Abnormal: phobia

        E.   Abnormal: post traumatic stress disorder

4.   A.   Mood disorders involve emotional, behavioral, cognitive and physical symptoms.

        B.   In bipolar disorder, mania alternates with depression.

        C.   Antidepressant drugs raise the levels of serotonin and norepinephrine.

        D.   There is no change.

        E.   Negative thinking seems to be both a result and a cause of depression.

        F.   Repeated failure can be a source of learned helplessness, a characteristic related to depression.

5.   A.   Josephine has delusions. The fact that she believes that airplanes dirty the streets and sidewalks by dripping oil, that pilots have a power called "telectic penetration" and that she is being used as a radar are all examples of delusions.

        B.   Josephine is experiencing hallucinations. She hears the pilots talking to her about her location.

        C.   Josephine is demonstrating incoherent associations, including "telectic penetration," her latitude and longitude, and airplanes.

        D.   Josephine's behavior is inappropriate in that she withdraws and is unable to speak.

        E.   From the description, it is unclear if Josephine is exhibiting emotional flatness.

ANSWER KEYS FOR CHAPTER SEVENTEEN

ANSWER KEY - PRACTICE TEST 1 - MULTIPLE CHOICE

1. A	2. A	3. D	4. D
5. A	6. D	7. D	8. A
9. A	10. B	11. B	12. C
13. D	14. C	15. A	16. C
17. A	18. B	19. C	20. C
21. A	22. D	23. C	24. B
25. A	26. A	27. D	28. B

ANSWER KEY - PRACTICE TEST 2 - SHORT ANSWER

1. schizophrenia; psychoses
2. tardive dyskinesia
3. antidepressant
4. Lithium carbonate
5. relapse
6. prefrontal lobotomy
7. electroconvulsive therapy
8. psychodynamic; free association
9. transference
10. systematic desensitization
11. exposure (or flooding)
12. evidence; interpretations
13. emotive behavior
14. client-centered; unconditional
15. Family
16. research
17. coercive
18. empathy; genuineness
19. cognitive; anxiety
20. behavioral
21. coercion
22. multiple personality disorder
23. Community; Rehabilitation

ANSWER KEY - PRACTICE TEST 3 - ESSAY

1.   Medical treatments feature drugs and other forms of organic intervention. Drugs are very useful for psychotic disorders, and, in combination with psychotherapy, are effective against other disorders, including major depression, bipolar disorder, some anxiety disorders.

Psychotherapies attempt to change thinking, emotional and behavioral processes. They are designed to help clients think about their lives in new ways in order to find solutions to the problems that plague them. They have been shown to be very useful with mood disorders, anxiety disorders, and eating disorders.

Community services tend to be problem-oriented and offer counseling, support groups, and skills training. They can be useful for those with mental or physical disabilities, including schizophrenia.

2.   A.   Anxiety disorders: minor tranquilizers
     B.   Mood disorders: antidepressants
     C.   Psychotic disorders: antipsychotics

Drug treatments are limited by the complications of side effects and finding the right dosage. They may not be effective for everyone or may work effectively only in the short-term. Often there is little research on the effects of long-term usage. Moreover, drugs relieve symptoms and do nothing to help people learn new coping skills.

3.   Psychodynamic therapies strive for insight into the unconscious processes that produce a problem. With insight and emotional release, symptoms should disappear. The goal of treatment is not to solve an individual's immediate problem, since it is only the tip of the iceberg. Techniques include free association and transference. Psychoanalysis was the original model proposed by Freud in which a patient was seen multiple times in a week for many years.

Cognitive therapy aims to correct distorted, unrealistic thoughts, beliefs and expectations. Techniques vary but revolve around examining negative thoughts, formulating reasonable responses and using realistic perspectives.

Behavior therapy attempts to eliminate maladaptive responses and behavior patterns. Techniques are based on learning principles and include systematic desensitization, aversive conditioning, flooding and operant strategies.

Humanistic therapy is designed to increase self-esteem, positive feelings and self-actualization. Approaches include client-centered therapy and existential therapy. Client-centered therapy utilizes unconditional positive regard, empathy and genuineness.

Family therapy aims to correct the forces in the family that are contributing to the expression of a problem. The family may be analyzed from a multigenerational standpoint, using a genogram, or as a social system.

The shared features include - support factors, which allow the client to feel secure and safe; learning factors, which allow the client to see and experience his or her problems in a new light and think about how to solve them; and action factors, which allow the client to reduce fears, take risks and make necessary changes.

4. Client features - commitment to therapy, willingness to work on their problems, and expectations of success; cooperativeness with suggested interventions and positive feelings during the therapy session.

Therapist features - empathy, warmth, genuineness and imagination; make clients feel respected, accepted, and understood; expressive and actively invested in the interaction with the client.

Therapeutic alliance: a relationship in which both parties respect and understand one another, feel reaffirmed and work toward a common goal.

5. Coercion by the therapist to accept the therapist's advice, sexual intimacies, or other unethical behavior. Bias on the part of a therapist who doesn't understand the client because of the client's gender, race, religion, sexual orientation, or ethnic group. Therapist-induced disorders can be harmful, such as when therapists so zealously believes in the prevalence of certain problems that they induce the client to produce the symptoms they are looking for.

ANSWER KEYS FOR APPENDIX A

ANSWER KEY - PRACTICE TEST 1 - MULTIPLE CHOICE

1. C	2. B	3. A	4. C
5. D	6. A	7. B	8. D
9. A	10. D	11. B	12. B
13. C	14. A	15. C	16. C
17. B	18. D		

ANSWER KEY - PRACTICE TEST 2 - SHORT ANSWER

1. frequency
2. polygon
3. mean; mode
4. central
5. range; deviation; mean
6. percentages; z-scores
7. normal
8. negatively
9. null
10. statistically

ANSWER KEY - PRACTICE TEST 3 - ESSAY

1.   A.   These descriptive statistics are measures of central tendency and describe data by a single, representative number.

     B.   These descriptive statistics measure variability and reflect the spread of obtained scores.

     C.   These statistical pictures are used to organize data in terms of an overall visual summary.

     D.   These transformations are used when scores are put in a standardized format for easier comparisons.

2.   A.   This statement is justified because the mean and mode are equal in a normal distribution.

     B.   This statement is unjustified because the normal distribution is symmetrical, with either side of the mean mirror-imaging the other.

     C.   This statement is justified because less than 16 percent of the population receives a score about one standard deviation from the mean.

     D.   This statement is unjustified because this curve is likely to be skewed to the right given that basketball players are chosen for their height.

3.   A.   The null hypothesis is rejected whenever results are statistically significant.

     B.   Statistical significance occurs when differences between the experimental and control groups are very unlikely to be caused by chance or random errors.